D0016229

TRUFFLE HOUND

BY THE SAME AUTHOR

*The Essential Oyster: A Salty Appreciation of
Taste and Temptation*

*Apples of Uncommon Character: Heirlooms, Modern Classics,
and Little-Known Wonders*

*Shadows on the Gulf: A Journey Through Our
Last Great Wetland*

*American Terroir: Savoring the Flavors of Our Woods,
Waters, and Fields*

The Living Shore: Rediscovering a Lost World

*Fruitless Fall: The Collapse of the Honey Bee and
the Coming Agricultural Crisis*

*A Geography of Oysters: The Connoisseur's Guide to
Oyster Eating in North America*

TRUFFLE HOUND

ON THE TRAIL OF THE WORLD'S MOST SEDUCTIVE SCENT, WITH DREAMERS, SCHEMERS, AND SOME EXTRAORDINARY DOGS

Rowan Jacobsen

BLOOMSBURY PUBLISHING

NEW YORK · LONDON · OXFORD · NEW DELHI · SYDNEY

BLOOMSBURY PUBLISHING
Bloomsbury Publishing Inc.
1385 Broadway, New York, NY 10018, USA

BLOOMSBURY, BLOOMSBURY PUBLISHING, and the Diana
logo are trademarks of Bloomsbury Publishing Plc

First published in the United States 2021

Copyright © Rowan Jacobsen 2021

All rights reserved. No part of this publication may be reproduced
or transmitted in any form or by any means, electronic or
mechanical, including photocopying, recording, or any information
storage or retrieval system, without prior permission in writing
from the publishers.

Parts of this book originally appeared, in different form,
in *Eating Well, Orion,* and *Smithsonian* magazines.

Bloomsbury Publishing Plc does not have any control over, or
responsibility for, any third-party websites referred to or in this book.
All internet addresses given in this book were correct at the time of
going to press. The author and publisher regret any inconvenience
caused if addresses have changed or sites have ceased to exist, but can
accept no responsibility for any such changes.

ISBN: HB: 978-1-63557-519-4; EBOOK: 978-1-63557-520-0

LIBRARY OF CONGRESS CATALOGING-IN-PUBLICATION DATA IS AVAILABLE

2 4 6 8 10 9 7 5 3 1

Typeset by Westchester Publishing Services
Printed and bound in the U.S.A.

To find out more about our authors and books visit
www.bloomsbury.com
and sign up for our newsletters.

Bloomsbury books may be purchased for business or promotional use.
For information on bulk purchases please contact Macmillan Corporate
and Premium Sales Department at specialmarkets@macmillan.com.

To whomever first took a whiff and thought, "Why not?"

Try to explain why you love her, and what the attic smelled like.

—RACHEL HERZ, *THE SCENT OF DESIRE*

CONTENTS

AUTHOR'S NOTE

About a dozen species of truffles play prominent roles in this tale, but two have starring roles: *Tuber magnatum*, Italy's celebrated white truffle, which is often called the Alba; and *Tuber melanosporum*, the queen of black truffles, also known as the Périgord, after the region of France that helped make it famous. Neither of these truffles is constrained to the region it's named for, so there's a growing consensus to move away from place-specific names. In this book, I follow current naming conventions and refer to them as the white and the black winter, and I use the most established names for the other species as well. Most truffles, however, have several aliases; for a cheat sheet of who's who, and what they're like, please refer to "The Dirty Dozen" photo insert. *Bonne route.*

Down the Rabbit Hole

C arlo Marenda and I pick our way through the cool, mossy woods by the light of his headlamp, his truffle dogs Emi and Buk just ahead, like ghosts at the edge of the dark. Emi sniffs the ground around each tree, a quick once-over for the slightest hint of the maddening scent of a white truffle, which lives several inches underground but is pungent enough to grab the attention of any mammal with a good sniffer.

It's late fall in northern Italy, and the white puffs of Carlo's breath catch in his headlamp. The Italians say the best time to truffle is when there's "a nip in the air and the trees are bare." They also say the best time is at night, when the air is cool, the wind is still, and truffle scents pool on the forest floor.

These trees aren't quite bare, but the nip is there. For hours we've been wandering a *Game of Thrones* landscape of dark forests and medieval hill towns, every one topped by the jagged silhouette of a castle, dousing our lamps and lying low whenever somebody stirs in a neighboring farmhouse. Carlo has assured me it's okay to hunt these scraps of woodland nestled between Barolo's famously steep vineyards, but I'm not 100 percent clear on what "okay" means. I'm intensely alert, my consciousness pushed out to the tips of eyes, ears, skin, nostrils.

We pad along, the only sound the trickle of the creek we are following and Carlo's soft, steady "Dai, dai, dai" as he urges the dogs onward. *Go, go, go.* Emi and Buk are Lagotto Romagnolos, an ancient Italian truffle-hunting breed. Lagottos come in various combinations of brown, white, and cream. Adorable mops with bright beady eyes and bonkers enthusiasm, they remind me of Animal from *The Muppet Show*. Originally bred centuries ago for retrieving ducks from the marshes of Romagna, they are believed to be the ancestors of other water dogs like poodles, which they resemble. Their intelligence and energy make them excellent trufflers, but the training takes years. A skilled Lagotto can set you back $10,000.

Insanity? Perhaps. But white truffles are the world's most expensive food. In Alba, the city a few miles north of here where the annual Alba International White Truffle Fair is in full swing, it costs €3 to €4 per *gram* to get them shaved over your pasta. In the United States, they can fetch $3,000 a pound. They command such prices because no other food produces such arresting aromas, a cascade of sensation that can bring first-timers to tears, and because they can be found only in the wild, growing symbiotically with the roots of certain trees. A good truffle dog pays for itself.

Pigs were humanity's original truffling partners. Pigs are natural and enthusiastic consumers of truffles, and truffling probably evolved from farmers observing their sows uprooting truffles with abandon. By the Middle Ages, and likely long before, farmers in France and Italy had trained their pigs for the hunt.

But pigs love truffles too passionately. It's difficult to stop them from eating the truffles they find (stories abound of nine-fingered truffle hunters), so by the 1700s people were already switching to dogs, which happily work for treats. Besides, truffling is a secretive affair; if you're loading a four-hundred-pound porker into the passenger seat of your Fiat, everyone knows exactly what you're doing.

Suddenly Emi doubles back on her trail and plants her nose to the ground, sweeping back and forth. "Piano, piano," Carlo coos to her. *Slow . . . slow.* She lingers at the base of a poplar tree, and I begin to get my hopes up, but then she pulls away and keeps hunting, and again I wonder what I'm doing out here in the middle of the night in a muddy forest at the foot of some of the most celebrated vineyards in the world, when I could be in one of Barolo's spectacular cantinas drinking those wines instead.

But I know. I'm here because a few days ago I walked into a restaurant, here in the peak of truffle season, when the whole region goes *pazzo* for the little white fungi, and there in the middle of the dining room was a fat one under glass like a bulbous pearl, and I lifted the glass and took a sniff and my world exploded.

I have smelled lots of yumminess before, but this was different. It was not the warm, cozy scent of chocolate chip cookies baking. Nor was it mouthwatering. It was hardly a food scent at all. It was more like catching a glimpse of a satyr prancing across the dining room floor while playing its flute and flashing its hindquarters at you. You think, What the hell was that? And then you think, I have to know.

That all went through my head in the seconds it took me to walk from the truffle display to my table, where I joined a distinguished group of wine writers and food aficionados. This was an important meeting, for which we'd all flown great distances, and I was supposed to be bringing my A game.

Instead, I sat there in a daze, experiencing something I've recognized many times since: I couldn't stop thinking about that truffle. This wasn't an intellectual exercise; I believe I had a look on my face like the one my dog gets when he discovers some exquisitely stinky carcass along the roadside.

Introductions were made, at which point I said, "I'm sorry, I have to go smell that again." I stood up, set my napkin down, walked back to the display, lifted the glass, and snorted like John Belushi.

Truffles have very little taste. Like flowers, their strength is their scent, and they wield it for the same purpose: to attract animals that will help them reproduce. Like mushrooms, truffles are the fruiting bodies of subterranean fungi that live their lives in the soil as netlike filaments attached to tree roots. But unlike mushrooms, which use wind and water to disperse their spores, truffles stay underground, wrapped in a protective coat known as a peridium, and keep their spores on the inside, like a mushroom that never unfolds. Most are about the size of a button mushroom, though they can get much larger.

Slice open a truffle and you'll see a beautiful marbled interior, with a fine honeycomb of white "veins" enfolding countless pockets of microscopic spores, which usually turn dark when ripe. Truffles depend on animals to dig them up, eat them, and spread these spores far and wide. To achieve that, they produce a dumbfounding array of aromatic compounds. The scent seems to emanate from every atom of the truffle, and it works: squirrels, slugs, mice, foxes, pigs, deer, bears, beetles, baboons, and many other animals go crazy for the things. And so do we.

No words can do justice to the scent of a white truffle, though much ink has been spilled in the attempt. Common terms include garlic, cheese, earth, sex, and gasoline, but they all miss the mark.

The late food writer Josh Ozersky may have come closest, describing it as "a combination of newly plowed soil, fall rain, burrowing earthworms and the pungent memory of lost youth and old love affairs." Not the kind of thing you easily forget.

I returned to the table and muddled my way through lunch, but I was useless. I kept asking my dining companions if they wanted to go smell the truffle. In my mind, I was trying to make sense of all the underwhelming truffle experiences in my past, the truffle fries and truffle salt that almost smelled synthetic, like freaky wax models of the real thing. Even the handful of pricey truffle dishes I'd had in American restaurants had been utterly drained of their mojo compared to whatever I'd just encountered. I'd never understood the truffle thing, and now, suddenly, I had to.

~~~~~

A few days later, my opportunity seemed to come. My companions and I signed up for a hunt with a famous *trifulau*, as truffle hunters are called in the Piedmont. These hunts have become ubiquitous in the area and, I would later learn, in other truffle regions as well. They have a remarkable sameness to them, and it generally goes like this:

You meet your truffle hunter and his dogs and learn the basics. Then you follow your hunter to his selected spot. Off go the dogs. Surprisingly quickly, they start digging. The hunter exclaims, pulls out his *vanghetto*—the long-handled trowel used by all *trifulau*—and begins excavating, surrounded by a penumbra of cameras. Just like that, a nice white truffle pops up, near the surface. Wow! Lucky day. It's even pretty clean. The goods are passed around, everybody sniffs and ooohs, and deeper into the woods you plunge.

For the next hour you don't find a thing, the dogs cruising through the woods on autopilot, but it's fine because you've already had one success and the hunter is fielding questions from everyone and regaling them with anecdotes in his broken English and everybody is having a grand time, including the dogs.

On your way back, the hunter pauses in a grove of trees near where you began. He seems almost to be lingering. Depending on the quality of the dogs, they may just mill around until the hunter actually starts telling them to search certain trees. And then—miraculously!—a second truffle is found. The dogs and hunter dig it up, more photos and sniffs, and then immediately you head back to his house or restaurant, where you have a truffle meal, or at least get to sample and purchase all the products the hunter's family makes: truffle oil, truffle honey, olive spread with truffles, and so on.

In recent years, these hunts have become a huge hit, and for good reason: watching dogs triangulate to a truffle, as if they can smell in stereo, is amazing. It's even more heartening to witness the mind meld between a good hunter and his dogs.

But the hunts aren't real. What sane *trifulau* is going to take a bunch of strangers to his best spots? And what stranger is going to want to do it through the mud and cold of a long November night?

To keep the tour buses happy, many *trifulau* now pre-bury truffles on their land in advance. Everybody gets in and out in an hour or two, everybody wins. It's hard to argue with the logic. Anyone who handles tourists on a daily basis learns fast that they are dealing with the shortest attention spans this side of kindergarten.

I loved watching the dogs at work, but I knew enough to know we were getting a simulation. And somehow that mattered. The old-timers say that the time to hunt truffles is "when the witches are out," but as soon as the tour bus pulls up at midday, the witches scatter.

Whatever elemental message had been encoded in the insistent aroma of that Barolo truffle, it had something to do with listening to dogs and trees and truffles, with the visceral wisdom of honoring senses over sense. And I wasn't finding the answer at Epcot.

Who would take me on a real hunt? After a little recon, I discovered Carlo. He was on a mission. We met for drinks at an Alba café so he could scope me out, and he gave me the scoop.

The average *trifulau* in Piedmont is more than seventy years old, but Carlo was in his thirties, making him one of the youngest. A decade earlier, he'd been taken under the wing of Giuseppe Giamesio, the eighty-year-old dean of Piedmont *trifulau*. For years Giuseppe had been watching the forests of the region diminish in the face of development and expanding vineyards.

Even the remaining forests were becoming less productive. Truffles do best in open woodlands with little undergrowth. In the old days, when most people were farmers and heated with wood, they would harvest the undergrowth and fallen limbs for their stoves, and graze their animals in the copses. Now everyone was a winemaker, and no one heated with wood. The forests were choked with debris. And the truffles were suffering.

Truffles need people, Carlo told me. It's an ancient partnership. We enrich each other. And we are forgetting that. For years, Giuseppe urged his fellow *trifulau* and winemakers to take better care of the remaining forests, but he got nowhere. In 2015, on his deathbed with cancer, Giuseppe summoned Carlo. You're the only one who cares, he told him. Take my dogs. Protect the truffles. A few days later, Giuseppe died. Carlo inherited Emi and Buk, and he founded the nonprofit Save the

Truffle in Giuseppe's honor. He speaks in the schools, trying to get a new generation to look up from their phones and embrace the tradition, and he tries to organize truffle hunters, winemakers, and local governments into a coalition to steward the forests, but it's an uphill battle.

The upshot: Carlo was more than happy to take an American writer on a night hunt. And now, after a muddy hour with no action, Emi doubles down on the dirt around an oak tree and starts scraping with her paw, and quickly Carlo pushes her away and gets down on all fours himself, nose plastered to the spot, searching for the slightest hint of funky gold, and then I've joined him, both of us snuffling like razorbacks, rumps in the air, and now I really have to wonder what's going on here. Sure, there's money to be made, but not enough to turn grown men into wereboars.

Somehow, the truffle has bewitched me. Its olfactory tentacles have reached out of the earth and into my brain, bypassing the circuits devoted to logic and language and wrapping themselves around the inner core where smell, memory, and emotion entangle.

And I'm thinking about all this as Carlo breaks out his *vanghetto* and we start to tunnel into the wet earth. What kind of force has brought men since medieval times to genuflect on their knees in this witchy ritual in the cold, dark woods?

And I'm realizing that Josh Ozersky may have nailed it after all, because there's a perfect word for that abstract thing you can't put your finger on but you can't stop thinking about, that thing that makes you stupid and invigorated at the same time, a thing as combustible as sex and gasoline. It's called *love*.

2

Black Magic Apple of Love

M y truffle obsession put me in good company. Truffles have captivated and mystified people since ancient times. What were these extraordinarily smelly things that looked like little hearts? Were they even alive? For a remarkably long time, no one had a clue. Classical and medieval authors fretted over their lack of roots, stems, or other functional parts. (The umbilical cords that connect truffles to their mother fungus are too tiny to see.) They just thought of them as something the earth spontaneously gave birth to.

The Greeks were among many cultures who believed truffles were born in "thundery weather" when a lightning bolt struck a tree and snaked through the roots. In *Table-Talk*, his account of awesome dinner party conversations, Plutarch recounts a first-century symposium in which huge truffles were served, and a debate began. Some argued that truffles were created by lightning. Others maintained that the lightning simply opened up cracks that gave the truffles somewhere to grow. Nah, Plutarch

countered, it's the rains that accompany the thunder. The lightning takes away the burning part of the energy, making the
rains that fall especially gentle and generative, "with a great
deal of warmth and spirit." When those generous rains soak the
earth, he argued, they create a truffle—which, he pointed out,
is not like a plant, having neither roots nor sprouts, but is "a
being in itself, having the consistency of earth that has been
slightly altered."

Close enough. Truffles do require abundant summer rain—
they come after the thundery weather—and they are, in a sense,
the earth come to life, fungal golems.

Whatever they were, they were always rare, expensive, and
noteworthy. Truffles featured in luxurious banquets in Greek
and Roman times, and played the same role in the 1500s, when
Catherine de' Medici introduced them to the French court.
There are no records of the lower classes consuming them, but
that probably had to do with who was keeping records. We
know that in the 1400s trained pigs were being used to hunt for
truffles in Norcia (now Umbria, still a truffle hot spot), which
was considered the source of the best. People with pigs must
have always known the deal. I wouldn't be surprised if the
Gauls had a healthy truffle habit long before Caesar arrived.

None of the ancient authors pointed out the captivating
scent. They knew only desert truffles, which are mild. (They also
did terrible things to truffles, involving hours of boiling.) The
first raves arrive in the 1700s and 1800s, when Europe's culinary
eyes were opened, and many gazes fell upon the truffle. The
Italian composer Rossini called it "the Mozart of mushrooms." It
was "the diamond of the kitchen" to proto-foodie Jean Anthelme
Brillat-Savarin. "Whosoever says truffle," he wrote in 1825, "utters
a grand word, which awakens erotic and gastronomic ideas."

To Alexandre Dumas, it was simply "the holy of holies."

To the French novelist and feminist George Sand, the "black magic apple of love."

But writers have always struggled to describe that crazy fragrance. William Thackeray gave it a shot: "Something musky, fiery, savoury, mysterious—a hot drowsy smell that lulls the senses, and yet enflames them."

Diane Ackerman worked much the same territory in *A Natural History of the Senses*, comparing the scent of the truffle to "the muskiness of a rumpled bed after an afternoon of love in the tropics."

The aphrodisiac thing comes up again and again, ever since Aristotle, though it has always been in dispute. Brillat-Savarin valiantly attempted to answer the question by surveying all the women he could, but gave up because "all the replies I received were ironical or evasive."

In reality, of course, no foods are true aphrodisiacs. The best they can do is set the mood, and here truffles excel. You might even say they are more mood than food. For this reason, the best accounts of first-truffle experiences focus on feelings. Alice Waters considered her first encounter with white truffles—in a rustic trattoria in northern Italy in the 1970s—one of the formative moments of her career. "I remember having someone come to the table and shave white truffles on top of a wide noodle pasta I had ordered," she recalled in the magazine *First We Feast* in 2015. "And I was struck with the thought that it was maybe the best thing I'd ever had in my whole life . . . After I ate it I kept pondering, why was that so good, what was that? I almost couldn't imagine that that sort of fragrance and taste could exist."

In *The Cooking of Southwest France*, Paula Wolfert described her first tryst with a black truffle in similar ways: "I felt at one with nature, that my mouth was filled with the taste of the earth. There was a ripeness, a naughtiness, something beyond description."

Even better: Sally Schneider, writing in *Saveur* about the time when she was a young chef, and someone slipped a black truffle into her pocket as she worked. As the heat of her body warmed the truffle, its scent enveloped her. "It was intoxicating—a smell I knew intimately, yet had no conscious memory of, triggering a flood of elusive associations, like flashbacks into some amnesiac period of my life, or some prenatal memory."

Prenatal memories and musky love beds are not generally the kind of thing one pays to have grated over one's pasta in Michelin-starred restaurants. The more I reflected on what others had written about truffles, as well as my own response, the more I began to suspect that centuries of snobbery had got truffles all wrong. High-end chefs and promoters had convinced us that they were the ultimate luxuries of civilization, fancy food to be savored in black tie, but I began to wonder if they were more like little Trojan horses, wheeled into the finest dining rooms in the world, only to discharge a scent that mocked civilization and its trappings.

And I was ready for it. To be honest, I needed it. After years of culinary writing, I'd been fortunate enough to experience many of the world's most wonderful foods and drinks. But no matter how delicious, how artfully created, after a while you notice that most share a certain sameness, as if all our gastronomic poetry is written with the same small set of words. This was something different, a chthonic yawp from a different kingdom of life. I didn't know this story.

As it turns out, it's a story that often circles around yearning and disappointment—lost youth and old love affairs, as Josh

Ozersky so insightfully put it. The truffle is a bit of a trickster, always promising gratification, only to stay just out of your grasp. You can't find it, or you can't afford it, or you spring for one and the smell is inescapable right up to the point that you grate it over your food, when it suddenly disappears, like a dim star in the night sky when you try to stare right at it. If the core emotion of the truffle dynamic is love, all too often it's unrequited love.

To wit: Carlo and I get skunked that night. *Niente.* Four hours of bombing through the woods, dodging eye-gouging twigs and ankle-flipping snags, mud-splattered and soaked, all for nothing. We dig a small crater where Emi indicates, but no truffle, just loose dirt. Somebody has been there before us. Emi has caught the last lingering scent of loss.

Sometime in the wee hours, Carlo drops me back at my hotel and I collapse on my bed, no longer feeling so high and mighty about visceral wisdom. I'm just another tourist junkie. I have two days before I have to fly back to the States, and I desperately need another fix. And I know what that means. I'm going to have to reach for my wallet and throw myself on the mercy of the marketplace.

3

The Alba Connection

If truffles are drugs, then Alba is Bogota. From October to January, white truffles are the lifeblood of its cobblestoned streets, beckoning from every shop window and trattoria menu. The apotheosis is the Alba International White Truffle Fair, a huge bash in an exhibition space in the center of the old city held for three successive weekends every October.

I walk to the festival through pouring rain. Fog is normal in late fall in the Piedmont, but this is an absolute deluge, and everyone agrees it's weird. Hurricane-strength winds on the Ligurian coast. Dark murmurs about climate change.

On the street, I pass a remarkably hefty truffle dealer sitting outside his shop at a card table under a tent, like you'd find at a farmer's market. His truffles are each covered with a clear plastic disposable cup, like some weird version of three-card monte. "Annusare il profumo, Signore!" he urges me. *Smell the perfume.* Most *trifulau* look like craggy tortoises, but this guy has a gray beard and a rumpled cowboy hat and reminds me of Jerry Garcia. *Late* Jerry Garcia.

My loose plan is to cruise the fair, take in the scene, and come home with a truffle of my very own. Tasting a truffle in Alba is not hard. Virtually every restaurant in town offers truffles—the best places bring a scale to your table, weigh the truffle in advance, shave with abandon until you say uncle, then weigh the truffle again and charge you the difference—but I'd done that a few times and decided the answers I sought were not going to be mediated by an overworked waiter. If I'm going to tease out the truffle's secrets, I need to play with it, to get to know it. I need to bring it home.

I huddle under the tent with my friend, rivers pouring off the awning. "Annusare il profumo!" he says again. So I lift a cup and lean down to the truffle.

No, no, he pantomimes, just lift the cup to your nose.

I do, and boom, there it is, garlic and fried cheese embedded in the plastic. "Bellissimo!" I offer.

He gestures over his wares. *How many would you like?*

I scan the prices and gulp. A hundred euros for a marginal truffle. "I'll think about it," I say, and duck out into the rain, ignoring his appeals.

The theme of the festival this year is "Terra e Luna"—the earth and the moon. The sign at the entrance displays a large white truffle and a full moon side by side, pockmarked twins. It's haunting and effective. Every truffle hunter in Italy believes that truffles ripen a couple of days before the full moon, though the scientists remain skeptical.

The truffle fair was launched in 1928 by Giacomo Morra, a restaurateur and entrepreneur who made it his life's work to put the Alba white truffle on the map. At the time the French black truffle got all the love, but Morra was a natural promoter. He put out the word that *Tuber magnatum* was the truly great truffle (he had the Latin to back him up), and that it was to be found only in northern Italy.

By 1933 the *Times* of London had dubbed Morra the King of Truffles. The fair grew fast. In 1949 Morra sent the finest truffle of the year to Rita Hayworth. That garnered so much attention that he continued the practice in the following years, gifting Harry Truman, Winston Churchill, and the king of Saudi Arabia, among others.

Today, white truffles sell for three times the price of the best black truffles. Exceptional specimens go for much, much more. In 2007 a 3.3-pound white truffle sold to a Macau casino mogul for $330,000.

I step inside the festival space and am staggered by the locker-room bouquet, the air thick with garlic and hormones. Near the entrance, bored truffle dealers display their goods under glass cases. Around the perimeter, local wineries peddle glasses of Barolo and Barbera. On one end, celebrity chefs are showing off at a demonstration kitchen. On the other, an ad hoc restaurant churns out plates of the canonical dishes: white truffles shaved over eggs, tajarin pasta, tiny ravioli called plin, tartare, or Robiola cheese fondue. Prices run about €10 for a serving, plus an extra €30 to get ten grams of truffle shaved over the top. Lines are long.

I wrestle with the math. Hundreds of thousands of visitors. Tens of thousands of truffles consumed. More every year. It doesn't seem to square with what Carlo told me about the declining forests. How can a few septuagenarians in Piedmont possibly supply the world?

The center of the fair is a warren of booths offering tastes of every imaginable truffle product: oils, pastes, sauces, spreads, pâtés, salumi. I walk the aisles, scarfing samples, but pretty quickly I realize I'm not loving the flavor of any of this stuff. It seems a little heavy on the old socks and a little light on the holy of holies. It will be a long time before I finally understand why.

I decide to buy my truffle and escape. At the entrance, the *trifulau* open their glass cases so I can peruse their wares. The truffles are displayed on traditional blue-checked cloths. Mottled and khaki-skinned, with the slightest tinge of chartreuse, they look about as sexy as ginger bulbs, but the little paper disc beside each truffle, with a weight and a price, makes it clear this is no ginger. Small truffles for €200. Quarterpounders for €500 and up. Way up. The vibe seems familiar. Precious glass cases. Proprietors just going through the motions because they're pretty sure you don't have the cash. Jewelry by any other name. Receptacles of desire.

People have warned me that the truffle business is rife with fraud. Ersatz species of truffles get passed off as the good stuff, sometimes doused in synthetic scent to make them more convincing. The Alba fair screens all its truffle sellers, and for further guarantee, three stern old men with badges sit on a dais in the center of the room beside a sign that says "Have your truffle checked by the Truffle Inspectors!" So I have no doubt these are *Tuber magnatum*, but I also have no doubt they're overpriced. Carlo has already explained to me that truffles are at their best for just a few days after they come out of the ground, and only if you keep them refrigerated at all times. In my mind, I keep hearing his words about the fair. "It's nice," he said with a shrug, "for tourists."

More important, the excess is dimming my desire. It occurs to me that white truffles are like nudes. One's sexy. Three thousand's a crowd.

I slip out and trudge dejected through the rain, splashing through low spots in the cobblestones. Already I'm second-guessing myself. What's a hundred bucks to mainline a little lost youth and love in the tropics?

And suddenly there's Jerry Garcia at his booth. "Annusare il profumo, Signore!" he says, clearly not remembering me from an hour before.

I don't mess around. I point at a small truffle and fork over a handful of €20 notes. "Quello."

He leaps to his feet in surprise, wrapping the golden nugget in a paper towel and sticking it in a bag before I can reconsider. He throws in a tiny black truffle as a freebie, perhaps racked by guilt for what he's doing to me.

I thank him and slosh back to the hotel, shielding my treasure under my coat.

I'm staying at the Hotel Savona, a spot with a 1960s Euro vibe that has been on the piazza near Alba's main gate since 1863. The Savona has deep truffle bona fides; it was Giacomo Morra's hotel and restaurant, where he dazzled decades of visiting VIPs. It was here in 1961 that Marilyn Monroe showed up to accept a giant truffle from Signore Morra himself. It seemed an appropriate place for my experiments to begin.

I take out my truffle and sniff it. Nothing. Maybe it has to be shaved.

I borrow a truffle shaver from the hotel bar, whittle the entire nubbin over a hunk of buttered baguette, and chow down. Nothing! Only the faintest bit of must. Had the smell been all in the plastic cup? I have no idea. Only much later will I realize that the truffle was either old, unripe, or both.

The black truffle is even more unimpressive, with all the aroma of a piece of painted cork.

There's so much I don't understand. All I know is I have twenty-four hours to solve this increasingly existential dilemma.

Carlo, I know, is truffle-less at the moment.

But what about the old truffle-hunting legend who took us on the simulated hunt? He moves dozens of truffles through his restaurant every day. I reach out and play the desperation card. Might he have any to spare?

Si, he says. Nice ones. One hundred euros apiece. How many do I want? Four? Five?

Umm, maybe three, I say in a panic, wondering what the maximum ATM withdrawal is.

Excellent. Where am I staying?

Alba, I say. Hotel Savona.

My daughter Giulia works near there. Meet her in the lobby at 8:00 A.M. tomorrow. Bring cash.

The only things moving in the Hotel Savona lobby the next morning are me and the desk clerk, who has just made me a cappuccino. Behind the clerk hangs a bank of room keys, each attached to a hunk of brass with the heft of a railroad tie, discouraging any guest from even thinking of walking off with one. The lobby has a polished marble floor, red art deco armchairs, and disconcertingly pink walls that match the lilies on the coffee table. If Wes Anderson shot a John le Carré novel, he might well choose the Hotel Savona for his set.

I sit in one of the low red chairs, legs crossed and knees high, sipping cappuccino, doing my best Adrien Brody impression. The glass door slides open. In steps a woman in high heels and a red pantsuit. This is not the rustic I've expected. She walks over, heels clicking on the marble. "Mr. Jacobsen?"

"Giulia?" I ask, as if other strange Italian women might be looking for me that morning.

She lowers her voice. "I have your truffles."

"I have your cash," I murmur in equally low tones. I'm not sure why we're whispering, since as far as I know buying truffles is perfectly legal, but I also have the feeling that the *fisco* will not be getting his cut of the taxes on this particular transaction. The concierge eyes us suspiciously from behind the front desk, but this can't be the first truffle deal he's seen go down.

I pull out my three crisp €100 notes and fan them out for Giulia.

"Excellent," she says. Then she leans in a little closer. "Would you like to . . . smell first?"

I'm trying hard not to reveal myself as a truffle virgin, so I nod and say, "Of course."

From her pocketbook she pulls out a clear plastic box with a fastening lid, like a tiny treasure chest. Inside are three perfect white truffles, smooth and suede-skinned, not a speck of dirt. She cracks open the lid and holds the box to my nose.

I lean in and inhale. It's like the universe has shoved smelling salts under my nose. Everything I've been looking for. "Oh, yes!" I blurt. The concierge rattles some keys uncomfortably behind the desk.

I hand over my money, and she hands me the box. We smile awkwardly. "Well," she says, "I'm late for work." She clicks back across the foyer, then turns briefly at the door. "I hope you'll have good memories of Italy."

I hold up the box and rattle it. "Me, too."

~~~~~

Do I declare my truffles at U.S. customs? I do not. There's so much ambiguity about the rules. Raw fruits, vegetables, and meat are definitely banned, as is soil, but fungi are theoretically fine. I've been told customs will probably not object, as long as there's no soil on my truffles, but €300 is on the line, so I stuff the plastic box into a sock, stuff that in another sock, stuff the whole thing in my boot in my pack, and hope for the best.

Running the gauntlet of the customs line in Newark feels interminable. (I've already lost my fancy new truffle shaver at the Milan airport security line, as if I was going to microplane my way into the cockpit.) I can smell truffle stink radiating from my bag and assume everyone else can, too. Sure enough, the drug dog's head jerks as I pass. Our eyes lock. He's a no-nonsense German shepherd, and he looks at me like I'm some sort of deviant, but apparently fungus is not in his job description. I sail into America with my truffles.

Back home in Vermont, I don't try anything outlandish; I want the core truffle experiences. I shave them over pasta al burro. I grate them into slowly shirred scrambled eggs. I make a risotto alla milanese for friends that leaves us all burping truffle fumes for hours.

By then, I'm feeling pretty satisfied with myself. I'm convinced that I know where to find the best truffles, what to do with them, and why it matters.

And I couldn't be more wrong.

4

Remembrance of Truffles Past

The first time it happens, I'm pumping gas. Standing beside my car in the December chill, clouds of exhaust dancing behind the other cars, and suddenly an intense impression of truffle crackles through my mind like a fork of lightning. It's less a memory than a flashback, just as Sally Schneider described. I stand transfixed, chills on the back of my neck.

It's been weeks since I polished off my truffles. The fumes subsided long ago. Clearly the scent-memory was triggered by the gasoline vapors in the air, but it's not gas I'm smelling. It's truffle. I glance around the service station. Definitely no truffle. Somehow my perceptions are short-circuiting.

The flashbacks keep hitting at random moments through the following weeks. Truffle ghosts flare from an empty glass of wine, the musty corners of my desk, the paws of my dog, the woodstove. Every time, I'm momentarily slain by the eruption out of the past, the poignant sense of lost moments. I can't help but think that if Marcel Proust had been haunted by a truffle instead of a madeleine, he'd have collapsed in on himself like an old French farmhouse.

Eventually the flashbacks subside, but the obsession doesn't. What is this organism that has such a hold on me? Why can't I stop thinking about it? Or not even *thinking*, really; it feels like it's operating at a lower layer of cognition.

Which turns out to be the case. Smell is our original sense, the only one that harkens back to our primordial past as single-celled creatures. Before there was such a thing as vision or hearing, simple organisms learned to detect molecules in their environment and react accordingly. Is it yummy food? A scary predator? An appealing mate? Memory and emotion evolved from our need to respond to these cues: love, fear, remember.

When signals come in through our eyes and ears, they go to the thalamus, the brain's gatekeeper, which relays them to various parts of the higher brain for processing. The experience is analyzed, interpreted, and labeled, and only then does it get routed to the limbic system, the primitive brain, where memory and emotion are housed. But smell is hardwired straight into the limbic system. Scents bypass the higher brain, instantly imprinting on emotion and memory without interpretation. They are pure experience, unmediated by language, which explains why they're so hard to describe with words. Our rich repertoire of feelings evolved from a system designed to respond to scent, and in a sense we each recapitulate this evolution: smell is the one sense that forms fully in the womb; it may be how the awakening of consciousness begins.

However the mind chooses to unpack it later, every scent is a prelinguistic mote of meaning. Words or no words, truffles get

in your head. And you can't get them out. And whether you're a
flying squirrel or a food writer, you keep going back for more.

~~~~~

The myco-guru Paul Stamets has a nice online video of a squirrel
eating a truffle. It looks like it's thinking something very similar
to Paula Wolfert when she ate her first. *My mouth is filled with
the taste of the earth. There's a ripeness, a naughtiness, something
beyond description.* To achieve these Jedi mind tricks, a truffle
has to concoct a cocktail of compounds so potent and compel-
ling that even distant animals will heed the call.

If you could don glasses that allowed you to see invisible
vapors, you'd realize that a truffle is a volcano, "blowing gas," as
truffleheads say, in all directions. That gas is a simmering
mélange of volatile organic compounds, or VOCs. More than
two hundred different VOCs have been identified in various
truffles. In a typical whiff, you are probably inhaling fifty.

Some of these VOCs have scents we know well: pineapple,
salami, garlic, blue cheese, sweat, kerosene, airplane glue. Others
are more exotic. Half of these compounds are manufactured by
the truffle itself, in its tiny cellular gasworks; others are actually
made by microbes that the truffle nurtures within its body for
that purpose. Long before cheesemakers and winemakers, truffles had mastered the art of fermentation.

Those microbes also mean that, as with cheese and wine,
terroir plays a huge role in truffle flavor. The same truffle will
harbor different microbiomes in different soils, regions, or
seasons. Every environmental factor, from the temperature to
the partner tree, is going to affect the smell.

Some truffle VOCs aren't meant to register as smells at all;
they're hormones and pheromones, chemical signals meant to

affect plant and animal behavior subliminally. Truffles make androstenol, a sex hormone produced in the saliva of male boars and the armpits of male humans. There's no proof that pheromones play a role in human behavior, but all you have to do is watch a roomful of frisky truffle eaters to suspect that something is going on.

Some truffles also produce anandamide, a cannabinoid naturally produced by the mammalian brain. The word *ananda* means "bliss" in Sanskrit, and anandamide is used as a neurotransmitter to produce blissed-out states during sex, eating, and other peak moments. (The cannabinoids in cannabis, such as THC, affect us because they lock into the receptors designed for anandamide.) Anandamide also affects memory and suppresses stress, anxiety, and pain. Recently scientists discovered a woman in Britain with a genetic mutation that gives her twice the normal level of anandamide; she has never experienced pain or distress.

The function of other truffle VOCs is unknown, but they may well operate on that fundamental level Sally Schneider touched upon, triggering intimate floods of elusive associations, almost like false memories. However they do it, it's a more effective formula for chemical seduction than any human perfumer has hit upon. The truffle seems to know us better than we know ourselves.

But that has always been fungi's game. They are masters of mutualism. Unable to make their food from sunlight, as plants do, or to move quickly, like animals, they have had to strike partnerships with organisms very different from themselves. Time and again, through evolution, they have figured out what makes other organisms tick and how they might exploit those needs for their own purposes.

Truffles provide animals with valuable minerals—they're sometimes called the salt licks of the forest—and a gustatory thrill in exchange for spore dispersal, but their relationship with trees is even more vital. Truffle fungi live as mycelia: mats of microscopic filaments that feel their way through the soil, mining nutrients. They partner with trees for their daily existence, sheathing the root ends in a net of hyphae, like a glove on a hand. The fungal threads actually penetrate the root, snaking into the interstices between the cells so they can share resources. This tangle of intimacy is known as a mycorrhiza, literally a "fungus root."

Both partners benefit. Fungal hyphae are a hundred times finer than the finest plant roots, twenty-five times thinner than a human hair. With more surface area, and an array of enzymes at their command for dissolving rock, they are far better at harvesting water and micronutrients from the soil. They become the extended root system of the plant, feeding these nutrients to the tree in exchange for sugars, which plants make through photosynthesis. It's a beautiful, and essential, relationship. Mycorrhizal fungi will die if they don't connect to a plant root shortly after germinating, and most plants can't survive without fungal partners. If not for mycorrhiza, plants would still be stuck in the sea.

Although both sides depend on the partnership, it's up to the fungus to make it happen. As they creep through the soil, fungal hyphae detect—smell—molecules seeping through the soil, and move toward the interesting ones. They are, in a sense, all nose. When they find a tree they want to partner with, they spray the root in a mist of plant hormones and other molecules known to control plant growth and behavior. In a sense, they hack the tree's operating system. These compounds shut down the tree's immune response, so it doesn't treat the fungus like an invading pathogen, and commandeer the root's cellular development, forcing it to shorten, branch, and send out lots of small root hairs—the perfect hand for the fungal glove.

"Evolution" is the easy way to explain away this amazing ability. But you could just as well say the fungus exhibits sophisticated problem-solving abilities over geological time scales. Or you could just say it's smart.

~~~~

Soil fungi are generally off our radar, being microscopic and subterranean, but they are extensive; a single teaspoon of soil contains *miles*. That makes them one of the dominant forest organisms. The soil fungi in a typical acre of forest weigh as much as a couple of cows, and individual fungi can get huge. The largest organism on earth is a honey fungus in the Blue Mountains of Oregon that spans 2,400 acres (1,364 soccer fields), weighs around 100,000 pounds (two blue whales), and is thousands of years old.

By such standards, mycorrhizal fungi like truffles are tiny, but their role in the ecosystem is outsized. That became apparent in the 1990s, when scientists discovered the extensive nature of the mycorrhizal networks that connect trees. Although some mycorrhizal fungi partner with just a single tree, most connect to multiple trees, often more than one species. And because most trees will also have more than one fungal partner, most trees in a section of forest will be connected and able to share resources through these common mycorrhizal networks.

In 1997 the journal *Nature* dubbed common mycorrhizal networks the Wood Wide Web, launching a thousand *Avatar* comparisons. Big trees shared carbon with seedlings that couldn't get enough light to make their own, "nursing" them. Dying trees bequeathed their resources to the network. Birches shared with firs. And these trees weren't just sharing carbon. Other experiments found that a tree attacked by bugs could alert other trees through the network so they could prepare their chemical defenses. The networks could transport all sorts of information, sometimes by moving actual molecules, sometimes through electrical signals, as in a nervous system.

After the German forester Peter Wohlleben published his bestseller *The Hidden Life of Trees* in 2015, new ideas about the communitarian life of the forest soared in the popular culture. But they never quite made sense. Why would a birch slide its hard-earned sugar to a fir, its direct competitor? Why would any tree donate its resources to any individuals other than perhaps its own seedlings? Altruism is vanishingly rare in the natural world. It gets squeezed out of the gene pool every time.

The answer, of course, was right under our feet. All the Wood Wide Web pundits virtually ignored the fungi doing the connecting, treating them like dumb plumbing. The observers were, as the mycologist Merlin Sheldrake puts it in *Entangled Life*, his brilliant 2020 chronicle of fungal exploits, "plant-centric." That's understandable. We see plants every day; we build our lives around them. Fungi are ever present but mostly invisible, like dark matter. We forget they exist.

But who is pulling the strings of this web? Aren't fungi the likely puppeteers? Plugged in to many different plants, sometimes many species, they probably get different resources from each. It's in their interest to keep the whole suite alive. Part of the reason our forests contain as much diversity as they do may be because mycorrhizal fungi like it that way.

In recent years, the evolutionary biologist Toby Kiers has discovered that mycorrhizal fungi do indeed have control over the resources that flow through them. Far from being a commune, a mycorrhizal network functions more like the Wall Street trading floor. Fungi hoard their nutrients and information, driving hard bargains with their tree partners and striking deals to get the best price. The trees also have control over what they trade, but the fungi are the ones that hold the whole thing together. Like a neuronal network in a brain, they allow the forest to function at a higher level of cognition. They give it executive function.

In *Entangled Life*, Merlin Sheldrake calls mycelial networks "the living seam by which much of the world is stitched into relation." To me, that sounds a lot like Obi-Wan Kenobi's description of the Force to a young Luke Skywalker: "It's an energy field created by all living things. It surrounds us and penetrates us. It binds the galaxy together."

With threads of mycelia and tendrils of fragrance, truffles bind not just tree to tree, but tree to squirrel to truffle hunter. The more I learned about truffles, the more I realized they were the living seam that stitched together a rich web of traders, trees, chefs, dogs, boars, hunters, microbes, and me. And they weave it all out of scent and psyche.

5

Hocus Pocus

For months I try to slake my longing with cheap imitations. I pound truffle fries. I drizzle truffle oil on my asparagus. Every time, I regret it. The smell is a grotesque caricature of truffle, as subtle as a Yankee Candle store.

It doesn't take me long to figure out why. Truffle oil has no truffle in it. It's just olive oil spiked with a synthetic chemical known as 2,4-dithiapentane. That compound is one of hundreds of aromatic molecules produced by a white truffle, but it's an important one, so a shot of dithiapentane gives a crude and heavy-handed impression of truffleness.

As such, it's been widely employed by chefs since the 1990s. Most chefs didn't even know there was no truffle in their truffle oil, as Daniel Patterson confessed in a 2007 *New York Times* piece titled "Hocus-Pocus, and a Beaker of Truffles":

> When I discovered truffle oil as a chef in the late 1990's, I was thrilled. So much flavor, so little expense. I suppose

I could have given some thought to how an ingredient that cost $60 an ounce or more could be captured so expressively in an oil that sold for a dollar an ounce. I might have wondered why the price of the oils didn't fluctuate along with the price of real truffles; why the oils of white and black truffles cost the same, when white truffles themselves were more than twice as expensive as black; or why the quality of oils didn't vary from year to year like the natural ingredients. But I didn't. Instead I happily used truffle oil for several years (even, embarrassingly, recommending it in a cookbook), until finally a friend cornered me at a farmers' market to explain what I should have known all along. I glumly pulled all my truffle oil from the restaurant shelves and traded it to a restaurant down the street for some local olive oil.

But many chefs did not trade in their truffle oil, with good reason. A lot of people love 2,4-dithiapentane. To them, that's what truffle is. And because it costs so little, it can be used without restraint, a bawdy "slap in the face," as the Los Angeles food critic Jonathan Gold put it. Replace that with the delicate flavor of real truffles, and many people are disappointed.

The same goes for truffle products—the truffle butters, oils, sauces, honeys, salts, zests, potato chips, and popcorn that are the backbone of the industry. The flavor of real truffles is much too volatile to preserve. Instead, virtually every product on the market gets its truffle scent from dithiapentane or another chemical. On the label, this gets listed as truffle "aroma," "flavor," "essence," or even "natural truffle flavor." (It can be called "natural" if the raw material used to make the chemical came from a plant, usually corn.)

That was the impetus for a class-action lawsuit in the United States in 2017 that charged the major truffle companies with "false, misleading, and deceptive misbranding" for calling their truffle oil "truffle oil." After a flurry of press coverage and theatrical outrage, the suits were later dismissed. As long as the ingredients lists were accurate, judges ruled, it was up to the consumer to know the deal.

To me, the use of synthetic truffle aroma in these products was no freakier than the "natural flavorings" used in other packaged products, but the products themselves had no appeal. Anthony Bourdain called truffle oil "about as edible as Astroglide, and made from the same stuff" on *The Tonight Show* in 2017, which seemed about right to me. It was the antithesis of my innocent pas de deux in Barolo. And what was missing, of course, was nature.

The tragedy of truffles is that the sensual thrill of this subterranean wonder has been commodified into a mass-market signifier of luxury. It struck me as no coincidence that truffles are always compared to diamonds, another scintillating denizen of the underworld that has become so tied to its price tag that the original thrill is almost beside the point.

The De Beers of truffles is Urbani Tartufi, the Italian giant that controls about three-fourths of the global truffle enterprise. That's what Urbani says, anyway, and no one else is in a position to call them on it. Truffle people do not keep very good records.

In the mid-1800s, the Urbani family began buying truffles from local hunters in Umbria and exporting them to France, which was already consuming more truffles than its own hunters could supply. At first the business was all fresh truffles, but Urbani soon embraced canning and bottling to solve its transport challenges. Urbani kept expanding, hiring more and more buyers to acquire more and more truffles from hunters throughout Italy and France, and selling them across the globe. It even acquired Tartufi Morra, Giacoma Morra's original Alba truffle company.

Urbani is helmed by Olga Urbani, the great-great-granddaughter of company founder Constantine Urbani. For a taste of Olga, just check out the *60 Minutes* piece on the company, twelve minutes of cringe that embraces every myth in the book and features dialogue seemingly written by Dr. Seuss. ("Trafficked like drugs! Stolen by thugs!") The alarmingly tan and raven-haired Olga, holding forth in a truffle patch in a lavish fur coat and black leather gloves, seems straight out of central casting, and the movie being cast is the latest Bond flick, with Olga as SPECTRE mastermind. It's easy to see how Urbani epitomizes what most people think of when they think of truffles: luxury, decadence, retro Europe, and above all, money.

Urbani's reputation as the SPECTRE of truffles was sealed in the 1990s, when two species of truffles from China—*Tuber indicum* and *Tuber himalayensis*—began turning up in the international supply. *Himalayensis*, in particular, was visually indistinguishable from *Tuber melanosporum*, but both Chinese species were flavorless. Mixed into a shipment of *melanosporum*, however, or in packaged products augmented by synthetic truffle oil, they were hard to spot. (One experienced Italian hunter told me to scratch the skin: *melanosporum* should have a fine layer of brown beneath the surface; *himalayensis* will be all black.)

Chinese truffles are found in the high reaches of southern China and Tibet. Ripe, they have a decent, if mild, aroma. They were never popular in China, but once their export value was discovered, they were rampantly overharvested with rakes, hoes, and plows, instead of dogs. The truffles were completely unripe, but they shipped well, which was more important to buyers. Unfortunately, such evisceration of the soil, sometimes a foot deep, tends to wipe out the fungi that make the truffles.

In the 1990s the going rate for Chinese truffles was about $25 a kilo—a tiny fraction of what *melanosporum* commanded—so mixing them into a shipment was, as many people observed, like cutting baby powder into cocaine. Highly profitable—and highly illegal in Italy, where the Chinese truffles were banned altogether.

For years, rumors existed that Urbani dabbled in Chinese truffles, and in 1998 those rumors were confirmed when Italian police raided Urbani's Umbria warehouse and confiscated forty-seven tons of Chinese truffles.

Forty-seven tons! Let that sink in. All of France, spiritual center of the black winter truffle, produces less than thirty tons a year. Urbani had forty-seven tons of ersatz truffles in its warehouse at one random point in time.

According to testimonies, Urbani began by cutting Chinese truffles into its mix 30/70, but later it got greedier and sloppier—the usual *Goodfellas* arc. The company paid some big fines, but everyone avoided jail until 2001, when they were convicted of dodging millions of dollars of taxes. Even then, Olga's father Paolo just had to trundle around his palazzo in an ankle bracelet for a while.

To be fair, since 2001, Urbani has kept its nose clean. It gets a lot of truffles into the hands of a lot of people around the world. It isn't bad. It's just *big*. And the unfortunate truth is that it doesn't matter if your product is caviar or corn flakes, as soon as it becomes big business, it turns into a widget, and all you can think about is how to make it a more profitable widget.

If any food could resist this tendency, you'd think it would be truffles, every one of which represents some moment of grace for a hunter and a dog. Little balls of poignancy, their provenance and authenticity should be integral to their specialness. And yet, because white truffles are wild foods, hunted in secret and traditionally sold through informal networks, they have always had about as much backstory as people in the witness protection program. They just show up at chefs' back doors, dealt by large companies, small ones, and random dudes who just happened to have a few fall into their laps. Somehow the farm-to-table revolution that transformed almost every aspect of gastronomy bypassed truffles. There was a big black box between the Carlo Marendas of the world and the restaurants and festivals where these truffles appeared.

That seemed odd to me. Were chefs who could spot a subpar sea urchin at twenty yards really being fooled by ersatz or second-rate truffles? I didn't know. I'd never been a part of the truffle business.

But as luck would have it, I knew someone who had.

I knock on the former truffle dealer's Brooklyn door at 8:00 P.M. sharp. I'm packing wine and vanilla ice cream, as ordered. She has the pasta, the "banging good" Italian honey and sea salt to go with the ice cream, and the truffle I've shipped. I've brazenly proposed that we eat our way through a truffle dinner at her place while she spills her secrets. I promised to do dishes.

Deal, she said.

It's a bleak fall night in New York, and I shiver on the stoop as a wet wind mists me, but I'm feeling excited. I can't believe my luck. I'd no idea that this woman I've worked with, a hotshot in food media circles, has a past in truffles. I randomly found out, and now she's agreed to tell me about it.

Zelda (as I'll call her) opens the door. "I don't have a table or furniture yet," she says. "New apartment. Sorry."

"Did the truffle arrive?" I ask. I splurged. It seemed a small price to pay for primo intel.

"Yep. Smells great."

"That's all we need."

I follow her upstairs, hustle my ice cream into her freezer, pour some wine, and grate truffle into melted butter while Zelda boils linguine. Effortlessly urbane, she's one of those people who can be equally at home in a five-star restaurant or a roadside snack bar. "I started selling when I was twenty-four," she says as she stirs. "I'd worked in the restaurant world for five years, and I was really tired of waiting tables." She'd helped open Milk Bar. She'd been a line cook in New Orleans. She knew food. She'd also been freelancing for food magazines. But none of that was paying the bills. She needed dough.

Then she saw an online ad: LOOKING FOR TRUFFLE DEALER/ SORTER. Well, that got her attention. "I'd never had a truffle, could never afford it, but I'd always been fascinated by them," she tells me. "I mean, Aristotle? Byron? The magic. The mystery. I liked that no one can describe why they love it. And I liked the connection to nature."

Zelda looks up with a funny smile. "There was also this tragic beauty to it, because it's literally the plight of the female pig. She gets aroused, she's digging toward her lover, and then no one's there. The more I learned about them, the more I thought, 'This is really strange.'" She sips her wine. "And if it's strange, I'm in."

"Why?"

She thinks for a minute. "It reminded me of orchids. This organism that specializes in deception. We think we've got truffles. But it seems like they've got us."

She called the number listed. Yes, the position was still open. The next day, she took the PATH train out to Hoboken for an interview. She had to walk a mile through increasingly sketchy neighborhoods to reach the equally sketchy warehouse. "It looked like the kind of place where someone would be held hostage," she says. The office in the warehouse had 1980s brown carpeting that reminded her of her elementary school and shelves piled high with boxes that looked like they could topple at any moment. The smell was almost incapacitating.

It was a small Italian truffle company trying to survive against the Urbanis of the world. It seemed pretty shady, and Zelda's instincts told her to get out, but she didn't. She wanted to become a writer, and she could already tell this was good material. It was strange, and she was in.

I pry Zelda for scoops about creepy characters and dangerous deals, but she says she never encountered any. "The truffle people I met weren't like that."

"What were they like?"

She looks me up and down. "Dorks," she says. "Truffle people are dorks."

Every week, a Styrofoam box of white truffles, maybe thirty pounds, would be overnighted from Europe. It was Zelda's job to pick them up from the cargo hangars at JFK. "It was surreal," she says. "You'd walk into the cargo hangars, and there would be live puppies in one corner and dead bodies in boxes in the other—people who'd passed away overseas. And over on the side there'd be truffles and bananas." While she waited for her paperwork to clear customs, she'd hang out in the waiting room with the undertakers. They had cigars and nice leather shoes.

The next day, she'd try to sell the truffles to chefs in New York. She found herself riding the subway with an insulated camo backpack filled with thousands of dollars' worth of truffles and a little pink coke scale. "People would literally be saying, 'Who farted?' And I'd just think, 'What am I doing with my life?'"

But wasn't it romantic to be walking into famous restaurants with an ingredient that makes people swoon?

Zelda scoffs. "I never enjoyed it. It was always a hustle. The chefs were assholes. They'd say, 'Urbani was just here, and their price is half of yours.'"

And then she shocks me with information many others would confirm: nobody buys truffles based on smell. The ultimate aromatic ingredient sells on looks alone. Everyone wants smooth, round, golfball-sized truffles that they can shave tableside into perfect wafers for their big-spending clients.

She also found that truffles were victims of the dysfunction of the restaurant world. "The famous European truffle companies have a tradition of hiring women with big boobs to deal their truffles. And these dudes will buy whatever, because it's all about the dick-measuring. They want to show off. Well, I'm five-foot-one, and I look like the babysitter just walked in. How was I going to compete?"

She tried educating chefs on quality and freshness, urging them to just *smell* her best truffles, but that just wounded their pride. "One thing truffles taught me is that chefs are vulnerable,"

Zelda says. "They rarely have the chance to learn about ingredients like the people who are selling those ingredients." That's especially true with a rare, expensive ingredient like truffles. "Even the best chefs don't see really good truffles very often. They think they know, but they don't. So they're being sold bullshit every day." And they are at the mercy of the trade.

Worn down after years of trying to sell this precious ingredient to people who couldn't have cared less about the magic or mystery or the plight of the female pig, Zelda burned out. "It was such a rat race. My phone was blowing up all the time. I'd get texts from chefs at two in the morning, at the end of service, saying hey, we need four hundred grams of white by eleven A.M. And I knew that if I didn't get to them in time, someone else would."

And if she didn't get it to someone, it was going to die. White truffles last just a few days, and they lose water weight all the time. "Every day I didn't move things, I was losing a ton of money."

Truffles can also break apart, which doesn't change their aromatic power at all, but it renders them useless in the eyes of chefs. Once, says Zelda, that provided her with a rare moment of bliss. She was driving down to the New Jersey warehouse, and hadn't had breakfast, and happened to have some useless shards of white truffle in the cooler. So she bought a bagel—toasted so the cream cheese was warm enough to awaken the truffle vapors—and grated the broken truffle shards all over it. Zelda sighs wistfully, summoning her inner Proust, and maybe her inner Byron, too. "That may have been the best thing I ever ate."

But that was it, she adds. "For three years, I was dealing a product I could never afford to eat. And I was still broke." That aspect of the job—pawning a product for the privileged few—began to bother her more and more as time passed. As Zelda puts it, with a wistful nod toward her bowl, "Who gets to eat truffles?"

Long after our dinner is over, that question stays with me. Who does get to eat truffles? Is their status as edible jewelry a necessary result of rarity, perishability, and byzantine supply chains? Or is there room for a grassroots revolution that connects truffle lovers with truffle hunters—or with the woods themselves?

I don't know. But I do know that before I can answer, I need to understand more about Big Truffle. And for that, all arrows point toward Italy.

6

Big Truffle

The central Italian region of Umbria sits between Le Marche, to the east, and Tuscany, to the west, and in everything from economy to spirit it occupies the same middle ground. Not quite so much forest as Le Marche, but not nearly so many vines as Tuscany. And while its medieval stone towns draw more visitors than Le Marche, they don't get the full Tuscan crush.

Truffles are one of the few areas where Umbria has eclipsed its rock-star cousin, though it wasn't always so. The Tuscans brought truffle culture to Umbria in the 1800s, after having learned it from the Piedmontese. They'd stay in Umbrian houses, borrow Umbrian pigs, then venture off into the rich Umbrian oak forests with said swine, never explaining what they were up to.

At the end of the season they'd head back to Tuscany, bags stuffed with some mysterious fruit of the forest. "We're going to leave the pigs here," said the Tuscans. "On one condition. You must promise to eat the pigs."

Sure thing, said the Umbrians.

Well, the Umbrians did not eat all the pigs. And soon they were trufflers, too. The wives learned to follow the pigs into the forest with a bucket of grain. When the pigs began to dig, they would bang on the buckets and throw some grain, and the pigs would leave the truffle just long enough for someone to grab it.

Umbria's forests were especially rich in black truffles, both the summer and winter varieties, and soon Urbani had cut out the Tuscans and carved out a nice business for itself, buying local truffles and selling them to France. In the 1900s, other Umbrians got in on the game, and the region became an unlikely truffle powerhouse.

Today, Urbani Tartufi claims to control 70 percent of the truffle trade. Sabatino Tartufi, its archrival, calls itself "the world's largest truffle company." You do the math.

But the more important math is fairly easy: the biggest players in Italian truffles are not located anywhere near Alba or Piedmont. They are in central Italy. From their respective redoubts in rural Umbria, just a couple of valleys apart, the two companies have waged a battle for truffle dominion. Urbani had a huge lead, and probably still does. It's the one company, according to truffle hunters, that buys so many truffles that it can manipulate the price. When Urbani buys hard, the price goes up for everyone. When they take a week off, people scramble to unload their truffles.

Sabatino is the smaller player with the friendlier reputation, the Lyft to Urbani's Uber. Several people pointed me in their direction for an honest accounting of what the truffle business was like. The company got its start in 1911 when Sabatino Balestra opened a store in Montecastrilli, a tiny hamlet in the green heart of Italy, as Umbria is known. At first it was a general provisions store, selling wine, wheat, olive oil, truffles, whatever they could grow or purchase locally, but by the 1980s the company had become a truffle specialist, and it launched its American operation in 2000.

Sabatino's big coup came in 2014. Oprah Winfrey had been obsessed with truffles since 2008, when she received a gift basket from Lisa Marie Presley that contained truffle salt. She fell hard for the seasoning, and made no secret of it. "When I travel," she wrote on her blog, "I have a jar, my assistant has a jar, security has a jar, and it's the one thing we request in a hotel: 'Can you make sure there's truffle salt in the room?'"

In 2014 Oprah publicly pined for a truffle hunt. "I'm a truffle freak," she declared. "I want to go to Alba and hunt with the pigs." Sabatino smartly swooped in and invited her to join them—even though it would be neither Alba nor pigs.

Oprah spent three days hunting and feasting in Umbria with the Balestra family and their dogs, and a fast friendship grew. They made sure she was never without a supply of their Truffle Zest—a mix of carob powder, truffle flavor, salt, and dried black summer truffles, in that order—and she made sure the rest of the world knew about it. Truffle Zest quickly became Sabatino's bestselling product. Oprah used it on television, tossed it into recipes in the magazine, and generally helped kick off a truffle-products frenzy in the United States that is still going strong. Today half the country seems to be lubed in truffle oil, and America has become Sabatino's stronghold.

The Sabatino mothership is a low-slung, flat-roofed, modern stone rectangle set into a sloping hillside in Montecastrilli, more Frank Lloyd Wright than Michelangelo. The top-floor lobby plays all the luxury truffle tropes: gleaming marble, polished oak, a glass-walled tasting room, and a giant fake tree rising from the floor and extending its branches into the ceiling. Shelves in the lobby display jars of Sabatino products like truffle olive oil, truffle sauce, truffle cream, truffle zest, truffle salt, and truffle honey, along with menus from multicourse truffle blowouts in the past.

A long-haired blond in a blue Mini Cooper pulls up outside, bounds up the steps, and introduces herself as Giuseppina Balestra, one of the five Balestra siblings—Sabatino's grandchildren—that run the company. She manages the Umbria factory while her brother Federico runs the U.S. operation from New York. "We speak every day," she says. "It's like he's here. We have a big fight one day, and the next we're back to normal."

Giuseppina wears jeans and sneakers and has a throaty laugh that makes me think of cigarettes and good times. She's no SPECTRE operative. "I'm a country peasant trapped in a corporate life," she confesses. "I used to get to hunt a lot, but not anymore." When I ask if she eats a lot of truffles, she waves off the question as absurd. "A baker doesn't want cake!"

Every week during truffle season, thousands of pounds of fresh truffles flow into the Sabatino factory. Some come directly from locals, but like other big operations, Sabatino buys from hunters and middlemen throughout Le Marche, Umbria, Tuscany, and Molise—the Appennino Centrale, the mountain range that bisects Italy. "That's really the heart of Italian truffles," Giuseppina says.

What about Alba? I ask.

A shrug and a smile. "My hat's off to them."

Her phone rings. It's a truffle hunter looking to sell. "I'm here," she says. In addition to managing the factory, Giuseppina handles the buying of the local whites directly. At €1,500 a kilo, it's too risky for an inexperienced eye. Every truffle must be haggled over. Although Sabatino has long-standing relationships with some hunters, there are no contracts. "Just trust. If I haven't seen them in a while, I wonder who they're selling to."

As we wait, Giuseppina wonders if the hunter's truffles will be decent. The summer in Italy had been crazy dry, and the truffles—which depend on summer rain to ripen—were behind schedule. Late October should have been the beginning of prime season, but the hunters were reporting very few biancos in central Italy. Everyone hoped it was just a slow start.

The hunter arrives, carrying a small blue vinyl bag. Renzo is a portly grandfather type with a white beard, a torn blue sweater, and muddy hiking boots. Trailing him is a younger hunter in camo, who never says a word. They shed a trail of dried mud as they trudge across the glossy white marble floor.

Renzo has been selling to Sabatino for decades, and he and Giuseppina have their choreography down. After much cheek kissing, Giuseppina steps behind the green marble buying counter and produces an electronic scale, while Renzo unzips his vinyl bag, removes two frozen bottles of water serving as ice packs, and lifts out a small paper bag. "Seco, seco, seco," he says, shaking his head. *So dry out there.* "But I found some good stuff." He dumps the bag on the counter. Out tumble a dozen shriveled white truffles.

Giuseppina scowls. "Boy, are these ugly," she says in her smoky rasp, digging at them with a green-handled paring knife and rolling them around as if she's trying to find their good side. "Who did you sell the good stuff to?"

Renzo turns to me in operatic exhaustion. "Don't be fooled just because she's blond and blue-eyed. She's a ball-breaker."

She cackles as she scrapes dirt off the truffles. A fine layer of duff covers the gleaming counter. "Oh, sure," Renzo says, "you take the dirt off now, but after I leave you're just going to put it back on when you sell to the next guy."

She cackles again, gouging soft spots. "Mamma mia, so ugly." Although the group includes a couple of large truffles, all are deeply furrowed. One is mottled with pinholes. She slices it open and white grubs wriggle out.

"That's a beauty," Renzo said.

"Fantastico," she says, moving it to a reject pile.

White truffles fall into three classes: Second, First, and Extra. First class, or Primo, means a normal good truffle: more than twenty grams, firm and round, good color, no rot, no mouse carnage, no wormholes. The kind chefs can use in the kitchen to produce pretty discs atop plates of tagliatelle. They usually sell for €2,000 per kilo or more.

Second class is for the bits that can't make nice slices but still can be used for cooking or products. If downgraded simply for size or incompleteness—not bugs, stink, or rot—they can be a steal.

Extra class are the showstoppers, the ones reserved for dining room theater. They have to be big and pretty. For that, they bring at least an extra €500 per kilo.

But Giuseppina confirmed what I'd learned from Zelda: scent is not a consideration.

Giuseppina gouges more and more gunk from the truffle furrows, adding each to the scale after cleaning. "These are definitely all Seconds."

"No, there's a couple of Primos in there," Renzo protests, pulling the best of the bunch off the scale.

Giuseppina holds up the truffle to show him where a snail has chewed a hole into one side. "Secondo."

"That just shows it tastes good!"

She returns it to the scale and glances at me. "He's a good friend, but his truffles are shit. Seriously, Renzo, where are the good ones?"

"Oh, wait." He smacks himself in the head and digs into his blue bag. "I almost forgot." Out comes a second paper bag yielding half a dozen fat, round truffles, aroma pouring off of them. On their website, Sabatino describes this scent as "deep-fried sunflower seeds or walnuts," which is the kind of unexpected description that only comes after long exposure.

Giuseppina chuckles appreciatively and takes her knife to the truffles, but there's much less to remove.

Renzo points at my pen and pad. "Tell everyone I brought good stuff." I lean in close, snort, and exclaim happily. He turns triumphantly to Giuseppina. "See!"

She glares at me and wags a finger. She clears the Secondi off the scale and replaces them with most of the new batch, removing the most questionable. Renzo gingerly grabs the two best of the Seconds and adds them to the scale with the Primos. "I'd say these make the cut."

"And I'd say they don't," she replies, pulling them back off. Back and forth they go.

"What about this one?"

"No."

"This one?"

"No."

"Not even this?" It's a small, pretty truffle, though far from perfect. With a hint of a smile, Giuseppina allows it to stay on the scale. Conveniently, it brings the Primos to an even 300 grams. She records that number in her ledger, removes the Primos, and adds the rest, for another 844 grams.

While Giuseppina and Renzo disappear into a back room for payment, I take a stab at the math. At €1,500 a kilo for the Secondi, that would be €1,266. Plus another €600 for the Primi (at €2,000 a kilo), for a total of €1,866. Not bad for a week of hunting in a crappy season. Renzo has to split his take with the young guy, so he certainly isn't getting rich, but it seems like pretty great beer money to me. As Italy struggles with high unemployment—especially its youth unemployment rate, which has hovered around 30 percent for years—truffle hunting has become an increasingly important, if undercounted, way for many guys to make a few bucks. Grab your dog, get lost in the woods, walk out richer than you walked in.

But that has led to new problems. "There's so many more people in the woods now," Giuseppina tells me upon her return, "and a lot of the new people don't know the forests. They don't close up their holes properly. The environment is getting compromised."

Not only that, but with so many more people finding and selling fresh truffles, profits are disappearing. "Anybody can sell fresh truffles," she says. "There are no regulations. And there's always somebody willing to sell a truffle a euro cheaper than us. Even the hunters themselves sell straight on the internet now!"

And then she surprises me. With such impossible margins, white truffles have become an almost insignificant part of their business. In fact, all fresh truffles combined make up only a small percentage. The important stuff?

"Follow me."

〜〜〜

We pull on hairnets and head downstairs to the factory floor. Whatever fantasies I've had about the seamy netherworld of the "real" truffle business are immediately dispelled in the fluorescent glare of spotless, antiseptic tiles, floor drains, stainless steel walk-ins, and gleaming German cooking and bottling machinery. It looks like every other factory I've toured—with good reason, Giuseppina explains. While there are no restrictions on the fresh truffle trade, regulations for conserved products are becoming stricter and stricter. "We have to be FDA certified for most international accounts now," she says. "We get inspected all the time."

So much for noir romance. What about the backroom deals? The rakish smugglers? She rolls her eyes and laughs. After the Urbani kerfuffle, Italy forced most of the truffle underground into the light years ago with the inspections, the paperwork, and a law requiring truffle companies to name the hunter they bought each truffle from. Does this law get flouted? *Naturalmente.* Is it still turning Big Truffle into something almost disappointingly normal? *Certamente.*

On the factory floor, women in white coats and hairnets are meticulously cleaning black truffles before feeding them into the Rube Goldberg apparatus where they are canned, jarred, and transmogrified into sauces, oils, and powders. "We do more R&D than anyone in the industry," Giuseppina says. "We invented Zest right here. It was the first powdered truffle product. Then everybody copied us."

The best truffles are sold fresh, but most are frozen, canned, and used in products, and nothing is wasted. "In Italy, we say the truffle is like a pig," Giuseppina tells me. "Every part of it gets used." Even the wash water from black truffles, which is full of truffle spores, goes back onto Sabatino's *tartufaia*—their cultivated black truffle grounds—to make future truffles.

Another surprise: most of the truffles Sabatino uses are black summers, *Tuber aestivum*, a species that grows wild throughout Europe, as far north as Sweden and as far east as Iran. Black summers are common as dirt. A million kilos come to market annually, with Bulgaria alone supplying somewhere around 300,000 kilos. A few years ago, Iranian dealers discovered the West's insatiable demand and dumped so many black summers on the market that the price plunged from the usual €200 per kilo to just €30–40.

And that's what makes black summers the backbone of the industry. Black winters and whites smell great, but they are far too expensive and rare to use in products. The only truffle that can keep the factory pipeline filled is the black summer.

The only problem? It has very little aroma. But that turns out not to be a problem after all. Any truffle is going to lose most of its prized aromatics during the canning process. The scent is going to be supplied by 2,4-dithiapentane and other chemicals, which is what most consumers prefer anyway, just as they prefer artificial strawberry flavoring to real strawberries. So there's no need to use any real truffles to make your product smell right to people.

But then there's the question of looks, ingredients lists, and authenticity. People do expect real bits of truffles in their truffle salt, truffle mac and cheese, truffle risotto, and truffle oil. And that is where *Tuber aestivum* shines. Its value is its ontological status. It's a real truffle, it looks great, it holds up, and unlike the Chinese truffles, it's legal. Part of the reason Chinese truffles are rarely seen today is because they've been displaced by black summers.

None of this is what I expected, but I begin to appreciate its necessity. The money that Urbani, Sabatino, and other large truffle companies make off their products allows them to stay in the fresh truffle game. And that's important. In my mind, I keep going back to the moment when Giuseppina allowed Renzo's obviously second-rate truffle to stay on the scale with the first-class group. There are webs of relation that no outsider is going to easily grasp.

So I'm willing to grant Big Truffle its zests and oils. But at the same time, I've spotted my first sign of a shakeup in the Truffleverse. Apparently some hunters are beginning to realize they don't need the big guys anymore. Now I just have to find them.

7

Tartufi Town

The name Acqualagna has a lovely ring to English ears, but it translates as "water slaughter" and refers to an ugly incident during the Gothic Wars of the 540s, when the Byzantine Empire and the Ostrogoths battled for control of Italy. The little town of Acqualagna had major strategic importance back then, straddling the Flaminian Way, the road that connected Rome and Ravenna through the limestone gorges of the Apennine Mountains, and for a while the waters of the Candigliano River ran red.

Today the Goths are gone, there are much faster routes to Ravenna, and Acqualagna has zero strategic import—unless one plans one's life around truffles. In that case, Acqualagna looms much larger than you'd expect for a town of four thousand sleepy souls in Italy's little-known Marche region, an hour north of Umbria. As the town VIPs are quick to tell me as soon as I arrive for the fifty-fourth Acqualagna National White

Truffle Fair, they, not those rich grandstanders up in Alba, are the center of the Truffleverse.

Hmmm, hard to believe, I counter. I mean, come on, *Alba?* Ninety years. Big names. International fame. And soooo many truffles.

We're standing in the main piazza, where the fair is centered. Truffle purveyors are setting up their booths on the cobblestones around the piazza, beneath the olive trees. At the high end of the piazza, the Urbani booth looms over them all. The unmistakable tang of white truffles mingles with the scents of coffee and cigarettes as people stream into the piazza from the side streets. It's a throwback crowd: men in sport coats, women in leather pants and catty sunglasses. Surely Marcello Mastroianni and Sophia Loren are lurking at a table just around the corner, drinking Campari.

I'm mingling with the mayor, the former mayor who still kind of thinks he's the mayor, the Chamber of Commerce people, and the tourism director. I've come because I've heard that this little-known fair is the small-town antithesis to Alba, and thus perhaps a little closer to the heart of truffle goodness, but I've just said the perfect thing to incite them all.

"Marketers!" That's the former mayor, Bruno Capanna, looking sharp in a black coat and tie, his graying hair slicked back. Admittedly, very good marketers. "Our local bank gives us two thousand euros per year for our festival. You know what Alba gets from their bank? A hundred and twenty thousand. But where do you think all their truffles come from?"

I shrug, playing dumb.

He tries another tack. "Look around the Alba countryside. What do you see?"

"Vineyards?"

"Look around Acqualagna. What do you see?"

I literally look around, even though that's not what he's suggesting. The two-story buildings surrounding the piazza are low enough to reveal green hillsides looming over the terracotta roofs. And beyond them, I know, are the vast forests of Le Marche.

"Trees," I say.

He smiles, resting his case.

It's true. Le Marche doesn't meet my cliched visions of Italy. No vineyards, no castles, no walled towns. Just mountains and forests and streams. Hiking trails and horseback rides. Farms and karst. It could be the Cumberland Gap.

Bruno presses his point. "We have the limestone, the high-pH soil, the climate. Most important, the clean and pure land. This is why the people in Le Marche live to be a hundred, longer than any other region in Italy."

Really, longer than anywhere else?

"Well, us and Sardinia. But of course they're more famous for it."

This has been Le Marche's beef for at least a thousand years. They're just too deep in the sticks. No one comes. So they send their truffles to Alba, and Alba gets the famous fair.

Le Marche was always the producer, Bruno explains, and it never got any respect. There are a thousand truffle hunters in the region. Seventy percent of Italy's truffle dogs are trained here. Two-thirds of Italian truffle production flows through Acqualagna. "You know all those products for sale at the Alba festival?"

Sadly, I do.

"Who do you think makes those? Alba has one company that makes its own products. We have ten."

The whole group is working itself into a well-rehearsed pique. Admittedly, Piedmont has sandier soil, not rocky like here, so their truffles are nice and round. But Acqualagna's have more aroma—truffles that have a hard life smell better.

Besides, Alba has no truffle but the white. Acqualagna is the only place in the world where you find truffles year-round: the white, the black summer, the black winter, and the spring white. In the past, the old truffle hunters would look at the houses in an area to tell what kind of truffles grew there. If they saw sandstone houses, they knew it would be good for white truffles. If redstone, that was a black truffle area.

As I take this in, I scan the piazza. Half the storefronts are truffle shops. The other half are restaurants serving truffles. We're standing outside the Museo del Tartufo di Acqualagna. The window of the blacksmith shop displays an assortment of *vanghetti*, which in Le Marche feature a sharp notch cut out of one corner of the blade for severing tree roots. The town used to have an official public truffle scale. (Though nobody used it.) It still hosts the National Truffle Exchange, which sets the official price for white truffles each day. (Nobody pays attention.) When Prince Albert wanted to put in a truffle orchard in England, he consulted with Giorgio Remedia, Acqualagna's most famous truffle hunter.

In other words, Alba is a wealthy city that happens to throw a big truffle festival for a few weekends each fall, but Acqualagna is a small town whose entire existence depends on *tartufi*. For too many decades it has toiled in Alba's shadow. And now, it believes, it has what the world wants.

The Acqualagna brain trust has actually been working on this since 1966, when its hunters and producers formed an association to establish the Acqualagna brand, launching the festival in partnership with Urbani. They've had some success. Today, Acqualagna is known for truffles among Italians, thousands of whom make the trek out to Le Marche for the festival. International recognition, on the other hand, has been elusive. As far as I can tell, my presence raises the grand total of native English speakers to one.

Now the truffle booths are filling up with tantalizing lumps, so I excuse myself and walk over to sniff a beautiful pile of black summer truffles. Great looks, bland as wood.

The Tartufi Tofani booth is showing off some monster whites atop mossy beds under glass bells, like fungal terrariums. The booth is staffed entirely by blond women of various ages but singular features, all members of the sprawling Tofani family, which, it turns out, cofounded the fair in 1966 and is a behind-the-scenes powerhouse in the truffle world. They've got baskets of golfball-sized truffles, displayed on traditional blue plaid cloth, just like in Alba, for €50. Racquetball truffles are €100, and baseballs are €300.

The rock stars are under glass. In the center of them all is a bowling ball of a truffle, a beige mass of spheroids melded into a grooved meteorite, both horrifying and spectacular. When I ask Signora Tofani the weight, she grabs my notepad and jots down "1,143 grams." Two and a half pounds.

Biggest this year?

Biggest in *ten* years.

Who found it?

She sizes me up. A local guy, she says, and that's enough on that subject. I ask how she'll sell such a thing. Who can afford it?

Already sold, she replies. To an Italian client in America. It leaves for New York in an hour.

She lifts the glass so I can have a smell, but the first sniff almost knocks me backward. Size matters with truffles. The little ones tickle your consciousness. The big ones wrap their tentacles around your face like the thing in *Alien*.

Signora Tofani snaps me out of my daze and waves me away so she can recap her truffle. She points toward the theater bordering the piazza. Sorry, time for its big moment. She hefts the truffle and its glass bell and staggers toward the theater. I follow, curious. Outside the door, she confers with the town VIPs, who wave me inside.

I grab a seat in the dark theater, which is filling up fast. Projected onto the big screen behind the stage is a surprisingly artistic image of a hound with drooping oak leaves for ears and a body composed of truffles, dirt, moss, and leaves, a *vanghetto* crossed in front. A harpist plucks the notes of Pachelbel's Canon while luminaries gather onstage.

It's an impressive lineup: the mayor of Acqualagna, the president of the truffle-producer association, the president of the province of Pesaro and Urbino, and the president of the whole Marche region. Each puts in their two cents on the awesomeness of Acqualagna truffles. Then the Italian secretary for economic development weighs in. Everybody is excited about Lonely Planet, which has just named Le Marche its No. 2 destination for the year.

Then the harpist fires up Pachelbel again, the lights go up, and down the center aisle comes Signora Tofani, hoisting the giant truffle terrarium in her upturned arms like a chalice. She plows through a gauntlet of camera crews from the national television networks, feels her wobbly way up the steps to the stage, and gets a standing ovation, in part because we're all relieved she made it. Gold medals with red, white, and green ribbons are draped around every neck, we get a few final words on the joys of truffles, and then the crowd breaks up and Signora Tofani hustles away to Cryovac her package and hand it over to DHL.

Out in the light, the crowd is sampling truffle products and munching on fried olives stuffed with pork and served in paper cones, a local specialty. I duck into the surprisingly hip Museo del Tartufo di Acqualagna, which features a floor-to-ceiling cardboard truffle, all abstract triangles, emerging from one corner of the lobby.

The next room holds a lush diorama showing how truffles grow amid tree roots. There's an extensive truffle history going back to ancient times, highlighted by the creation of the dish tagliatelle alla Benito Mussolini, to honor the night Il Duce stopped in town for a truffle dinner while traveling from Rome to his home town of Predappio. (In 1936, locals actually sculpted Mussolini's giant profile out of the face of the Furlo Gorge, just down the road from Acqualagna, but it was destroyed by partisan bombs a few years later.)

In the basement, projected against an ancient stone wall, a short film documents an imaginary debate over the merits of black and white truffles between local boy Gioachino Antonio Rossini and French truffle fiend Alexandre Dumas. (If you can't guess who was championing which truffle, you haven't been paying attention.)

In the next room, two giant sensory wheels, complete with sniffing tubes, break down the experience of black winter and white truffles as if they were chardonnay and pinot noir.

Black winter: Hay, black olive, hazelnut, walnut, Emmentaler cheese, cocoa, glutamate, honey, licorice, leek.

White: Butter, sulfur match, hydrocarbon, shiitake mushroom, honey, star anise, vanilla, garlic, celeriac, acacia, hazelnut, underbrush.

Spot-on. Somebody at the truffle museum knows their shit.

Seized by a sudden hankering for acacia-scented underbrush, I head back out to the piazza. But as I wander, snarfing samples of crostini with black truffle sauce and focaccia dipped in white truffle oil, it isn't garlicky acacia I smell so much as the sulfurous match of 2,4-dithiapentane. The square is an orgy of synthetic truffle, just as Alba was.

Although each booth has a pile of fresh truffles in the center, the rest of the space is piled with jars and packages of truffle oils, truffle sauces, truffle creams, truffle salts, truffle bruschetta, truffle cheese, truffle pâté, truffle pasta, truffle salumi. Every jar I check lists aroma or flavor in the ingredients. As charming and authentic as Acqualagna is, business is business, and the business of truffles is done in boxes and jars.

And so I say my goodbyes, slam an espresso, and head for Tuscany. There, I have a date with a guy who is most certainly not part of the truffle establishment, a purist who wouldn't be caught dead near a bottle of 2,4-dithiapentane, and would be equally unlikely to be seen at a table with Marcello and Sophia. In fact, from what I've been told, he's barely domesticated at all.

8

Moon in Crescendo

E xactly one year after my fruitless hunt with Carlo Marenda, I find myself standing in yet another Italian night, this time in a chilly drizzle, awaiting a guy I hope will bring me better luck. I've asked Matteo Giuliani, my truffle date, for authenticity: No pre-burying, just you and the dogs and fate, do what you always do. No problem, he replied. Hope you like to get up early.

The villa I'm renting is down a long gravel driveway, shrouded by trees, and the darkness is absolute. Standing there with water pouring off my hood at 5:00 A.M., it feels very unlikely that anyone is about to pick me up.

But I'm wrong. At 4:55, lights hurtle down the driveway. A beat-up blue Nissan four-by-four, rain coursing across its headlights, skids to a stop on the gravel, inches from my toes. I hop in, sharing the passenger seat with a vicious-looking *vanghetto*.

Matteo shoots me a vigorous grin. He seems Marine-like, in camo gear from head to toe, with a headlamp pulled over his buzz cut. Over the camo gear he's got a vest and chaps made from some sort of industrial-strength mesh. I glance at my flimsy Patagonia rain gear and wonder what I'm in for.

"Lucky day!" Matteo says, pointing toward the shrouded sky. "Moon in crescendo!"

I nod. That's good for truffles?

"Crescendo moon, crescendo truffles," he says. "No moon, no truffles."

Good year so far?

"No. No truffles."

None?

"Very bad," he says. "Very bad." It's the dryness. Truffles begin to form after summer rains and fungal snogging, nurtured on a slow IV drip from the roots. But the summer was parched, and so far the truffles are a no-show.

"But today," Matteo says, flashing that optimistic grin, "lucky day!"

We speed into the Tuscan night. Matteo drives like someone who wants to get the driving part of the trip out of the way as quickly as possible, the suspension on the jacked-up Nissan bouncing like a toy. From the green metal box in the back of the truck, I can hear the scrape of claws seeking purchase as we careen around corners, the *vanghetto* rocking beside me.

We blow past all four hundred meters of Ghizzano, a ridgetop strip of stone and stucco houses dominated by the Venerosi Pesciolini estate and winery, trace a twisting side road down through vineyards, and drop into the fog. The vineyards are part of Tenuta di Ghizzano, an acclaimed biodynamic wine made by Ginevra Venerosi Pesciolini—a twenty-sixth-generation contessa whose family has been in Tuscany since the year A.D. 1000, give or take, and in the tiny burg of Ghizzano, pop. 312, since 1370—and who, through a wine-importer friend, was how I found myself in the Terre di Pisa, as this off-piste corner of Tuscany is called.

Ginevra's family has always made wine. Like most wine-makers in Italy, they embraced chemical-intensive conventional farming approaches in the second half of the twentieth century, but in the early 2000s Ginevra looked at the poor condition of the land and decided to convert to organic and biodynamic production.

Biodynamic farming is all about balance. The birds and the bees, the vines and the trees, the minerals and the mycelial threads all play a role in strengthening the system. To maintain that balance, only 20 of Tenuta di Ghizzano's 280 hectares are planted in vines. Another 15 hectares are olives for the estate's excellent oil, 100 are chickpeas and farro, and the rest are preserved as wood-lands and poplar groves. And from those woods come what may be the world's only certified organic white truffles.

Ghizzano sits on a fold of limestone, ancient seabed, which gives it the ideal conditions for mineral wines and white truf-fles. Half the people in Ghizzano go truffling, with Matteo foremost among them. Matteo is a hunter to the depths of his soul, Ginevra told me. His father was a hunter. His grandfather. Truffles, boar, you name it. They don't always hunt when and where they're supposed to, but hey, good energy.

In recent years Matteo has channeled that energy into his truffle business, I Tartufi di Teo, selling to a few restaurants around the Terre di Pisa. But it was dicey, for all the reasons Sabatino had already explained to me: low margins, unreliable supply, dodgy restaurants, always some sketchball willing to sell his truffle for a euro less.

Ginevra had a better idea: Transform Ghizzano into a biody-namic truffle destination, and maybe bring some income to the locals. She was helping Matteo turn a villa on the estate into San Luigi Farm, a truffle shop, hunting ground, and guest house all in one. They envision people coming to Ghizzano for a guided truffle hunt on the estate, then a tasting in the Taverna del Tartufaio and maybe a bottle of vino in the Tenuta di Ghizzano cantina—*agriturismo* at its finest.

Ginevra's land isn't producing right now, Matteo explains, so we're headed for the deep woods. Soon we're barreling down dirt roads through a Tuscan landscape no tourist office has ever promoted, not a Lombardy poplar in sight, just thick green brush flashing past in the headlights and whipping the truck as we tunnel through.

I notice that the odometer on the truck is well over 300,000 kilometers and point admiringly. "All truffle hunting," Matteo says proudly. "Tutti!" He holds up two fingers. "Two autos for Matteo. One for family. One for truffles." On email, we'd been corresponding in long, comfortable paragraphs, but it's clear that his English is as limited as my Italian. Google Translate has fooled me again. For the rest of the day, we gesture and grunt like cavemen.

Matteo thumps his chest as we drive. "Three generation truffle hunter." He counts on his hand, starting with the thumb, while driving with the other. "Grandfather. Father. Matteo." He has a soul patch under his lip and big brown eyes that hide nothing.

I ask about his earliest truffle memory. "Five years old!" he says without hesitation. "Grandfather come home and give me truffle. I smell and say, 'Ahhhh, this is my life!'" He turns those brown eyes on me with startling intensity. "For me, every truffle is same emotion. Every time!"

That's a lot of emotion, I say gingerly, suddenly remembering that his brochure promised guests would get to experience the "emotion" of truffle hunting. It's clearly an important word for him. I ask how often he eats truffles.

He makes a fist and shakes it in the cab between us. "Every day!" he says, conviction jumping off him like sparks. "Every day!"

You had me at crescendo, I think, heart melting. It isn't hard to see the five-year-old who fell for truffles. All that's changed is his *vanghetto* is much bigger now.

We rattle down a dirt rut, pull off the side, and hop out. I've no idea where we are; dripping black woods that could be almost anywhere on the planet. Matteo clicks his headlamp and opens a door in the green box on the back of the truck, and two midsize dogs leap out, one black (Artu) and one white (Miro). If anything, they're even more amped than Matteo.

In most parts of Europe, hunters generally keep their truffle dogs kenneled outside the house. It's a more formal relationship than in the United States. The dogs are working dogs. They know their role, and the rules and rewards are fairly rigid. Many hunters have several dogs. They think of them almost like golf clubs—you need different ones for different tasks. Some find black truffles. Some don't. Big ones for long-distance hunts. Small ones to check under brush. And sometimes it's nice to have a tiny one that you can just carry around and point, like a metal detector. The hunts are some of the few times the dogs get out, and they lean into it like huskies strapped to the sled.

Artu and Miro tear into the woods. Matteo slings his *vanghetto* over his shoulder and charges after them like Rambo. I snap on my own headlamp and try to keep up, thorny vines tearing at my clothes and occasionally my face.

"No facsimile, eh?" Matteo calls over his shoulder.

It's a Google Translate word, for sure, but a good one. *Si*, I reply. No facsimile.

Our lights fall on the dogs exploring a stream bank. The terrain is remarkably similar to where I'd hunted with Carlo: forested river bottom, rain-slicked clay, a creek trickling nearby. I'm starting to get a sense of these truffles: the whites like the wet lowlands, the blacks the well-drained highlands.

Matteo calls to the dogs every few seconds, a low, guttural "Hey," as if he's trying to intimidate a bear. It's impossible to keep our lights on them as they dash through the fog and undergrowth and scramble under fallen trees. The vines are vicious, like pushing through a hanging curtain of raspberry bushes.

Matteo's light falls on Miro, who has stopped to explore the mud at the foot of a stump. "Hey, hey!" he shouts, tearing ahead through the prickers. I race after him. But as soon as we arrive, Miro lifts his head and moves on. Matteo's shoulders sag.

No truffle?

Matteo shrugs. "Animal smell, maybe."

So it goes for two hours. Lots of false alarms. No truffles. Weariness creeps in. A sickly gray light suffuses the forest. The rain has overcome my Patagonia. Mud splatters my legs. My cheek is wet with blood. And I have nothing to show for it. People do this for a living?

Even Matteo's bravado is crumbling like a sandcastle in the rain. But then, hope: the dogs seem excited about a spot on the vertical bank of the stream. He pushes them aside, sticks his own nose in the dirt, and shouts, "Yes, I think!" He yanks his *vanghetto* off his shoulder, excavates, sticks his nose in the hole again, digs some more, smells again . . . and pauses.

He calls Artu back over for a spot check. Artu gives the hole a once-over, shoots Matteo a "get real" look, and moves on.

And that's it for Matteo. "No truffle," he whispers, pulling himself to his feet. He looks at me sternly. "You see," he says, "this is no facsimile." He closes his eyes, face crumpling, and leans his head against the handle of his *vanghetto*, murmuring almost inaudibly, "No facsimile."

It's a dark moment, there in the first light. As promised, I'm experiencing the emotion of a real truffle hunt. It's just not the emotion I'd bargained for.

"No good year," he whispers to the tool. "No lucky days."

First Carlo, then Matteo. I'm beginning to wonder if I'm a truffle albatross. They just don't like me, which is all the more hurtful, because I so like them. Perhaps they're taunting me on purpose. Perhaps that's just the nature of *Tuber magnatum*.

For a long time, we stand defeated in the forest, listening to the patter of rain on the leaves. The dogs gaze up at us, confused. I consider telling Matteo to go on without me, to save himself.

But then he raises his head and opens his eyes. "Espresso?"

Totally, I reply.

〜〜〜〜

Every bar in Italy serves more or less the same menu, but for some reason we have to go to one that's a good thirty minutes away. By now it's morning for normal people. Half the cars we pass give us a honk and a wave. The blue Nissan is famous. Matteo salutes, his smile creeping back into place. A passing truck flashes its lights. "Truffle hunter," Matteo says. As we drive, he keeps up a running minimalist commentary on the passing groves of trees. "Good. Good . . . No good."

I begin to discern a pattern. The good spots tend to be stands of poplars along the river, their pale trunks and yellow leaves standing out like Impressionist paintings. I see another stand ahead and point. "Good?"

"Very. In *Diciembre.*" He points at his noggin and winks. "Esperienza!"

I try again. "Good?"

A pained look crosses Matteo's face. "Yes. But *zona* not for Matteo. *Zona* for friend of Matteo."

Like lobstering, I think. Take a wild resource and enough time, and the locals will work it out, no government required.

The bar is packed with truffle hunters, winemakers, and grumpy old men. As we down espressos and dry ham sandwiches, they ask Matteo how the season is going. "Minimale, minimale," he says, shaking his head sadly, the lament of every forager and fisherman I've ever known.

By the second espresso our optimism is restored. "Secret spot?" Matteo asks.

Yeah, I reply, secret spot.

Secret Spot is down a pull-off just off the main road, tucked into high brush. But it holds another car. Matteo coasts up behind the empty hatchback, knuckles in his mouth, and considers the situation. "This hunter no good," he says. "Dog no good. No danger for truffles." He starts to open his door, but then stops. Knuckles back in mouth. "Can't see Matteo," he explains to me. "Other hunters see Matteo, then they know." He shakes his head in frustration and pulls out.

Matteo's phone rings, and he engages in a vicious argument while steering with one hand and one eye. Amid the shouting, I'm picturing divorce or worse, but eventually he hangs up and chirps, "My best friend! We say hi."

We follow a few kilometers of dirt roads and pull up beside another truck in the middle of Tuscan nowhere. Standing beside the truck, smoking, is a guy wearing the same boots, chaps, and vest as Matteo. He eyes my clothes skeptically. He and Matteo smoke a cigarette, compare truffle travails, and make plans to hunt *cinghiale*, wild boar, the "primary antagonist of truffle hunter," as Matteo puts it in Google-inflected English.

As much as Matteo loves hunting truffles, the boar hunt is the pinnacle of his year. And since boars will eat every truffle they can find—they can even tell which trees have mycorrhizae, years before the first truffles appear, and will eat those, destroying the mycelia—putting a little *cinghiale* in your freezer is a win-win.

We say our goodbyes, they jam out their cigarettes, and we head for our last hope.

~~~

"Here?" I ask, surprised. "Really?" It's a particular kind of place, very distinct, and of the many places I'd have thought to truffle, it would not have been one of them.

"Secret!" Matteo insists, jamming his finger into my chest, then holding it to his lips. "No one!" His brown eyes are wet with sincerity. "No one!"

Okay, okay, I'm not telling. But to my questioning look he explains, "Special permit with owner."

Righto. Soon we're cruising through a field, paralleling the edge of a wood. No thorns, no nettles. Heaven. Matteo exclaims delightedly, yanking a two-foot herb out of the ground and handing it to me. "Nepitella! Queen of *la cucina Toscana*!" It smells like a lively mix of oregano and horse mint, and I can't believe I've never heard of it.

In the open, it's easier to watch the dogs work. They're maestros, loping casually along the edge, nose low, zigzagging. Something catches one's attention and he turns on a dime and starts circling, slashing back and forth in a tightening cone, while the other charges over to get in on the action.

As the two converge far ahead, Matteo begins to accelerate, but their tails keep wagging slow and wide, they abandon the spot, and Matteo aborts his run, exhaling in frustration.

Minutes later, another convergence. This time the wags get tight and fast, and Matteo leans into a full charge, grunting, "Hey! Hey! Hey!"

Artu starts to dig tentatively with his front claws, nose right in the dirt, chuffing loudly as he works air across his sinuses—but then he blows it all out in an explosive sneeze and runs on.

Matteo slams to a dejected halt. "That," he says, "means no truffle."

That's our pattern. The dogs lope ahead, then dart to a random spot and start digging so often that we spend most of the next hour in a full sprint, Matteo waving his arms at the dogs but daring not shout. Eventually I forget we're truffling at all. It's more like we're just out for a weird run with the dogs, kind of nice, actually. The rain has ceased, the blood on my cheek has dried, and I'm trotting through Tuscany with a crazy man. No complaints.

And so I don't even notice when Artu starts digging harder with his paws and doesn't chuff. But Matteo notices, and he barrels across the turf in his camo like a recruit in basic training. He yanks Artu away, falls to his knees, plants his face in the hole Artu has begun, and squeals. "Yes, here!" he says, lifting handfuls of dirt to his nose like a cokehead. "Smell! Smell!"

I kneel beside him and stick my own nose in the hole. It smells like dirt. "Are you sure?"

"Yes, yes!" He eases his *vanghetto* into the hole and scrapes away a millimeter of dirt. "Smell!"

I lean in. I smell dirt. Grass. Moldy leaves. And then, peeking out of the interstices . . . a tickle of garlic? "I don't know," I say.

"Yes, yes!" he says again, pushing me aside and resuming surgery. Artu tries to dart in and help, but I pull him back. Matteo leans in and squeals again.

I stick my nose beside his. Now it smells like we're tunneling toward some distant underground trattoria. "Ecco!" I shout, hoping that's the right word.

Matteo ditches his *vanghetto* and switches to fingertips, whimpering softly. Something ivory crowns the surface at the bottom of the hole. Another moment of excavation and the thing yawns wide and fat, like an egg on its side. Matteo's whimpering rises an octave and his limbs wiggle like a puppy. He sits up and pats me rapidly on both shoulders, so I do the same back to him. We kneel there for a moment, thumping each other's shoulders and making happy noises. Then we yank the dogs away from the hole and go back in.

We spend the next five minutes digging around the truffle, until it sits on an earthen pedestal. White truffles have the lumpy, beige look of fossilized dinosaur bones, and this feels exactly like paleontology: the same thrill of discovery, slow reveal, and fear of a catastrophic nick.

Once we've gone deep enough to be certain the truffle doesn't continue downward, Matteo wiggles his *vanghetto* underneath and pops the truffle off its stand. I can smell the goaty garlic pouring off it, but it's shrouded in earthiness. Later I'll learn that the pure *magnatum* scent doesn't fully emerge until the truffle is cleaned and enclosed in the fridge for a few hours.

Somehow that truffle breaks the spell. The dogs sprint from success to success, and we fly after them, digging up the goodies. We pass a porcino the size of a bread plate, but Matteo just waves his hand. "Small money," he says without breaking stride.

True to his word, every time the dogs hit paydirt, Matteo is overcome. The fourth truffle we find is twice the size of the others, maybe eighty grams. By then it's clear we're going to have a big day, which is more emotion than Matteo can contain. He begins humming like a bomb about to detonate, brown eyes gone wide and urgent as he searches for an appropriate vessel to receive this eruption of feeling. He looks at the dogs, looks at me, and then his eyes fall on the poplar tree that hosted this truffle. He wraps his arms around the trunk, plants his lips against its bark, and gives it a long, sloppy kiss.

By late morning we've found ten truffles, and the dogs are mental toast. We load them back into the green box and pile our truffles into Matteo's lucky hat, a ragged, torn khaki ballcap from childhood. It's part of the ritual, he explains. "Grandfather of Matteo? Same."

Back at San Luigi Farm, we weigh them: 389 grams. A very solid start to the season.

"Lucky day," I say.

Matteo shakes his head and points skyward. "La luna."

I buy a small, ugly truffle with great smell, swap *ciaos* with Matteo, and walk back through Ghizzano toward my villa, my shirt pocket perfuming my walk like a censer. The last clouds are blowing off, and the air has turned crisp. The vines below Ghizzano are tinged with rust.

I feel the peaceful contentment of nonfailure. Maybe I'm not a truffle albatross after all. More important, my instincts have been validated at last. The essence of truffles is not to be found in jars or snazzy restaurants. The formula is quite simple, really: wood, dog, fungus, hope. And it still happens in Italy every autumn, just off-piste. Same emotions, every time.

9

Black Autumn

Back home, I find myself thinking about wine. For a long time, Bordeaux and Burgundy had a lock on the wine world. They were virtually the only places considered capable of producing great wine, the only ones worth collecting. The Continental love of hierarchy—what my truffle friend Zelda dubs "Classic European Bullshit"—had spent centuries establishing a clear pecking order, and the establishment had every reason to maintain it.

Then it turned out you could make great wine from cabernet sauvignon, chardonnay, and pinot noir in lots of places. And as the old rules fell, it turned out you could make great wine from lots of different grapes in lots of different places. Further, it turned out that a lot of people who hadn't been steeped in the rules had some very different ideas about what constituted great wine in the first place.

And the wine world got vastly more exciting for it.

I begin to wonder if I'm seeing something similar in the Truffleverse. It's clear that white truffles can be found all over central Italy. And not just whites—black truffles are rampant in Umbria and Le Marche as well. Might the same go for other places, and other truffles? Might we all be suffocating under a pile of Classic European Bullshit?

At first, Google is no help. Most online sources just parrot the old myths—tales of decadent Alba dinners and mysterious syndicates.

But finally I stumble onto a site unlike the others: A "family business" that hunts its own truffles in "a unique secret location," but also provides truffles to restaurants, promising unparalleled freshness and transparency. The company claims to source directly from hunters, skipping the middlemen. "We hunt truffles. We import truffles. We supply truffles. In fact we pretty much live, sleep, eat and breathe truffles." The Instagram feed is filled with images of huge, muddy truffles and a smoldering black Labrador with bronze eyes. Typical comment: "There is no such thing as perfect . . . but this dog and this truffle both come pretty close! Another great day in the woods."

I like the vibe immediately. But what really grabs me is the truffle list. The usual suspects are there—black winter and white—but so are four other varieties: black summer, spring white, honey, and black autumn. The black summers and spring whites come from Italy. The black winters from Spain and Australia. The honeys from Hungary. The black autumns from their own secret wood.

And the whites? Well, those are the subject of a jeremiad called "The Truth About White Truffles," which begins, "Many

people still think all white truffles come from Alba, but
actually . . . none of them do!"

Music to my ears. The claim is a bit of a technicality—Alba's
a city; truffles don't grow in cities—but the larger point strikes
home:

> I've been to Alba many times and, if you have too, you'll
> know that there are very few trees around Alba.
> Vineyards, yes. Woodlands, not so much. Of course,
> there always have been white truffles found in the wider
> region of Piedmont, including a very small amount that
> are hunted quite close to Alba. The world of white truffles
> is very secretive so there is no way to know exactly how
> many of Europe's white truffles come from this region,
> but my guess would be that it's much less than 5%.

Five percent! I hope Alba doesn't have this guy's address. But
he's just getting started.

> I've been lucky enough to smell and taste a huge number
> of white truffles. I mean a really huge amount. I obvi-
> ously couldn't afford to do so if I didn't work in the
> industry, but fortunately I do. I've also had the chance
> to go out hunting them with many of our partners. So
> I've been able to compare white truffles from many
> different sources.
>   I've had some delicious truffles which were definitely
> hunted in Piedmont, as I saw them coming out of the
> ground, but I would say the best Italian white truffle I
> have ever experienced came from Emilia Romagna, in
> the hills around Modena. I've also had excellent white

truffles from Tuscany, Lombardy, Marche, Umbria and Abruzzo.

Check, check, check. Truffles like limestone, and they don't read maps.

And the best white truffle I've ever had? Very hard to say, as so much of the aroma and flavour that one experiences is influenced by other external factors; but I would say the most incredible truffle I've ever held in my hands, smelt and eaten came from either the Croatian peninsula of Istria or from the huge oak forests of Southern Hungary. Or maybe from Serbia. So not from Alba, but also not from Piedmont or even Italy.

And now I imagine Olga Urbani throwing darts at a photo of this man from behind her very expensive desk.

Most of the white truffles in these other countries, the writer claims, get sold to Italian buyers and then sold as Italian truffles, for no reason other than that people will pay more for an Italian truffle. The myth self-perpetuates—at the expense of freshness. Price, too: cut out the middleman, and we could all be eating cheaper, fresher, better truffles.

But, thankfully, times are changing. The hunters in other countries are realizing that they can now openly export their truffles direct to the major markets . . . There is also now a new breed of honest truffle supplier—one that is deeply passionate about high quality truffles, but very keen to tell those that serve and eat their truffles exactly where they have come from.

His last point leaves me salivating over the possibility that the real truffle underground is even more colorful than I've imagined:

> None of the magic of white truffles is lost by knowing where they really come from. The main thing that makes them so utterly wonderful is their aroma; the second factor is their seasonality and rarity, along with the mysterious and exciting way they are hunted. The hunters, truffle dogs, trees, hills, woodlands and traditions of Croatia, Hungary, Serbia and other Eastern European countries are just as magical as their Italian counterparts.

Well. So many questions. Is the forest-to-table movement about to rock the truffle world? Is the Franco-Italian stranglehold going to collapse? And what the hell is a honey truffle? I fire up my email and send him a note, praising his emphasis on authenticity and traceability.

The reply comes twenty-four hours later. At first, it doesn't sound promising. "Thank you for your email and interest in what we do. As you suggest, we are very strict about the secrecy of the locations of where we hunt. Also we struggle with time as I'm run off my feet almost always running the business."

But then it turns out I was right to play the authenticity card. "That said, it would be nice to host you . . . I like to support serious, genuine and informative publications on truffles rather than the usual rubbish that one so often sees."

A hunt is proposed. Then lunch. An NDA must be signed. The last thing he needs is strangers poaching truffles. He's also seen enough journalists to have a dim opinion of the species.

I quickly agree to all conditions.

And so my journey through the truffled Veil of Maya begins. Appropriately, it takes me in a direction I'd never have guessed. I'm not headed to Italy. Nor France. I hop on Kayak and book my trip to the Wiltshire Downs.

~~~~~

My train leaves Paddington Station and drones through the bleak industrial penumbra of London. After a sleepless redeye, the morning light feels like an affront to all that is good in the world. But then, just as I feel myself succumbing to jetlagged hopelessness, the blight gives way to rolling green meadows. Soon there are mud-and-wattle cottages with thatch roofs. Sheep spotting the hillsides. Horses rolling on their backs for the sheer joy of being English on a soft autumn day. The leaden sky, threatening rain, just makes the colors all the brighter.

My heart leaps. I've left *Bleak House* for *Watership Down*. I can almost see the plucky bands of rabbits scuttling along the hedgerows. Tea from the porter restores me. I'm on my way to meet the planet's top truffle dealer, and life is good.

He's given me almost disturbingly precise instructions. Which train to take, what time, where to get off. "I will collect you from the station. When you arrive please walk out of the station, turn left immediately and go up the stairs. I'll be in a black Mercedes."

I can't say which station, beyond the fact that it's somewhere in the Wiltshire Downs of southern England. I can't say much. (*See:* NDA.) Not where he hunts, who he buys truffles from, or who he sells to, beyond the fact—obvious to anyone who stalks him on Instagram—that most of the London restaurants that care get their truffles from Zak Frost.

In terms of volume, Zak is far from the planet's top truffle dealer. The Italian heavyweights dwarf him. But in terms of the quality of his clients, his truffles, and even the information he puts out online, well, Zak is tops. Unlike dodgy dealers, he sends out an email with his price list every Monday, and he never haggles. "You're not selling cheap tracksuits," he says. "It's a high-end, magical, mysterious ingredient. You have to have a bit of class."

The day before was Zak's delivery day in London. Pushing my luck, I suggested tagging along. No way, he replied. "I am literally sprinting from restaurant to restaurant. My day is basically a series of rapid-fire meetings with the leading chefs in the UK, so it wouldn't be appropriate to bring someone else with me." Besides, he does it all on motorbike. I pictured Zak in black leather, a box of truffles strapped behind, slaloming between lanes of traffic and screeching to a halt at the back of the Fat Duck, dismounting just long enough to slide a few tubers into Heston Blumenthal's hands.

The Mercedes is right where it's supposed to be. It rolls forward, dark and sinister, triggering all my Bond goose bumps. I hop in, and we speed off toward the miracle grove. Zak is tall and bald, more Peter Boyle than Sean Connery. My Bond fantasies sag until Stanley the black Lab—strong, dark, and suave star of Instagram—pokes his head between the seats and revives them. "Instagram transformed our company ten times over," Zak says as we drive. "Chefs see me out with my dog. It's much more authentic than some dealer who doesn't really know anything about truffles or how they grow."

The twisting lane ambles through insanely quaint towns, all walls and pubs. We wind into the countryside and pass a group of pheasant hunters with shotguns and tweed caps. I can't help but mention *Watership Down.*

"Actually, it's quite close," Zak says. "I go walking there all the time."

Wiltshire. Not even remotely on my truffle map, but it probably should have been. To my surprise, the paper trail leads all the way back to 1693, when the English physician and naturalist Sir Tancred Robinson published a letter in the *Philosophical Transactions of the Royal Society* in response to some truffles that had been unearthed in England and sent to him for identification. They are, he wrote, "indeed the true French *truffles*, the Italian *tartufi or tartuffole*, and the Spanish *turmas de tierra* . . . I have seen them thrice as large at Florence, Rome, and Naples, where they eat them as a delicious and luxurious piece of dainty, either fried in slices with butter or oil, salt and pepper, or else out of pickle, and often boiled in their soup."

Robinson didn't quite realize that there were two true French truffles, *Tuber aestivum* and *Tuber melanosporum*, and that the ones popping up in England were *aestivum* that would never quite attain the gastronomic heights of *melanosporum*, which requires a more Mediterranean climate. But he did rightly observe that the English ones "are all included in a studded bark or coat . . . the inner substance is of the consistency of the fleshy part in a young chestnut, of a paste colour, of a rank or hircine odor, and unsavoury, streaked with many white veins or threads, as in some animals' testicles."

And then he cited the old thunder-and-lightning thing. "I conjecture that these *tubera terrae* were found after the late thunder and rains . . . they are most tender in the spring, though after showers and sultry weather they may be plentifully found in the autumn: The wet swells them, and lightning may dispose them to send forth their particular scent so alluring to the swine."

English enthusiasm for "trubs," as they called them, really took off after a Spaniard arrived sometime in the 1700s with a "pack of specially trained poodles"—Lagotto Romagnolos by any other name—and began hunting around Wiltshire. Between seasons he'd return to Spain and leave the dogs with locals, and pretty soon the English had their own line of truffle hounds.

The 1800s were the heyday of trub mania, with professional trufflers trawling the estates of nobles (who got their cut, of course). Queen Victoria even received two truffle hounds for her birthday in 1842.

Scandal flared in 1860, when a dog tax threatened to put the truffle hunters out of business. They protested to the House of Lords:

> We, the undersigned Poor Men of the parish of Winterslow, in the county of Wilts, do humbly solicit the attention of our honble. House to our humble Petition. Being poor labouring men, mostly with families and aged, and living in a woody district of the county, where there is a great many English truffles grow, which we cannot find without dogs, we do therefore keep and use a small pudle sort of dog wholey and solely for that and no other purpose; and, as it is in the winter season of the year when we gather them, when labourers is generally on the excess in our neighbourhood, we often are enabled by the aforesaid dogs to provide a subsistence for our families, otherwise we should often be a burden to the parish; and as it hath been carried on by our ancestors for generations past without paying any tax for the dogs; but as the tax is

now leveled upon us, viz. twelve shillings per year, and
as we have to keep our dogs six months when we have
no use for them, it presses so heavy upon us that without
redress we shall in most cases, be obliged to make a
sacrifice of our dogs, and thereby become a burden on
the parish.

Tax or no, English truffle hunting collapsed by World War
I, which was brutal on truffle hunters everywhere. England's
last truffle hunter, Alfred Collins, retired in 1930. An account at
the time described him hunting beneath beech trees on chalky
soil. "He carried an implement like a short-handled thistle
spud, but with a much longer blade, similar to that of a small
spade but narrower; he was accompanied by a frisky little
Frenchified dog, unlike any dog one commonly sees, and very
alert."

That's an apt description of a Lagotto Romagnolo, though
don't tell the Italians their truffle dogs are Frenchified.

Collins's expertise died with him, and for the next eighty
years, most of England forgot all about trubs. Then came
Zak.

≈≈≈

We pull up beside a handsome old farmhouse. Well-tilled fields,
all ready for winter, stretch away across the downs, punctuated
by small woodlots. "This grove really woke the whole interest in
truffles again," Zak says. "People started thinking, 'Well, if this
one place has them, it can't be the only place.' Now probably
fifty or a hundred people seriously hunt truffles in England, and
lots of other people are trying to train their dog. I get those calls
all the time."

The old farmer who planted these trees twenty years ago was not expecting truffles. He just wanted firewood and a windbreak. But the trees must have been infected with truffle spores, and they happened to be planted on perfect ground. Wiltshire's thin soil sits atop a big band of chalk that runs across southern England and into France (think Dover and Champagne), just the kind of high-pH environment truffles love. In addition, the land had been intensively farmed for decades and probably harbored few competing species of fungi.

The woods exploded with truffles. The farmer began collecting them and selling to a handful of local restaurants. Zak got wind of it and was instantly intrigued. He'd had a career as a dance-music DJ, traveling the world, and had settled in Tuscany for a while, producing music and falling hard for the local chow. "In the season, the aroma of truffles permeates whole towns across the region," he recalls. "From the first smell, I was hooked."

In 2004 he moved back home to start a family and heard about the Wiltshire truffles. "To find out they were growing where I grew up was so exciting." He tried them, loved them, and began helping the farmer, who hadn't been using a dog. "He'd just go to the right trees and feel around under the leaf mold. He'd miss a lot, but he'd find a few on the surface. And so I did that with him. It's really hard on your knees."

Stanley's predecessor, Wooster, always tagged along. "He went everywhere with me. At one point I just said, 'Why don't you go and find a truffle?' And he did straightaway. He just went and got one. So that's how I trained him. I literally said 'Find a truffle.'"

Zak pulls on a blue jumpsuit and red rubber gloves and grabs a Waitrose shopping bag. "This is what I like to use," he says, sounding almost apologetic. "When I do television, I have to wear nicer clothes and I get an old leather satchel, which is really annoying because I have to keep opening it."

Stanley makes for the woods at a jaunty trot. Zak lopes behind on long legs. Crossing the fields in that jumpsuit, he looks like a convict on the lam, and I'm back to Dickens, *Great Expectations* this time. *Keep still, you little devil, or I'll cut your throat!*

Once Zak began to rave to his chef friends about the truffles he was finding, they all wanted to try them. "Word went like wildfire. Everybody wanted English truffles." With the farmer's permission and Wooster's help, he began selling to a handful of top restaurants. Pretty soon Wiltshire Truffles was supplying most of London's Michelin-starred restaurants, all from this one extraordinarily abundant wood, which was yielding fifteen kilos a week. In a good year, Zak gets three hundred kilos. I'd already spotted his truffles for sale in London's Borough Market for £900 a kilo. Assuming he got half of that, it was a sweet little gig.

We slip into a beech grove. "Everyone's surprised when they come to these woods," says Zak. "They're expecting ancient oaks." Other than white truffles, most species do better under younger trees, which have a greater need for the fungi's nutrient-mining services. The wood is widely spaced, with minimal undergrowth and years of leaf litter. Diffuse light seeps in from the sides. Stanley cruises along, nose gliding just above the leaf litter, tail a steady metronome. In less than a minute he homes in on a spot, tail oscillations tightening, and pokes his nose into the litter.

"Have you got one, Stan? Is that a truffle? Let me see." Zak kneels beside him, parts the leaves, and pulls out a grape-sized nugget. "Nice! Good boy!"

Stanley gets a treat, and Zak hands the truffle to me. "I call this area Small Truffle Corner. For some reason, lots of little ones grow here."

I turn the truffle in my hand, half shocked at how fast we've hit paydirt. The truffle is coal-black, its coat like studded bark, just as Sir Tancred Robinson described. It looks a lot like the black summers I've seen, but when I hold it to my nose, a floral beauty seeps out.

"They're quite mild still," Zak says. "They don't get strong until the end of the season. But they actually smell a lot stronger once they've had a few days out of the ground."

Black autumn truffles, as Zak calls them, are known most places as Burgundy truffles. They're the same species as black summers, *Tuber aestivum*, as recent genetic analysis has proven, but while most black summers come from southern and eastern Europe, appear May through August, and have very little scent, the ones from more northerly climates—like, well, Burgundy, which is rightfully famous for them—don't appear until autumn and have the exquisite light fragrance I was currently trying to snuffle into my consciousness. Because of these differences, they used to be considered a different species and are still often known as *Tuber uncinatum*.

Stanley is already poking at another spot. Zak drops the truffle into his bag and hustles over. "Show it to me, Stanley." It's a near twin of the first. "Another tiny one. Small Truffle Corner strikes again."

In short order, Stanley nails another half-dozen residents of Small Truffle Corner, all barely beneath the surface. After the punctuated purgatory of hunting whites, I'm digging the immediate gratification. Zak hands me the bag so he can keep up with the collecting and treat dispensing. He carries a standard garden trowel with an orange handle ("It's not traditional, but you can find it when you lose it in the woods"), but he prefers to use his fingers for the easy ones, so as not to damage the mycelium.

Soon we've made our way to the other side of the grove. "This is a really productive spot," Zak says. "It's on the edge of the woodland, where the light comes in. That seems to be really important. The truffles from this area are usually the least flawed, the roundest, and quite dense. It's very localized."

Sure enough, the truffles start getting bigger and rounder. Stanley snuffles excitedly, then paws a fallen stick out of the way to show Zak the spot. Zak kneels down and pulls the leaf litter aside to reveal a fat truffle embedded in the earth like an errant golf ball. "Ahh, another beauty!" Then Stanley nudges aside more litter to unveil a twin. "Good dog! Clever boy!"

Soon the bag is heavy with plum-sized truffles, reddish dirt clinging to their crevices. "This is exactly what every chef wants," Zak says, holding one up in his gloved hand. "Good shape, flawless, nice color. If they were all like this, happy days."

These are destined for his top customer, a three-Michelin-star restaurant that orders big every week. "What they say goes. If they call me and say they urgently need some extra truffles, and I haven't got it, I'll put my boots on and go get it in the rain and drive it straight to them in time for lunch." Of course I want to know who it is, and of course he won't say. "I just think it's in bad taste to talk about your restaurants."

Oh, come on. I work him for a while, and finally he caves: the Fat Duck, which uses them in a celebrated dish on its tasting menu called Forest Floor.

Stanley has slipped ahead of us. "Wait up, Stan!" Zak hauls himself to his feet with a grunt. I'm hustling to catch up, scanning the ground for snags that could send me and my bag of truffles flying, when I spot something huge and black on top of the leaves, just sitting there like an offering. I grab it and show Zak.

"Good one!"

"It was just sitting there."

"Nice. I should give you a treat."

"What's it worth?" I like the idea that I'm not purely dead weight.

Zak hefts it. "It's about eighty grams. The current price is five hundred pounds a kilo, so that's about a forty-pound truffle. And that's selling to a restaurant. If you bought it at a shop, twice that."

Stanley has stayed on task while his assistants dilly-dally, nosing the wet leaves out of the way and flipping truffles out of the earth with his paw without nicking them. Sometimes he whirls around and trundles fifty yards to a spot as if it had a flashing beacon, as Zak watches in awe. "I understand dogs have a much stronger sense of smell than we do," he marvels, "but it's the directional aspect I find so amazing." Occasionally, when the bag of truffles has been sitting on the ground, Stanley has known there was a truffle *underneath* it.

How do they do it? The increasingly robust science of dog cognition—or, as it's often known these days, "dognition"—gives us some hints. While we live in the visual present, a micromoment built of ricocheting light waves, dogs inhabit smellscapes in which both past events and invisible players are profoundly present. For them, what walked over this fallen tree a week ago, or what is currently lurking beneath, may be more meaningful than what is right in front of their eyes. It's a Cubist way of seeing the world. Surfaces unfold. Time collapses. Everything matters.

This information is available to dogs because odors have physical structure and persistence. I always assumed an odor diffuses evenly through air, like drops of dye in water, but the aromatic molecules responsible for scents have a certain viscosity. They stretch like taffy, thin ribbons folding on themselves, meandering on the breeze, curling around tree trunks, pooling in low spots. When conditions are right, these trails rest along the ground, which explains why so many trufflers like to hunt at night or in the early morning, when the air is still and damp. Once the day begins and the wind kicks up, those traces fade like old contrails.

The lovely, wet, truffle-like lump of the canine nose is designed to lock on to one of these threads and reel it in, thanks to the slits on each side. A dog nose has inner flaps that control the direction of airflow. New breaths come straight in through the nostrils, but when a dog exhales, the flaps close and shunt the old air out the sides of the slits. In this way, a dog is able to continuously breathe in fresh samples of a scent trail—unlike humans, who contaminate and disperse the evidence with every exhalation.

When we breathe, all air goes up the sinuses, crosses a patch of olfactory receptors—nerve endings embedded in the top of the nasal cavity, each of which specializes in detecting one particular type of aromatic molecule—and continues on to the lungs, making the reverse journey a moment later. But dog noses have two channels: one leads to the lungs, the other branches off into a cul-de-sac of fine passages lined with a hundred times as many olfactory receptors as we have. Because this branch isn't en route to the lungs, dogs can give their olfactory receptors more time to process the contents of any particular sniff. It's like photography: dogs have a bigger lens that captures more light, a hundred times more pixels for recording the image, and a more observant photographer at the helm. That's why they're a million times better at finding any olfactory needle in the haystack.

And once they find the trail, they "bracket" it, as Stanley is doing now, nose to the ground, five quick sniffs per second, constantly changing position and doubling back, sampling the aroma's strength across many points to build a scent map in his head. Smelling in stereo, working each nostril independently, allows him to pinpoint directionality, the same way we do with sound.

However he does it, it works. Within a couple of hours we have more truffles than I can count, the bag is heavy, and my little truffle addiction is growing more acute.

"I've never seen another wild wood with this many truffles," Zak says. "Lots of people are puzzled. Truffles are native to Wiltshire, but the foragers I know would be delighted if they found a kilo in a week. The productivity here is just unique." He bounces the bag in his hand, smiling. "I love the feeling as it gets heavier. I'd say we've got four kilos. Current market rate, that's about two thousand pounds. Not bad for a half-day's work."

Although Zak is best known for the black autumn truffles he hunts personally, the season is September through November, and they make up just 4 percent of his business. The first few years he sold them, he kept his day job as a talent manager for dance DJs. One day, he was contacted by an Australian company looking to sell its black winter truffles in England. Might he be interested?

At first he was perplexed. Aussie truffles? Like most people, Zak believed that black winters came from France.

But the Australians set him straight. In the 1970s, French mycologists learned how to inoculate oak or hazelnut seedlings with black winter spores and trigger mycorrhization. Today virtually all black winter truffles are farmed. Spain is tops, France a distant second, but up-and-comer Australia produces the best of all—or so the Australians said.

Zak was skeptical.

Try them, they said.

He did. And he was amazed. Compared to the others he'd had, these were fruitier, richer, more perfect in shape. "I became totally fascinated," he tells me. "I kept flying out and meeting all the people who really knew, not the so-called experts that don't know. Now I basically live and breathe truffles all the time. My wife says I can't talk about anything else."

Zak learned that the Australians had brought a new scientific rigor to understanding what made a great truffle. "What's the best way to store truffles? How long do they last? When is the aroma at its peak? What's the best way to ship them and to keep the microclimate at the right conditions? They studied this, they got universities involved, and now they do it the right way."

Even better, Australia's seasons are inverted. Instead of December through March, the truffles are ripe June through August, when there's no competition. "I thought, Wow, these are going to be massive," Zak says. "So why not jump in and be the one to make them massive?"

He made them massive. By the time he added Spanish black winters to the mix in 2014, he had a year-round business on his hands. "At the time, nobody in London knew that truffles even came from Spain, because up till then all Spanish truffles had been sold by other truffle dealers as French Périgord truffles. So most people would say to me, 'Oh, I've never tried Spanish truf-fles.' And I'd tell them, 'Well, you probably have, you just thought they were French.'"

Zak discovered that most truffle dealers knew very little about the fungi they were peddling, and the chefs knew even less. "I'd be shocked when I started supplying a new restaurant, and I'd see the last stock of what they got from someone else, and it'd be this dusty, stale old crap. And I'd think, God, is this what you've been selling your customers up to now?"

He decided to make knowledge and authenticity the corner-stones of his business. "Because I do all my own deliveries, I'm in touch with most of the top chefs day to day. They were fasci-nated to hear where truffles are really coming from. In the past, people thought you had to say your truffles were from Périgord or Alba, or else you couldn't sell them. That was the big con that was going on. But we totally disproved that. Everyone bought them, and we took over the market for winter truffles that year. And ever since then, every other truffle company in England now openly sells Spanish truffles."

Zak later added white truffles to his line, seeking out small, trustworthy partners. "I noticed there are two different worlds in the truffle industry. There's a corrupt side to it, with lots of lying retailers and dodgy producers. And then there's this great network of lovely people, mostly family businesses. And I made a subcon-scious and then conscious decision to try to veer towards that."

To strengthen that commitment, he visits his suppliers every year. "It's partly for me to meet them, but it's more for them to meet me. The whole business is built on relationships and trust. I want them to pick up on my passion and obsession and under-stand that I'm someone that hopefully knows what he's doing, so they'll send the rubbish truffles to some guy in the States."

Although he found (and still uses) an excellent white truffle
supplier in Italy, most of the good stuff came from Croatia and
Hungary, which he openly advertises. The culture is ready, he
thinks. "It's changing rapidly. Even a couple of years ago, it
would have been inconceivable to go to Hungary and Croatia
and post on Instagram that all your white truffles come from
there. Now the majority finds it much more interesting."

Still, the diehards will fight him to the end. Zak mentioned
one old-school chef who'd long ago learned that white truffles
should only come from Italy. "He'd always say, 'Oh, when you
smell a real Italian one, there's nothing like it.'" So Zak brought
him a box of Italian and Croatian truffles, mixed together. "I
said, 'You're a truffle expert, you've been buying truffles for fifty
years. Pick out the best ones, and obviously they'll be the Italian
ones.' And he just gave me a look."

~~~~~

On the way to lunch, we swing by Zak's house to drop off our
bounty. The Mercedes rolls to a stop on a crunchy gravel court-
yard in front of a charming brick house with a slate shingle roof,
a bit of moss feeling its way through the cracks. Church bells
peal in the nearby village.

In the kitchen, Zak's eleven-year-old towhead son is making
cupcakes on a hoverboard, zooming back and forth between the
cookbook and the bowl. Zak hands his wife the four kilos of
truffles and asks if she'd terribly mind washing them, since he
has to take this journalist to lunch at the Red Lion. Her smile
is unconvincing.

Adjacent to the house is Wiltshire Truffles HQ, a squeaky-
clean tiled room with a gleaming steel fridge. Wiltshire Truffles
sold nothing but fresh truffles until 2020, when it added a

handful of products: truffle cream, truffle butter, truffle cheese, and truffle juice, all made without synthetic aroma, Zak's nemesis. "I liked truffle oil when I first tried it," he admits. "It was only gradually over the years that I came to hate it. Now I can't even bear it. And I can detect one drop of it in a dish. Chefs will say, 'Oh, I just added a touch to enhance the flavor.' Well, you've ruined it for me."

Zak yanks open the fridge door, and some sort of black autumn essence swirls out, tapping me on the nose ever so briefly before departing this world. The smell, Zak says, concentrates as the truffles sit in the fridge. He pulls out a big truffle and slices it open to expose the cappuccino-colored marbling. Then he slides another smoother-skinned black truffle into my hand. "This is probably the last black winter on earth right now," he says. "My Australian partners just sent it to me. It's very late in their season, so it may be the last on the planet until the Spanish season starts next month."

I hold it to my nose and a wave of wistfulness washes over me. Instead of hot and gassy, this is cool and introspective, a tall glass of *tristesse*. I think of beauty and sadness, blossoms in rain.

"To me, it's easily the nicest truffle," Zak says. "It's fun hunting *aestivum* and *uncinatum*, but realistically, they're never going to be as exciting as *melanosporum*. But it's too strong for some people. It smells a bit like feet or socks, too 'French,' as they say around here. Whereas *magnatum* is so ethereal and delicate."

I think back to the prancing satyr in Barolo. Ethereal?

Well, Zak demurs, "a good *magnatum* should feel feminine. Most women I know much prefer it."

I turn the truffle in my fingers, admiring its pebbly coat. Lovely. Is he giving it to me?

He is not.

He plucks it from my fingers, reseals it in shrink wrap, and returns it to the fridge. "I'm saving it for dinner with my Spanish truffle partner tomorrow night."

~~~~~

The Red Lion Freehouse—a white-walled, Michelin-starred pub with a mossy thatched roof and a snarling heraldic crimson lion guarding the exterior wall—seems to have been plucked from the back burner of my psyche where a lifetime's worth of cozy BBC programming has been quietly simmering. Inside, a brick hearth with a roaring fire and a wooden bar with hand-pulled pints. Zak hands his best truffle to Guy Manning, the chef, and we grab a table in the corner, Stanley settling comfortably beneath it.

Guy and his wife, Brittany, met as chefs at Per Se in New York and decided to decamp to Wiltshire to have a family and make the food they liked—country cooking executed to perfection using local ingredients. He and Zak became fast friends. They take hiking holidays together.

As we sip our pints, a procession of truffle-inflected dishes—pâté, gnocchi, poached cod in cream, crème brûlée—rolls out of the kitchen, black autumn fairies flitting playfully out of the steam. Other guests glance down at their fish and chips in confusion.

Zak catches the appraising look in my eye. "It's not all chef lunches and dog walks," he says.

Oh, really?

"Basically, I work seven days a week from now until Christmas. No breaks. The week leading up to Christmas last year we sold two hundred and seventy kilos of truffles. All delivered individually by me." Hence the motorcycle. He can hit forty or fifty accounts a day, spending just a few minutes in each one, versus maybe seven a day in the van.

"People have visions of me swanning around in restaurants, but I'm literally rushing around like a madman, trying to make sure everyone gets good truffles. I leave the house at three in the morning and get home at ten at night. When I get home from a few days in London I can barely talk. I can't even sleep. My mind's still going, 'I need two kilos here, one kilo there.'"

Zak sips his pint, reflecting. "It's an amazing job, but people don't see the insanely hard work that goes into it, or the incredible stress. There's two big stressors: not having enough truffle, and having too much truffle. And they can be serious. The profit margin on truffles isn't that great. If you lose one kilo, it can wipe out your profits. At the height of white truffle season, we import about twenty-five kilos of *magnatum* on a Monday. That could be worth sixty thousand pounds, and it's basically losing weight—and therefore value—at three to five percent per day. And people say, 'Oh, how can your job be stressful?'"

He reaches down and gives Stanley an affectionate pat. "My main hunting days are on Sundays and Thursdays. And the reason for that is my main delivery days are Saturdays and Wednesdays. Those are the hardest days, so then spending the next day hunting with Stan is essential for my mental health. Your stress melts away. You're just out with your dog on your own, the peace and the wind, the sanity. I genuinely could not do this job without the hunting part. Just selling truffles would drive me mad."

〰〰

I catch the last train back to London, the light fading, the downs darkening. As I listen to the rhythms of the wheels on the tracks, lights flashing by, I begin to think of truffles as small children in a round of hide-and-seek, scrunched down in their hiding spots, giggling hysterically as their pursuers close in, wanting desperately to be found, but still trying to hold it together to make the game last a little longer. So the game is afoot, and I can hear a lot more giggling. And it's all coming from Eastern Europe.

10

Mr. Big

The town of Motovun rises from the forest like a Tikal of truffles. Speeding along in my stick-shift Fiat Panda, enjoying how the roar of the tiny engine makes me feel like Mario Andretti (born in Motovun in 1940, when the Italians were still clinging to Istria), I've been following the bank of the Mirna River as it winds through the valleys of Istria when I swing around a bend and gasp. Miles ahead, a Fuji-perfect hill breaks the plain, its upper reaches terraformed into walls and towers.

Motovun. The Italians (who have not fully resigned themselves to Istria's loss) call it Montona. Both words derive from an old Celtic term meaning "mountain town," which is what it has been for five thousand years: defensible, good views of the surroundings, better air than the malarial swamps down below. The drier edges of those swamps were thick with massive oak trees, a gallery forest that stretched for miles along the river.

That was the big draw for the Venetians, back when the world was their oyster and the Adriatic their private lake. They called it St. Mark's Forest, and it supplied the timbers for their galleys. The Venetians learned to bend the tops of the growing trees with ropes, ensuring that the timbers would naturally form the curved lines of the galleys. Twenty thousand Istrian oxen—massive, marl-colored beasts that have been pulling plows across Istria's soil since Roman times—were employed to drag the logs the dozen miles from St. Mark's Forest to the coast.

The Venetians gave Motovun the first of what would become three rings of concentric walls, giving the five-hundred-person town a commanding position on the Mirna. Not that there was ever much to command. "This is the place between countries," a self-appointed historian named Ranko tells me over a liter of teran, the local red wine, shortly after I've parked the Panda at the base of the outer walls and hoofed it up countless stone steps to a cavelike tavern perched atop the innermost. "Always has been." Ranko means Istria, this shield-shaped peninsula jutting into the Adriatic on the far western tip of Croatia. "Nothing of importance has ever happened here," he says. "That's why it's so nice!"

Indeed, the tides of history have washed back and forth across Istria, changing little except the names. It was Illyria. It was a Roman outpost. It was Venice's woodlot. It was a forgotten backwater of the Hapsburg Empire. On the hill across from Motovun is a mansion where Hapsburg descendants bide their time, gazing out at their former property and waiting for the tides to again shift their way.

Istria was handed to Italy after World War I as a thank-you for joining the winning side just in time, then lost to the

Yugoslav Partisans during World War II. When Yugoslavia broke up and war broke out in the early 1990s, Istria was even then too far-flung to be strategic. No important battles have ever been fought here. No commercial hubs ever developed. That's why it's so nice.

I excuse myself before Ranko can delve any deeper into Croatian politics and walk the vertiginous maze of Motovun, hoping to catch the sunset on the far side of town, all of four hundred meters away. Each three rows of cobblestones are interrupted by a row set edgewise to form a lip to keep pedestrians and carts from sliding to their doom.

On the far side, a tortuous road switchbacks down to the valley through vineyards and olive groves. Istria is the shadow Italy, an oxbow in time. Roman ruins. Oxcart agriculture. Empty beaches peppered with wild rosemary. A plate of pasta con tartufo for €10. A jug of wine for €1. The limestone from the Apennines dips under the Adriatic Sea and rises on the other side, and in so doing leaves the old, familiar story of truffles and enters an alternate one.

At the base of the hill, the road meets Motovun Forest, as St. Mark's Forest is now known, the silver Mirna worming through the middle. That forest is legendary for its white truffles, many of which make their way to Motovun, which in the autumn is probably the most intensely truffly spot on earth.

The road crosses the river and enters the tiny outpost of Livade, where Istria's truffle story burst out of nothingness in the 1930s. Livade is still where the action is. The truffles may get served up in Motovun, but they get bought and sold in Livade, and always have. To understand Istrian truffles, one must come down from the heights of the walled city and mix it up at the forest station—and that's my plan. An early-morning truffle hunt, followed by a quick swing through Livade's very own truffle festival, and then an audience with Giancarlo Zigante, the man who has almost single-handedly put Istrian truffles on the map.

That part's got me nervous. There's the Trumpian proportions of his sprawling empire of restaurants and factories and festivals and trophy vineyards, not to mention the Trumpian aesthetic: bling, sons with slick hair, and a whole lot of name branding. There's the people in Motovun who quietly warned me to watch my step. And then there's the name itself: *Zigante* is old Venetian dialect for "gigantic." In other words, I'm literally meeting with Mr. Big.

~~~~~

The first thing I see when I roll into Livade is a curious roundabout. Out of a central circle of crushed white stone rises a giant copper cylindrical pedestal, topped by a sculpture of a white truffle the size of a beanbag chair. I strongly suspect it's a model of the "Millennium Truffle" Giancarlo Zigante discovered a few miles from here on November 2, 1999, which at 1.31 kilograms was the world's largest until 2014, when it got bumped off by a 1.79-kilo monster. Its grooves make it look strangely like the raised-fist logo of the Serbian Otpor resistance movement. Beneath the truffle, carved into the copper pedestal, are the words LIVADE: WORLD TRUFFLE CENTER, which seems like a big claim for a village of perhaps a dozen buildings.

To the right of the roundabout, a handsome square three-story Hapsburg-era building with tall shutters houses Zigante Tartufi's shop, restaurant, and headquarters. Beyond that, a tent where the truffle festival takes place. To the left, a warehouse from the same era, where the Istrian truffle industry began in the 1930s, along with the railway station where it continued during the Yugoslavian years. The entire story of Istrian truffles is within a stone's throw of the truffle fist.

This is also where K, my truffle hunter, told me to meet him. I'll call him K because, well, he was having a crappy day, and I wouldn't want him to be judged based on such a small sample size.

K rolls up a little later than our 7:00 A.M. rendezvous time in a clanking subcompact that's missing a hubcap and is smashed on one side from a recent collision. He throws open the passenger door. "Hop in!" He's a skinny young guy with rheumy eyes and cropped hair, dressed in a hoodie and vest. I try to place the extraordinary scent inside the car as we drive. It has elements of smoke, death, rubber, and prosciutto.

We clank up a dirt road into Motovun Forest. K seems agitated. His website promised a "true demonstration of truffle hunting"—wording, I thought, that beautifully shot the narrows of authenticity—but I begged him not to pre-bury any truffles. He grudgingly agreed, but now he's having second thoughts. "Season is terrible," he says. "Too hot. Too dry. Troffles need cold." He has a classic Croatian accent, midway between Italy and Dracula.

"That's fine," I reply. "I just want to know about the life of the truffle hunter."

"You want to know life of troffle hunter?" He nearly spits. "You hunt four or five hours, maybe you find one leetle troffle. Maybe you make ten euros. Not easy life." His phone dings. "Huh. My friend says he found half kilo yesterday." He stares at his phone in disbelief as the road rolls under us. "Not possible."

After a couple of miles we pull off by the side. K opens his trunk and three dogs pop out, like clowns from a box. The black

Lab and the white Lagotto immediately start sniffing, while the brown Lagotto bounds into the forest in hot pursuit of phantoms, ignoring K's shouts. He shakes his head glumly. "Guess which is young dog?"

We follow a path to a moldering wooden bridge that cuts across a brook ten feet below. The warped, mossy planks seem to be hanging on by inertia alone. It looks like a prop from an Indiana Jones movie. I hesitate.

"I am civil engineer," K says with a half smile. "I guarantee bridge."

He really was a civil engineer, hunting truffles at night only, but five years ago he quit to truffle full-time.

"Wouldn't you make better money as a civil engineer?" I propose.

K laughs. "This is Croatia." The path weaves between the mossy trunks of the towering oaks and into the dark forest. "Besides, here I'm never late for work."

I get the sense this may have been a problem back in the civil engineering days. K has a limp, a runny nose, and that profound aroma. As soon as we get into the woods he says, "Sorry, need toilet," and ducks behind a tree. Then he pops his head out. "Just follow dogs. They know everything."

I sidle up the path, giving him credit for dragging himself out here so early, and also for his excellent English. That was the hardest part of his civil engineering degree, he tells me when he catches up. "The math and physics were easy, but the English was so hard."

I was wearing boots and waterproof pants and three layers, still scarred from my adventures in the brambles with Matteo, but it turns out that hunting truffles in Motovun Forest is a walk in the park. Flat ground, trails everywhere, the ground a glowing carpet of freshly fallen poplar leaves. Lots of other people are in the forest with their dogs, too. Only K has the grungy truffle-hunter look I expected. Everyone else looks like the same people you see walking their dogs in any park. Smiling women in hiking boots. Bespectacled men with white beards and walking sticks.

Half of Istria hunts part time, after work and on weekends. It's something to do with your dogs that might, if you're lucky, make a little money on the side. There are numerous small dealers to sell to, and there's always Zigante. People used to go at night, and there would be so many flashlights panning the woods that it felt like a disco, but a few years ago the region passed a new law banning hunting from ten at night until five in the morning, to give the forest a chance to rest.

The main forests are all owned by the government, which charges €250 for a truffle-hunting license. In theory, hunters are also supposed to report to the Forest Department office, get their truffles weighed, and pay a tax, but according to official government records, not a single gram of truffle has been found in Motovun Forest in the past twenty years.

K knows all the hunters we meet. He chats them up while the packs of dogs skirmish and howl.

You finding anything?

No. Worst season in sixty years.

My friend says he found half a kilo yesterday.

Ha. Where?

I don't know. He wouldn't say.

Ha.

We veer toward a less tracked part of the woods. Nero, the black dog, doubles back to a tree and scratches tentatively with his paw. K limps over, urging him on, but Nero quickly abandons

the spot. K curses under his breath. "I think troffles will be late."
He checks his phone as we walk. "How he can get half kilo?
Where? Not possible." Then he excuses himself to duck behind
another tree. "Sorry. Follow dogs."

When he returns, I ask if he sells his truffles to Mr. Zigante.
"Sometime," he says. "But him and me fight over price. Mostly
I sell direct. People email me."

K started truffle hunting twenty years ago, when he
was twelve years old. It made him feel grown up, important.
But lately, he feels like the forests are changing. Too hot, too
dry. Too many truffle hunters. He's considered hunting in
Serbia.

"Serbia has truffles?" I ask, Zak Frost's manifesto ringing in
my ears.

"Really good troffles. And not so many hunters. My friend
hunts in Serbia. I said I wanted to come. But he said, 'No, they
smash your car and kill your dogs.' So I stay here."

I'd heard similar stories in Italy. Dogs get poisoned by other
hunters. Car tires get slashed. In one fight, a truffle hunter
sliced the fingers off a rival. Always these stories were told about
somewhere else, some truffle frontier where the hunting was
great but things were rougher.

After three hours of walk/limping through the lovely woods,
finding nothing, the dogs are clearly losing interest, and K
suggests calling it quits. "You pick right forest for book, but
wrong year." The Truffle Albatross strikes again. Either that, or
Istria isn't nearly the truffle paradise sources have led me to
believe.

On our way out, Nero suddenly darts off the trail toward an
oak tree and begins digging with purpose. K springs after him,
brightening at last. "Go, Nero, go!" Nero hits a mass of roots

and K cuts them out with his knife so Nero can continue. He flashes me a thumbs-up. "He's enthusiastic!"

But after ten minutes of tunneling, Nero is no longer enthusiastic. K leans down, grabs a handful of dirt, and sniffs in disbelief. "What you dig for?" He sticks his nose in the hole and sniffs all around. "Nothing! What this dog is doing? So crazy!"

K is in a full-blown funk by the time we load the dogs back into the trunk. "Can't believe you come and find nothing. Should have buried troffle." He flicks through the photos on his phone, showing me happy clients posing for trophy shots. "See. See! I find troffles. Big ones!"

K drops me off in front of the Zigante Truffle Days tent. I hop out and turn to offer a last word of encouragement, but he's already rolling away with urgency. "Sorry," he calls out the open window as the car clunks off, "just follow signs!"

≈≈≈

Zigante Truffle Days, which happens every weekend throughout the fall, is like an HO scale model of Alba. Tent, truffles, dealers, products. You can get a bowl of polenta with white truffles for $28 or black truffles for $16. If you want an extra five grams of white shaved over the top, that's a very reasonable $7. There's truffle pizza and truffle ice cream and truffle tiramisu. There are Slovenian tour buses. A jazzy funk blares through the speaker system. The best thing is the red-and-yellow-striped choo-choo trolley out front for taking attendees on simulated truffle hunts. Alba has no choo-choo.

I kill an hour marinating in 2,4-dithiapentane and then walk back to the truffle monument to meet up with Ivan Milotić, Zigante's Boswell. A noted historian from Zagreb, he's wearing a thin blue sweater and looks exactly like the public intellectual he is, a pale figure in frameless glasses.

A few years ago, Ivan became fascinated by Istrian truffle culture, but it was far too hermetic to allow entree to an outsider from Zagreb. "It's a mysterious world," he tells me. "It works very well. But they like their secrecy."

Zigante, on the other hand, was the nexus. He knew everyone, and was often their lifeblood. Key factor: he'd reached a stage in his career where he wanted the world to know the truth about Istrian truffles, but he wasn't a word guy.

Then along came Ivan. It took him two years to earn Zigante's confidence. In the process, he became something of a consigliere to the Zigante family. He and Zigante teamed up on a book called *Our Istrian Truffle*. It tells Zigante's life story, but also includes surprisingly detailed interviews with older truffle hunters, making it one of the best sources of true information on truffle culture. No one but Zigante could have coaxed them to open up, and his name is on the cover, but the book also includes extensive research into the region's archives, as well as expert translations from ancient Greek and Latin sources. One suspects Ivan's hand.

Ivan and I stand in front of the big truffle fist, and he says what I've already surmised: it all began right here. The settlement of Livade grew up around its railway station, where guests on the line from Trieste would disembark to catch a carriage to the famed St. Stephen's thermal spa, up toward the headwaters of the Mirna. By the 1920s Livade had a handful of shops and inns. The best was a tavern and wine cellar—the very same building where Zigante now has his headquarters—run by an Italian named Agostinelli.

One day, one of the local peasants brought Agostinelli a handful of ginger-colored tubers he'd found in the woods. *Good day, sir, do you have any idea what these stinky potatoes are? I found them underground. My pigs love them. Too bad they're so repulsive.*

Agostinelli rolled the things in his hands. He took a tentative sniff, then jerked his head away. Whoa. He had a hunch what they were, but he wasn't sure. Fortunately, he had the one phone in Livade, so he got on the horn and called his friend the Baroness Clara Ida Barbara von Hütterott.

The von Hütterotts were a noble German family that had settled in Rovinj, the fancy town on Istria's coast, during the time of the Austro-Hungarian Empire. Rich, educated, powerful, they had launched a number of enterprises, and Barbara, the free-spirited thirty-year-old daughter of the clan, was the most entrepreneurial and experimental of the lot. When Agostinelli told her some peasant might have just brought him a truffle, she thought that was mighty interesting and quickly mentioned it to another member of her social circle: Massimo Sella, director of Rovinj's Marine Biological Station, an important research outpost and collecting station for the Berlin Zoo.

Like Baroness von Hütterott, Sella was in his thirties, bearded, handsome, a well-known character given to bicycling around Rovinj in a white sport coat. He was the most learned man in Rovinj. He had a doctorate from the University of Rome, could speak six languages, and could bust out Beethoven and Chopin on the piano. Most important, he was from Piedmont. He knew exactly what truffles were, and what they were worth. When the baroness told him about Agostinelli's rank tubers, he must have freaked.

In the 1920s, white truffles were believed to grow only in the Po River Valley of northern Italy. Even then, they were worth a fortune. Among his many passions, Sella had a strong interest in transforming Istria from an indigent, malaria-riddled backwater into a flourishing corner of Italy. Truffles could help. Besides, he was super curious and always up for an adventure.

In 1929, on the train from Italy down to Rovinj, Sella met another Italian man from the Po River Valley. They got talking about truffles, of course. Sella mentioned what he'd heard. The man, named Testoni, agreed that the landscape of Istria seemed close enough to northern Italy that truffles might well lurk there, and he had half a mind to come back with a decent dog and find out.

Do it, Sella said, and I'll go hunting with you.

Late in the fall of 1929 the man arrived with a dog, and off they went. They found a few truffles of other species, just enough to whet their appetites, but they hunted in the wrong zones. They ran out of time and the dog had to be returned. In 1930 they tried again, this time with a pointer dog, but no luck. Maybe the spots weren't right, or maybe the dog sucked.

In 1931 they tried again with "two perfectly trained shaggy dogs" from Emilia Romagna, as Sella wrote in his seminal piece "The White Truffle in Istria," which he published in the *New Journal of Italian Botany* in 1932. They decided to ride to Livade and focus on the Mirna Valley, which they thought had the right vibe. (Oaks, willows, poplars, lots of streams.)

This time they nailed it. Everywhere they walked, the dogs found truffles. Everyone they met confirmed their presence. Those stinky potatoes? Sure, they're everywhere. They get stuck on our plows when we clear land. When our pigs come back from the woods, they smell like garlic. Disgusting.

With growing giddiness, the Italians realized they had discovered a virgin valley of truffles ripe for the picking. "Here is some information about the discovery," Sella wrote. "At the beginning of December, Testoni and I found four kilograms of truffles (that is, not even counting the badly damaged ones), among which there were some weighing 200 grams and more." That was in a single day of hunting.

They continued to find multiple kilograms most days, and by the end of the expedition had amassed fifty kilos, enough to have bought a couple of cars or ten thousand liters of wine. Sella knew they'd barely scratched the surface. He began dreaming of a brand-new small economy of truffle hunters and dealers that would lift the region out of poverty.

In 1933, the year after his article rocked the Italian truffle world, Sella and Baroness von Hütterott formed Azienda del Tartufo—Sella, Hütterott & Co. in a nineteenth-century stone warehouse in Livade, with the intention of buying Istrian truffles and selling them to Italy. Since there was no local truffle culture, they had to import dozens of hunters and dogs from the motherland, turning them loose in St. Mark's Forest. Unlike in France and Italy, this was purely a pursuit of *Tuber magnatum*. When they found black truffles, they'd feed them to the animals or throw them in the woods.

Soon they were shipping kilos of fresh truffles to all the major cities of Italy, as well as thousands of cans of conserved truffles. This means that even in the early 1930s, when Alba was first establishing itself as the sine qua non of truffles (and experts were already lamenting how Piedmont had cut down too many forests to make room for the mighty grapevine), Istria was already part of the fabric of the Italian truffle trade.

But things went south for Sella, Hütterott & Co. pretty fast. In 1937 they lost the exclusive concession to hunt truffles in St. Mark's Forest to a rival. Worse, in 1939 Italy went all-in on the wrong side of a dubious war. The truffle business collapsed. In 1943, with Italy capitulating and the Yugoslav Partisans closing in on Rovinj, the Marine Biological Station's boat was sunk, and Sella had to flee Istria on his bicycle. Barbara von Hütterott wasn't so lucky. She held on with her family at their Rovinj estate until 1945, when they were all killed in their home by the Partisans.

But during that brief period in the 1930s, truffle culture had taken hold in Istria. The men and dogs learned the trade, and they passed it down, though it wasn't widely accepted at first. Who were these grubby young men, wandering the woods with their dogs all day instead of putting in a decent day's labor in the fields? Only after it became clear that the grubby young men were earning several times as much as their farming peers did opinions shift.

As Yugoslavia got its wobbly legs under it, the State Forest Office set up a truffle-buying station in the old railway station in Livade, next door to Sella, Hütterott & Co's old haunts. A wealth of truffles continued to flow from Istria to Italy. But prices were low and fixed, and soon Italian smugglers were also flowing back and forth, offering twice the Forest Office's rate. Some were women, buying truffles for their husbands in hopes of an aphrodisiac boost. Most serious hunters learned to sell their good stuff to the smugglers, reserving just enough to sell to the Forest Office so the authorities wouldn't get suspicious.

That all collapsed in the 1990s, along with Yugoslavia itself. Wars broke out among its republics, including Croatia, though once again Istria was safely out of the way. And out of this truffle-economy chaos arose a figure who would soon amass a truffle enterprise larger than the nation of Yugoslavia's had ever been. From his beginnings as a part-time truffle hunter, he became a legitimate competitor to Urbani and Sabatino. And he runs everything from little Livade.

~~~~~

Ivan and I head for the Zigante Tartufi store and restaurant to meet the big guy himself. A hulking black Mercedes SUV sits on the street out front, two wheels pulled up on the curb at an angle. I have no doubt who it belongs to.

The restaurant is heavy on Eastern European gilt. Black and gold seem to be the official colors of the Croatian truffle industry. The gleaming wrought-iron lampposts in the dining room match the Mercedes perfectly. Dudes in suits glide through the dining room, trying to look important.

We slip into Zigante's office, where my assumptions are quickly upended. In contrast to the surroundings, the man himself is downright grandfatherly in jeans and a simple black cardigan. At age seventy, he has inky hair and a comfortable girth, and his office is little more than a wooden table and a mini fridge.

He pulls a paper bag out of the fridge and dumps a dozen truffles on the table, next to the golden life-size replica of his Millennium Truffle. I ask where he got the truffles, and Ivan tells me he's not going to translate that question.

Zigante puts on his readers so he can see the truffles, grabs a paring knife, and gives me a quick education in grades of truffles and how to tell an Istrian truffle from an Alba one. Wormholes, fine shades of color, shape . . . it turns out to be the kind of thing where you have to see ten thousand of them before you pick up on it.

Zigante has seen many times that. He started hunting in the 1970s, when he was in his early twenties. A machinist by training, he was working in a metal molding factory and truffle hunting at night for extra income, sleeping just a few hours a night. Through the 1980s, with the state in control, there was no room for innovation, but once the state collapsed and capitalism rushed into the void, Zigante was ready. He started buying and selling truffles far and wide. When the rural hunters saw his signature Mercedes cresting the hill, they raced to break out the good hooch.

Then he found the Millennium Truffle in 1999. So many times before, he thought he'd found a huge truffle, but it always turned out to be five or six smaller truffles nested together. This one was in soft soil, so he reached in his hand to feel it, and it just kept going down and down, beyond anything he could have dreamed. He threw a feast for his friends and business associates, but not before calling the press.

International recognition came his way, and he leveraged it like a pro. He opened his store the following year. Then the restaurant. Then the festival. Then the factory. Now he's up to a hundred employees. Heck, he's got a whole town; suck on that, Alba.

And yet, how does he spend his days? Driving through the Istrian countryside, stopping at the houses of the hunters he's known for decades, picking up their latest finds and unrolling bills, as if it were still 1999.

Zigante's latest mission is to free the Istrian truffle from its Italian bondage. That's what the restaurant and the festival and the book are really all about. He and Ivan have filed the paperwork to establish protected designation of origin (PDO) status—the same recognition given to place-specific foods like Gorgonzola and Champagne—for the Istrian truffle. They're even looking into tagging their truffles with QR codes so buyers can trace the entire path—an audacious shot across Italy's bow. Slowly but surely, they will show the world the unique flavor of Istria.

And in a way, they already have. When someone asks me where they can get the ultimate white truffle experience, I have an easy answer. Go to Motovun, I tell them. Inhale the funky madness oozing out of every shop. Walk the twelfth-century walls. Trace the oak canopy along the Mirna, some of the same trees that yielded Massimo Sella's first truffles a century ago. Grab an outdoor table along the walls and order some food as the light fades. Note the tendrils of grapevines silhouetted against the sky as they reach from the terra cotta tile rooftops, striving and timeless at once. Keep your senses sharp. You're in the heart of truffle culture.

11

Family

The village of Paladini has a population of forty-seven people and ninety-nine truffle dogs. To reach Paladini, you follow an ever-narrowing series of roads from Motovun, the route climbing past a sparkling reservoir to a cluster of stucco homes overlooking the forest.

Radmila Karlić, the matriarch of Karlić Tartufi, the multi-generational family business that has agreed to take me truffle hunting, is cleaning truffles outside when I arrive. Three huge amphorae mark the front yard. Ancient olive trees pepper the back.

Radmila greets me, and I immediately put my foot in my mouth. "Beautiful lake," I say.

A cloud darkens her sweet round face. "The best truffle grounds in all of Istria," she says, pointing a finger in the direction of the offending reservoir, "are at the bottom of that lake. That was my father's favorite place to hunt truffles." On further questioning, she concedes that nobody in central Istria had fresh water until the reservoir was built in the 1970s, but it still bugs her. *The best truffling in Istria.*

Radmila began hunting truffles with her father fifty years ago, when she was a young girl. Now her kids, Ivan and Ivana, who are in their twenties, hunt as well. When Ivan was six, his class had to draw pictures of what they wanted to be when they grew up. He drew himself as a truffle hunter. There was never a question.

As we chat, Radmila's phone rings. It's her seventy-four-year-old mother, Danica, needing a ride home from the truffle forest. She's recently taken up truffle hunting as well but she doesn't drive, so she and her tiny dog are shuttled back and forth.

"I still can't believe it," Radmila says. "When I started hunting with my father, my mother said, 'Don't do it! That's a job for men. Who will marry you if you become a truffle hunter?' Now guess who's hunting truffles every day?"

In fact, Karlić Tartufi is kind of a sprawling superorganism of truffle hunting, with half a dozen humans and twice that many dogs, any combination of which might be in the woods on a particular day, funneling truffles back to the Karlić manse, which includes a small shop, a state-of-the-art demonstration kitchen, a solar-powered dog kennel, and a glass deck cantilevered over the hillside. Karlić hunts truffles, buys from other Paladini families, and sells to dealers throughout Europe. I liked that Zak Frost was one of their loyal clients, but I especially liked that at least three different family members had participated in my email exchanges with them. It gave a sense of barely controlled family chaos.

Ivana's boyfriend, a strapping young Croatian with a black beard and ample tattoos, loads four dogs into the back of a

Citroën minivan. When I ask him his name, he says, "Call me Ban. It's my last name, but you can't pronounce my first." (It's Hrvoje, if you want to give it a shot.)

Radmila and I look out over the vigorous woods of Istria, glinting in the October light. The reservoir below us is the exception that proves the rule. A great patch of truffle forest got sacrificed for drinking water, but now any attempt by the Forest Service to hack into the truffle forests for a lesser cause is met by a swarm of local resistance.

Truffles saved Istria, everyone here keeps telling me. When many parts of Yugoslavia were depopulated during Communism, Istria wasn't. You could always make a living off truffles. When other regions lost their youth during the Balkan Wars of the 1990s and the globalization that followed, Istria didn't. Ivan and Ivana Karlić stayed, tethered to forests and family.

Truffles brought bigger houses. Running water and electricity and television. The truffle hunters were the breadwinners for their families and maintained self-respect, when that was breaking down across Eastern Europe. You can tell what people do for a living by their houses: the farmers have one story, the truffle hunters have two.

We pile into the minivan and snake down the road through the Karlić family vineyards. Radmila proudly points to a stand of oak and hazel seedlings. "In a few years, we'll have our own black truffles here."

At the edge of the valley forest, right below the dam that holds back the reservoir, we park and release the dogs. Candy and Betty, both nine-year-old white Lagotto Romagnolos, charge into the woods like pros, but three-year-old Istra (named for the local word for Istria), another Lagotto, begins frantically digging mini-holes to get attention, then looking up hopefully.

"My other dogs are excellent," Radmila says wearily. "This one, nothing. But she's young." Most dogs need about three seasons before going pro, so there was still hope for Istra.

Radmila is still in mourning for Blackie, her treasured truffle dog who died last year at age seventeen. "My pockets were always full with that dog," she sighs. "One year I bought a new car entirely with Blackie's truffles."

The current ace is Lela, a thirteen-year-old German short-haired pointer with a profound schnoz and a detached air of sagacity. Nose twitching, she plods calmly up the dirt path, and we dutifully follow.

"My best dogs are females," Radmila says. "Males don't listen. They get distracted by other dogs. They chase animals. Females are much easier to work with."

When I ask if certain breeds are better, she shakes her head. "You can pay a lot for a fancy dog, and it can't find its own nose. Or you can pick up a dog off the street, no mamma, no pappa, and it's perfect."

Each licensed hunter in Istria can have two truffle dogs, plus a trainee. Every member of the Karlić clan, including Ban, has their own license. Technically it allows you to hunt in any public forest in Istria, but by unwritten law, hunters from Motovun hunt in Motovun Forest, and those from Paladini hunt here. When I ask Ban the name of this forest, he shrugs. "The Forest."

The woods feel more jungle-like than Motovun Forest, thick vines drooping from a high oak canopy in the filtered green light. Ivy covers the ground and moss carpets the trunks. Cuckoos squawk, unseen. We pick our way through the underbrush, our boots squelching in the clay, the heavy scent of wet earth and chlorophyll in our noses.

ISTVÁN BAGI

Five species of truffles (clockwise from lower left): black autumn, *macrosporum*, *brumale*, white, and black winter.

ŽELJKO ZGRABLIĆ

All the ingredients for a banging good truffle hunt: Oak forests, limestone, and a Lagotto Romagnolo on a mission.

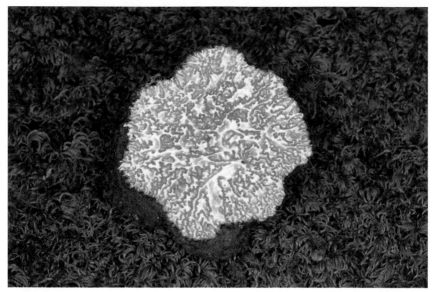

ŽELJKO ZGRABLIĆ

Black summer truffle.

ŽELJKO ZGRABLIĆ

Brumale truffle.

ROWAN JACOBSEN

A tree root thick with Appalachian truffle mycorrhizae.

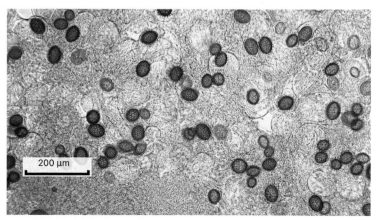

ANTONIO IZZO

Bianchetto truffle spores under the microscope.

ROWAN JACOBSEN

Truffle sellers at the Acqualagna National White Truffle Fair.

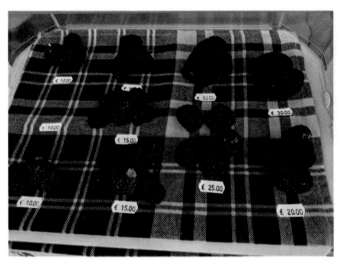

ROWAN JACOBSEN

Summer truffles for sale at the Acqualagna National White
Truffle Fair.

LAURA SABATTINI

The author with a monster 1,143-gram white truffle at the Acqualagna National White Truffle Fair.

ROWAN JACOBSEN

The Museo del Tartufo di Acqualagna in Acqualagna, Italy.

ROWAN JACOBSEN

Giuseppina Balestra of Sabatino Tartufi buying white truffles in Umbria.

ROWAN JACOBSEN

Truffling by night, Tuscany.

ROWAN JACOBSEN

Matteo Giuliani and
Miro find a big
white truffle.

Good day for
Matteo's lucky
truffle cap.

ROWAN JACOBSEN

ROWAN JACOBSEN

Motovun, spiritual heart of Istrian truffles.

ROWAN JACOBSEN

Livade, commercial center of Istrian truffles.

ROWAN JACOBSEN

Hunting truffles in
Motovun Forest.

ROWAN JACOBSEN

Ivana Karlić and Hrvoje Ban hunting truffles in the Istrian forest with Candy, Betty,
and Lela.

ROWAN JACOBSEN

A black autumn truffle in the Wiltshire Woods, with Zak Frost and Stanley working in the background.

ISTVÁN BAGI

A white truffle in Hungary, with Emil in background.

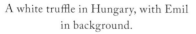

ISTVÁN BAGI

A Hungarian white truffle emerging from the earth.

ROWAN JACOBSEN

István Bagi and Mokka hunting truffles in southern Hungary.

ROWAN JACOBSEN

Zoltán Bratek, Grand Master of the Saint Ladislaus Order of Truffle Knights.

ROWAN JACOBSEN

A medallion from the Hungarian Federation of Truffling.

ROWAN JACOBSEN

A bianchetto truffle emerging from the loblolly pine orchard at Burwell Farms in North Carolina.

ROWAN JACOBSEN

Mycologist Omon Isikhuemhen and Burwell Farms manager Richard Franks in the bianchetto orchard.

ŽELJKO ZGRABLIĆ

A Lagotto Romagnolo
with two nice black
summer truffles.

ROWAN JACOBSEN

Oregon white truffles
being weighed at the
Oregon Truffle Festi-
val in Eugene.

ROWAN JACOBSEN

Charles
Lefevre and
Dante in
the Oregon
woods.

ROWAN JACOBSEN

Jérôme Quirion, first person to
successfully cultivate the Appalachian truffle, with Merguez.

ROWAN JACOBSEN

Truffled beet carpaccio, salad with truffles and chicken livers, truffled scallops crudo, and truffled eggs in shell, made with Oregon black truffles by Vitaly Paley at Paley's Place in Portland, Oregon.

Gustave, surprise winner of the 2018 Joriad North American Truffle Dog Championship.

ROWAN JACOBSEN

"Šu pokazati, Lela," Radmila calls to her pointer in Croatian, reeling her back in. *Show me the truffle.* "Ovdje, ovdje," she coos, pointing at the ground beneath promising trees. *Here? Here?*

Candy and Betty start digging at a spot halfheartedly, as if they aren't sure what they've found. Radmila brings in Lela for the final go/no-go. "Pokazati, Lela." Lela touches her nose to the ground once, twice, then chuffs in exasperation at our ineptitude and moves on.

The dogs mud-bog through puddles, having a blast but finding nothing. I try to distract myself from my rising fear of getting skunked again by closely watching Lela as she raises her nose to sample the air. She reminds me of a shaman, mediating between worlds, letting invisible presences old and new filter through her consciousness while we, the rest of the tribe, hang on her every gesture. It strikes me as charmingly absurd that this entire industry balances precariously on dog noses. For all their genius, they're still dogs. One minute they're visionaries; the next, they're eating deer poop.

Lela likes to slip away when we're not looking, and has to be regularly reeled in. "She's always disappearing," Ban says. "She's in her own world. You can tell she's doing it for herself. She'll take a treat, but she'd rather eat the truffle."

Radmila sighs. "Many times, that dog has had truffle lunch."

We slip down into a channel made by a seasonal stream to "sniff the walls," as Ban puts it. "The walls of the channel can be really good. The truffle thinks it's deep down, but not from the side." Candy points us to a spot, but it turns out to hold a tiny, rotten truffle.

"Listen," Radmila tells me, holding it to her ear like a seashell. When I do, I hear methodical crunching, an unsettling sound I associate with mice in my farmhouse walls. Tiny white things poke out of the truffle, wriggling. I'm about to toss it when Radmila stops me. "For dog practice," she says.

Suddenly Istra charges past us with something pale and round in her mouth, and everybody screams. Ban wrestles her to the ground and extracts the prize—a wild apple. As Istra revels in the limelight, Ban shakes his head. "Our little pig. She eats so many."

As we walk, I notice Ban has coordinates tattooed on his arm. He tells me they're the location of Srebrenica, his hometown in Bosnia and Herzegovina, and the site of a 1995 massacre during the Balkan Wars. He still has lots of family there, but he was too young to remember the fighting. He mostly grew up in Zagreb. "I've always lived in cities," he says, ducking under curtains of vines. "I'd never been in the country. I didn't know anything about nature."

One day, he met a cute blond girl outside a nightclub in Zagreb. They hit it off, but she wouldn't give him her number. It took him two weeks to track her down through Facebook. Her name was Ivana Karlić.

They went on a couple of dates. When it started to get serious, she said she wanted to cook him dinner. He came to her apartment. She made pasta dough, rolled it out, cut it into squares, and rolled them on the diagonal around her pinky into *fuži*, traditional Istrian pasta. She also made scrambled eggs and shaved something black into them.

"I wondered if they were truffles," Ban says, "because I knew she was from Istria. But she hadn't told me much about her family." If they were truffles, that made him nervous. "The only gourmet food I'd ever had was caviar, and I hated it. I thought maybe truffles would taste like caviar."

She served the eggs with their mysterious black flecks, and the fuži with butter. At the table, she shaved a white lump over the pasta and pushed it toward him. "Eat," she said. She looked nervous too.

He took a bite of the pasta. And his world opened. "I'd never tasted something like that. It changed me." He finished his pasta, then the eggs, then had more.

"Do you like it?" she asked.

"It's the best thing I've ever eaten," he said.

Her face relaxed. "Good. Now we can go out. My whole family is in the truffle business. If you didn't like truffles, it wouldn't work."

It worked. Not only did he love truffles, he loved truffle hunting. "We go hunting every chance we get," he says. "Hours at a time. Sometimes twice a day." He couldn't believe there were forests where you could explore freely and find amazing things in the ground. "The best part is just being in the woods with the dogs. The smells. The quiet. To me, in the fall, the whole forest smells a little bit like truffles. I think I'm more sensitive to it, because I didn't grow up with it."

Soon he was working full-time for Karlić Tartufi, even when Ivana was away at school. "But I'm still learning," he admits. "I've learned that dogs dig for three reasons: for truffles, for moles, and for cool ground." Many times on blistering summer days he's grown increasingly excited as one of the dogs excavates a giant crater, only to watch crestfallen as she plops her belly down on the cool earth and takes a nap.

Suddenly Lela does a head-check and zips off the path, her tail oscillating fast and tight. She doubles back on her trail, circles a tree, nose touching everywhere, then begins scrabbling slow and determined with her front paws.

Radmila charges after her, brandishing her *otka*, the Istrian version of a *vanghetto*. It's flat-bladed with a short wooden handle—a little more practical than the Italian *vanghetto*, though with less flair. She nudges Lela out of the way and takes over. A single nick from a claw can shave a hundred euros off the price of a truffle. She brushes the loose dirt from the top of the hole the dog has started.

I crane my neck for a glimpse into the hole, but all four dogs collapse on the spot and chaos ensues. There's a lot of shouting in Croatian. Candy flops down sideways on top of the hole, like a dog about to roll in a dead skunk, and has to be dragged away. Ban lifts Istra from the hole so Radmila can gently pry away dirt from the edges with her otka.

Radmila keeps scraping away layers of dirt, continuously pushing dog noses out of the way, and then sticks her own face in the hole. "Yes, for sure a truffle," she says when she comes back up, dirt on the tip of her nose. Her face is flushed from exertion and her hair has come loose.

She tunnels deeper, and something pale begins to breach the soil. She circles again, widening the hole, then widens it again. Judging by the slope of its shoulders, it's the size of a baseball. "Mamma mia!" she breathes, confirming that whatever your native tongue, you switch to Italian for emphasis.

When she's certain she's reached the bottom of the truffle, she wriggles her otka underneath and pops it out. "Brava, Lela," she murmurs, sliding a treat into the dog's mouth. Then she passes me the truffle, and I take a sniff. Through the scrim of fresh soil comes a beguiling collage of impressions, playful and strange. Ban's right; it smells like the whole forest.

We find several more truffles, mostly small, but a couple of nice ones. I buy the smallest scrap. It's too small and ugly to make it into the trade, but it smells great and costs me just €4. Who gets to eat truffles? People who think with their nose.

Back in Paladini, we reunite with Danica and we hose down the dogs and our boots. Ban decides I'm lucky and invites me back out the next day with him and Ivana, and I readily accept. Watching him return the dogs to the kennel, it occurs to me that the Istrians have become postmodern hunter-gatherers, and that the sprawling superorganism extends far beyond the immediate family. It includes chefs and truffle traders, hunters and dogs, oaks and poplars, all knit into relation by the evolutionary ingenuity of a species whose existence now depends on healthy forests and happy humans.

12

The Saint Ladislaus Order of Truffle Knights

S hame on me for not knowing there's a Hungarian Federation of Truffling. Or that it has Truffle Knights. (And truffle nights, now and then.) And a Patron Saint of Truffling. (That would be Saint Ladislaus, a big player in Hungarian history.) And a museum, complete with truffle folk art: truffle clocks, illuminated truffle saints clutching oak branches and warty black truffles, a handsome woodcut of a mustachioed man in an oilcloth coat leading a pig on a leash. Double shame on me for not knowing that Hungary produces eight species of edible truffles.

Eight! A truffle paradise, and nobody knows it. Most Hungarians don't even know it. With few exceptions, they aren't the ones eating the truffles.

I certainly didn't know it when my truffle odyssey began. But as it became clear that Eastern Europe was an important and overlooked part of the truffle story, a few things pointed me toward Hungary. One was Zak Frost, who raved about the beautiful whites he got from Hungary. Zak also was big on honey truffles, a nontuber species found only in the Carpathian Basin and almost always used for desserts because of its profound sweetness.

In addition to Zak, a respected truffle expert in the United States told me about a truffle virtuoso in Hungary named István Bagi. When I stalked István online, I liked what I saw. His name turned up on a few scientific papers ("No Radioactive Contamination from the Chernobyl Disaster in Hungarian White Truffles"), and LinkedIn had him listed as "Head of Truffle Department" for something called NEFAG Zrt., after a previous five-year stint as managing director of Truffleminers Ltd.

When I reached out to István via email, he told me to come in November, when the seasons for several edible species overlap. "Get ready for an intense couple of days and lots of secrets will be revealed."

That alone was enough to warm my heart, but the kicker came when I unearthed the Hungarian Federation of Truffling online. There I learned that Peak Truffle in Hungary was during the Austro-Hungarian Empire, and things had been pretty much downhill ever since. But like their Templar brethren, the Truffle Knights were valiantly keeping the flame alive. The federation offered golden information on the eight species of truffles, on truffle gastronomy, and on the rules for truffle collecting in Hungary. (Use a dog, and keep a journal with all your finds, which the police can check at any time.)

All in all, it seemed quirky, colorful, sui generis. Something was happening down on the Danube, and knowledge of it wasn't crossing over to the West. Perhaps that was an Iron

Curtain artifact, or perhaps it was just language. Magyar is a goulash of *y*'s and *z*'s peppered with enough diacritics to short-circuit the English-trained brain. It's impenetrable to outsiders, so what happens in Hungary tends to stay in Hungary.

Thus I went to Hungary.

As soon as I arrive in Budapest, I cold-call the Hungarian Federation of Truffling and the affiliated First Hungarian Truffling Society. Its president, Dr. Zoltán Bratek, says he can meet with me at his university office starting at 6:00 A.M. on Saturday morning. I swallow hard and say great.

My taxi driver dumps me in front of a Soviet-era monolith surrounded by vast plains of dead grass. Three lonely cars dot the giant parking lot.

Inside I ride the elevator to the fourth floor and find Zoltán peering at spores through a microscope. By day, he's a mild-mannered mycologist with wizardly eyebrows. But when the need arises, he transforms into the Grand Master of the Saint Ladislaus Order of Truffle Knights.

What that means, in practical terms, is that he has a closet in his office full of robes, truffle shields, truffle medallions, truffle art, truffle books in every language, photos of past Order events, and piles of truffle paperwork. (There are eight member bodies in the HFT, from the Hungarian Mushroom Growers' Association to the Transylvanian Truffle Gatherers' Society.) There's a bronze Master of Truffling medal of honor showing a relief of a man and a dog crouched over a hole, which I immediately covet. There's also a photo of gold-robed Truffle Knights closing their eyes and caressing a giant black truffle in a way that makes me think uncomfortably of Kubrick's *Eyes Wide Shut*.

It's pretty exciting stuff, though it doesn't exactly give me the sense that the Knights are crawling through the mud every day in search of tubers. One of the main things their pamphlet mentions is that "matching wines to the flavor of truffles is a great challenge for our Order of Knights."

The overarching goal of the Order is to restore Hungary's proud tradition of truffling, Zoltán explains as he bumbles around his office, searching in vain for interesting but misplaced paraphernalia. But despite all the Knights' labors, it isn't working. Even in Budapest, bastion of ruin bars and wrecked hipsters, just try to find a restaurant that can do justice to a truffle. Worse, try to find a forest where you can hunt!

The problem actually started well before Communism. In the nineteenth century, when the Hapsburg Empire was astride the world and Budapest was a capital of gastronomy and mustaches, virtually every book of Hungarian cookery included truffles. Then World War I came along, the Hapsburg Empire made like the *Hindenburg*, and Hungary never really recovered. Half the truffle hunters were dead, and most of the forests were razed. The knowledge was lost. The tradition died.

World War II, of course, did the country no favors either, and by the time Communism congealed in 1949, playing around with truffles was verboten. "It was considered too aristocratic," Zoltán says. "Like tennis." I consider objecting to this observation, having grown up playing some serious redneck tennis, but I see his point.

In the 1990s and early 2000s, the truffling societies tried to jump-start the tradition. They had a few minor successes— some good dinners, a few hunts, the museum—but the culture at large never really took off, in large part because it was getting harder and harder to hunt truffles in Hungary.

Zoltán is beginning to explain why when a colleague pops into his office. Young and tall, with a long ponytail, an excellent mustache, and a straw basket on his arm, the guy is a hard-core forager, and he's packing truffles I've never seen before. A few are gray-fuzzed *Tuber excavatum*, a common and (some say) tasty species that has never been commercialized. Others are tiny and redolent of cured meat.

Zoltán exclaims, grabs one, and puts it under the microscope to check its spores. "*Pachyphloeus!*" he announces. "A rare find. We have only a handful of specimens."

"In your lab?" I ask.

"In the world."

I take a second sniff. It's inarguably seductive. But it's also the size of a marble, and Zoltán says they never get much bigger. *Pachyphloeus* will not be storming culinary circles any time soon.

"We must celebrate!" Zoltán says, disappearing into his truffle closet. I'm nervous he's going to emerge in full Grandmaster regalia, but he comes out carrying a golden bottle of pálinka, the local brandy. "This is very special," he says, pouring shots. "It's made from apples, aged in oak for four years, and infused with truffles." He and his colleague knock back their shots and hand me mine.

I beg off. "I don't think I can do it. It's seven in the morning, and I haven't had breakfast."

Zoltán's eyebrows droop. "But . . . I've never opened this before."

I drink. It's delicious, truffly as hell, but I immediately feel the horizon dipping like a flight simulator.

While I struggle to get back on plane, Zoltán and his colleague catalog the new find. Zoltán is so jazzed that he again disappears into his closet, and this time the Grandmaster really does emerge. He wears a golden truffle medallion over a green velvet robe, his Birkenstocks peeking out underneath, and he carries a shield almost as large as he is. On a blue field, it features three black truffles, one topped by a golden crown, with a cross and a sickle moon overhead. The lights flicker. Somewhere in the heavens above Budapest, an ancient force opens one sleepy eye.

"Now," says Zoltán, "we're ready to truffle."

〰〰〰

Budapest is divided by the Danube into two cities: Buda and Pest. Pest, on the east side of the river, is flat, and like flat places everywhere, it used to be for the hoi polloi until commerce followed the hoi polloi and made Pest the throbbing heart of the city. Buda is a pile of limestone hills, topped by palaces, parks, and oak forests, and that makes it the only metropolis I know with decent truffle grounds within the city limits.

In the park, we rendezvous with a middle-aged guy named Imre Lencsés, who has a braided beard held together with tiny plastic hair clips, which reminds me of my hippie-farmer friends in Vermont, as does his long-suffering air of activism against the system. He's launched a business called Tuber Traders that hasn't been trading many tubers, for lack of both supply and demand, and is now trying to build up his business of taking tourists truffle hunting in the park. He thinks I'll be good practice.

Imre has a very chill one-eyed black Lab named Sailor. Sailor plods through the woods without urgency, nosing the brown carpet of dry leaves. When he finds a truffle, he scrapes away the leaves, carefully picks it up in his mouth, and brings it back to Imre. That would be disastrous with a thin-skinned white truffle, but it's common practice with black summers, which is what you find in the Buda hills. Black summers have such tough peridia that a conscientious dog isn't going to wreck them.

We angle away from the peopled paths toward the more remote sections of the park. In places, the ground looks like a deranged rototiller has rampaged through. "Wild boar," Imre says. "Big problem."

Zoltán (who, sadly, has traded his robe for fleece) is distracted by a stump sprouting white shelf fungi like wings. "These fungi are highly medicinal," he says. We all load our packs. I'm feeling more Hungarian by the minute.

After a bone-chilling hour in near-freezing temperatures, we have a dozen black truffles, a lifetime supply of medicinal mushrooms, and numb fingertips. "Let's have lunch," Imre says. "I made a picnic." There in the woods, he produces ham sandwiches with white truffle butter, salad with truffle vinaigrette, and tiramisu made with honey truffles. He hands us all tiny bottles of Hungarian wine. "This is what all the tourists will get," he says. "What do you think?"

I flash him a thumbs-up, my mouth stuffed with salad. The vinaigrette has a nutty funk and a sweaty attack. "What truffle is this?" I ask.

"*Tuber macrosporum*."

"You mean *melanosporum*?"

"No, *macrosporum*. It's the best truffle. It looks like a black truffle but tastes like a white. I rarely find one, but when I do, I never cook it. I always put it in salad."

Tuber macrosporum, I later learn, is sometimes called the large-spored or the smooth black truffle, but more often it's simply known as *macrosporum*, and it's the under-the-radar fave of many trufflers.

Unfortunately, the cold air is putting a damper on the aromas. The ham sandwich is a rock. I power through it quickly, shivering and eager to get to the tiramisu.

"This is for you," Imre says, handing me a whole honey truffle. It's heavy, white, and stippled with black, like a hunk of old cauliflower. Inside, it's starkly beautiful, with white veins against off-white spore sacs. *Mattirolomyces terfezioides* isn't technically a truffle (not being part of the *Tuber* genus), but it's one of thousands of mycorrhizal fungi that pursue the same life strategy. It's found almost exclusively in spongy, sandy soil along the Danube floodplain, under stands of young black locust trees. (Black locusts are an invasive species from North America, which begs the question: Where were the honey truffles living before the black locusts arrived?) Because of this habitat, the Hungarians call them sand truffles, but honey has become the dominant term in English.

The truffle smells mildly of Camembert and tropical fruit. Not a canonical truffle moment—none of the primordial *Altered States* fireworks go off—but I can see how the little vertebrates of the Carpathian Basin might get a thrill, especially once I set a forkful of tiramisu on my tongue. The honey truffle is sweet as stevia, and almost as cloying. That insane sweetness survives freezing and processing, and everyone in Hungary thinks it has great commercial potential. It's already become the next big thing in Hong Kong. And Hungary has a lock on it.

It seems like one more sign that the country is primed to break out as the next truffle star, and I say as much to the group. They exchange nervous glances and tell me it's not that simple. Yes, Hungary is rich in truffles. But it's no paradise for truffle hunters. In fact, other than a few parks like this one, it's increasingly difficult to find places to go truffling.

"But I thought Hungary had lots of forests," I say.

Yes, they reply, but who gets to use them? There are those on the inside, and those on the outside, and if you're a regular schmo, most forests are now off-limits.

I ask more questions, but they aren't comfortable saying more, so I let it drop. We pack up our picnic and make our way back to the parking lot, and I wish Imre luck with his truffle endeavors. He asks if I have other plans while in Hungary.

"I do," I reply. "I'm supposed to meet another truffle expert. Perhaps you know him. István Bagi."

I may as well have uttered the name Voldemort. As one, they draw in their breath, fall silent, and the temperature in the park drops another ten degrees. In that case, they mumble, this conversation is at an end.

"Let me guess," I offer. "István's on the inside?"

Actually, they say, he's on the *inside* of the inside.

≈≈≈

That evening I receive a mysterious email from Zoltán containing the phone number of a Truffle Knight who wants to speak with me. I dial.

"I've been awaiting your call," says the man on the other end, in crisp English enriched with Carpathian undertones. "There are things you need to understand. Meet me for dinner at seven thirty tonight. I'll text you the coordinates."

Which turn out to involve a long train ride into the Budapest hinterlands. I step out of the car onto the tracks of an unlit Socialist-era train station and walk down a long, dark street, every footstep clicking off the stone walls as if I've stumbled into *The Third Man*. After a lonely mile of nothing-ness in which I become increasingly convinced that Google has lost its mind, I come to a pool of light and a sign for the restaurant: Kakas Étterem. Per Google, I already know this means Rooster Restaurant, or maybe Cock Diner, and sure enough, old Chanticleer is crowing on the sign.

Relieved, I step inside and find Deep Throat. His name is Laszlo, like pretty much every man in Hungary not named István, and he's Transylvanian, which explains the accent. He's lived in Budapest for years and had been a notable architect. Did I know the big glass thing on the Danube, with all the curves? That's his, self-financed, but the state took it away from him. Yes, they do that kind of thing all the time. They just write new laws in Parliament. Dark times.

"As bad as the media makes out?" I ask.

"Worse," he says. "Much worse."

Laszlo, who is a vice president in the Truffling Federation, and also has a little truffle export business on the side, places a small bronze medal on the table. Over an image of angels lifting up a summer truffle, it reads PRO GLORIA TUBERIS. The other side has an image of Saint Laszlo on horseback.

"What would it take for me to become a Truffle Knight?" I ask, because why not.

One step at a time, Laszlo replies. And then we get to the business at hand. Did I know that the state has privatized the forests? That it's handing them to the oligarchs and pushing guys like him out of the business?

I don't, but I soon do. We're joined by two colleagues he's invited: another Transylvanian truffle dealer, and a caviar guy who's hoping to launch the first line of honey truffle bonbons. (His samples are delicious.)

When the waiter asks for our orders, I look to Laszlo for help.

"That's the best dish on the menu," he says, pointing. "They're famous for it." The English translation of the dish reads "Cock Stew with Testicles."

"Seriously?" I ask. "Cock-and-Balls Stew?"

"It's a classic."

I search his face for a hint of a smile, and find none. "Fine, I'm in."

Everyone else gets the fish soup.

Over the next two hours, as orange waves of paprika break over the table, the Transylvanians paint a dark portrait for me. Ever since the Communist era, vast amounts of Hungary's forests and farmland have been in state hands. When the state announced that it wanted to privatize those resources, the original idea was to empower a new generation of small farmers, Jefferson style, but with the last embers of democracy fading in the Hungarian hearth, Viktor Orbán's Fidesz party auctioned off much of the land to a handful of oligarchs and European syndicates, the only ones who could afford the soaring prices.

In the old days, they tell me, you could hunt truffles almost anywhere. Now you had to lease the rights from the forest's owner. Rates exploded. Soon only the most well-funded and well-connected players could play. More often than not, that player was Voldemort. Which left everybody else scrapping for crumbs.

I tell them that sounds a lot like the United States, where public resources like timber, mineral rights, and even fishing rights are usually auctioned off to the highest bidders, often in sweetheart deals. Capitalism, warts and all. I say that it sounds complicated.

This is Hungary, they reply. Of course it's complicated. How's your stew?

"Delicious," I say, which it is, rich and fatty and a touch gamy. I give it a stir, watching bits of meat that look like burst grapes float by. If the things are testicles that I think are testicles, roosters are ridiculously well-endowed. That, or balls swell a lot when cooked.

Dinner ends late. The last dishes cleared, Laszlo slides the medal across the table to me. I pocket it with solemnity. "Pro Gloria Tuberis," I offer. "What can I do?"

"Just tell the world what goes on. Nobody knows."

13

The Inside of the Inside

Voldemort picks me up in Budapest, buys me an espresso, and we drive south in the early light, headed for a forest near the Serbian border for two days of truffle hunting. When I ask if I need to line up lodging, he's cryptic. "It's okay, I know a house."

István Bagi has a sharp nose and a black goatee and would actually make a decent bad guy on TV. He's soft-spoken and focused in a way that can imply either spiritual advancement or supervillainy. He knows I've been truffling in Italy and Croatia and asks how the season has been.

"Not good," I say. "Too dry."

He nods and strokes his goatee. "Too bad for them," he says. "But good for us." He has a hunch that climate change is slowly pushing white truffles out of their traditional Mediterranean home toward cooler, wetter places like the Carpathian Basin.

Traditionally, Hungary has been considered black summer country, but István puts less and less stock in it. "I don't think that truffle has a future," he says. Too cheap, thanks to dumping by countries like Iran and Bulgaria. István also thinks consumers will eventually sour on synthetic aroma, which would be deadly for black summers.

"What about *melanosporum*?" I ask. I've heard that farmers in Spain and France, the two countries that produce the most, are struggling mightily with drought. "Are you cultivating that here?"

"*Here*?" he replies. "No."

I rephrase the question. "Are you farming *melanosporum* . . . somewhere?"

He shrugs, but his eyes are twinkling like St. Nick's. "I have lots of dreams," he says.

The truffle experts I know in the United States consider István Bagi a prodigy. He has an uncanny ability to find truffles, and in a country that never lost the Soviet-era habit of hamstringing its entrepreneurs, he's somehow managed to keep the apparatchiks at bay and build a successful truffle business. He's become, as one Budapest journalist put it to me, "The Pope of Truffles," though István downplays this as the suburbs give way to the rolling oak forests of southern Hungary. "It's a little bit me," he says, "but it's mostly Mokka."

At the sound of his name, István's eleven-year-old black Lab pops his head over the back seat. He's a puddle of Zen, and over the next two days he'll put on a clinic that sets him atop my personal truffle-dog pantheon.

Mokka's predecessor was also a black Lab. When István got him, back in the late 1990s, there were virtually no truffle dogs in Hungary. That whole 1949–1989 thing really took the starch out of the local truffle culture, István says. "It seemed too decadent. Like golf." I again hold my tongue.

By the 1990s, decadence was back in the Hungarian air. A few hobbyists—mostly mycology types—began to hunt black truffles,

István among them. "I always liked nature as a kid," he tells me as we drive. "I did a lot of mushroom hunting and birdwatching camps." Truffles were a natural extension. He didn't have a dog, but if you were very observant, you could sometimes find a few black summers, which often break the surface when ripe.

As he learned more about the truffle world—and the prices traders would pay—István began to wonder if Hungary might have white truffles as well, even though they'd never been documented. "I knew the southern edge of Hungary had a more Mediterranean climate. The vegetation looked kind of right. I thought, if there are any white truffles in Hungary, that's where they'll be."

In October 1998, he borrowed a loaner dog from a businessman friend who liked to hunt truffles in Italy. He had no car, so he and the dog rode down on the train and walked to the forest. Without knowing it, he was reprising Massimo Sella's celebrated foray up the Mirna seventy years earlier, with similar results: they stepped into the woods, and within minutes found a nice white truffle.

"I couldn't believe it!" István says. "It was too easy." They quickly found several more. "Just like that, I had half a kilo of white truffles. I thought the forest was going to have tons and I was going to get rich."

He didn't find another all day—he'd been duped by whites' predilection for edges and for messing with people—but he was hooked anyway. He bought a Labrador puppy (Mokka's predecessor), read the classic French truffling books to educate himself, and became a full-time hunter.

His timing couldn't have been better. The world wars had left Hungary with just 10 percent of its original forests, but in the 1970s it began planting new ones on a large scale. For a few golden years, he was able to live the truffling dream, walking the woods all day with his dog and scratching out a living. Black truffles in summer, whites in fall.

But in the 2000s, the rest of Hungary caught on, and István watched the Tragedy of the Commons playing out. "I'd visit a small forest, and there would be fifty cars there!" Most of the newbies didn't have dogs. Instead, they just raked the topsoil to get the black truffles near the surface, which tears roots and mycelia and disrupts the network of organisms needed to make more truffles and to support a healthy soil biome. Raking is an ongoing problem in Romania, Bulgaria, Iran, China, Oregon, and probably other places still under the radar.

But this is where the story of Hungarian truffles takes an unusual turn. Unlike those other places, Hungary stopped its raking problem cold. In 2010, new laws went into effect. "Very serious," István says as we drive. "Maybe too serious." I can't help but wonder if he had a hand in creating those laws. In 2013 more laws were added, and the leasing system began.

Today in Hungary, you can hunt truffles only with a dog. Both you and the dog need your own license. To get those licenses, you both have to pass an exam involving buried truffles. (István and Zoltán both occasionally administer the tests.) When you do hunt, you must keep a log with a record of every truffle you find—where, when, who you sold it to, and for what price. Police can demand to see a log at any time. The hunters I met took it very seriously.

All of this makes Hungary the most tightly regulated truffle country in the world. "Hungary used to be a traditional gray market for truffles," István marvels, "and now it's almost white."

Even with a license, you can't hunt most places without that permit from the landowner. Whether an oligarch or the state, most landowners like to auction off the truffling rights to a single entity in multiyear leases. István agrees that prices have skyrocketed. Typical leases might run €10,000 or €20,000 a year for a piece of forest. One forty-hectare parcel went for €60,000.

And this is where the gripes of the Truffle Knights come in, I point out. "Doesn't that mean you need money and connections to get in on the game?"

István raises his hands skyward. "In Hungary, you need connections to do *anything*." But there have been no sweetheart deals, he insists. He and his partners acquired their rights the old-fashioned way: they paid through the nose. István is the only one with the acumen to make it work. Even that €60,000 parcel paid off.

Admittedly, that left little room for hobbyists or newcomers. István agrees that Hungary needs more reserves where people can truffle for fun, but the number of professional trufflers in Hungary has fallen from about five hundred to less than one hundred, and he thinks that's about all Hungary's small forests can support.

"It's finally stable," he says. "The system is working." Multiyear contracts mean that both landowners and hunters are incentivized to manage the forests for long-term productivity. "It's good for the landowner, who gets paid. It's good for the hunter, who can control his resource. And it's good for the forests."

When I ask about the root of the trouble with the Truffle Knights, István shrugs. "They just don't like me." He worked with Zoltán years ago, but he had no time for robes or fancy wine dinners. He'd shown up for the first meeting of the Truffling Society, but none of them even had dogs, so he went his own way. He just wanted to be in the woods, hunting.

He started selling some of the truffles he found, and slowly it became a business. He estimates he's involved in three-quarters of Hungary's truffle trade. He leases about twenty-five forest parcels for his operation, working with a team of ten other hunters, all old friends he's known for years. "We have to be able to trust each other," he says.

István has truffled in twenty-five countries. He's even taught clinics in Japan, which has good native truffles but very few dogs, and where a burgeoning and uniquely Japanese-style truffle culture is emerging. He shows me photos of people in parks in Japan wandering around with parasols and bending down to observe truffles in the grass. "Sometimes I think that's my Plan B," he says. "If this country gets really bad and I have to leave, I'll train dogs in Japan."

István is also the Pope of Truffle Dogs. "I can train a dog to find truffles in thirty minutes. Just throw a truffle in the grass and let your dog fetch it. Over and over. Be very happy when they bring it back." Then start burying it and do the same thing.

The harder thing, he says, is finding a dog who loves to work hard, day in and day out. So many hunters told me their dogs were toast after two or three hours, but István and Mokka hunt six hours a day, five days a week. He rattles off his advice:

1. Buy a year-old dog. Its personality will already be evident.

2. Hunting and retrieving breeds are best. Water retrievers can be really good. He's not a fan of Lagottos. "Too much energy."

3. Don't get a dog that's too smart for its own good. They have to like doing the same thing over and over and over.

4. Train your dog *alone*. Not with an older dog. When dogs are together, they pay attention to each other, not you. The mind meld happens when you spend a lot of time alone with your dog.

With the best dogs, sometimes you co-create a new kind of mind. István was once hunting in Italy with friends. The first truffle they dug up had a hibernating frog next to it. Everyone exclaimed over the frog. The dog was watching their reactions closely. After that, it raced through the woods, digging up frogs.

≋

We leave the highway and follow small roads through flat plains near the Serbian border, endless wheat fields interrupted by patches of forest. This is Hungary's bread basket, but most of the farming has been mechanized and outsourced by the oligarchs, and the villages we pass look grim: empty houses, moldering roofs, a few stooped citizens on the sidewalks. White vans with speakers cruise the villages, playing ice-cream-truck jingles, but they aren't selling treats. All the stores have closed in these towns. The vans go village to village, selling everything.

Here and there, orange columns of fire light the sky—flares from oil rigs. Big oil reserves have been found in southern Hungary, which is having its North Dakota moment. "It's funny," István says. "This is the poorest part of Hungary, and they're sitting on top of tons of oil and white truffles."

We finally roll down a dirt road and park at a gate on the edge of a forest. A huge, addled German man emerges from a ruined house next door and begins circling us on his bicycle. "No one is allowed in this forest!" he shouts. "By order of the state!"

"Remember me?" István replies gently. "We've met several times. I'm the one leasing the forest. I paid you for the use of this parking area."

The German man doesn't remember. After a long argument, he rides away, muttering.

István opens the back of his car, and Mokka hops out, pees, rolls in the leaves, runs around the woods to loosen up, and gets to work, making a beeline for certain trees. "Experience is important in a dog," István explains. "They know to check their old spots."

By now, I recognize the classic signs of a *magnatum* forest: poplars and oaks, a few hornbeams, green ivy covering the floor and snaking up the trunks. The trees are still clinging to their leaves, turning the forest into painterly bands of yellow and green. Just as in the forests in Istria and Italy, a small, slow riverbed cuts through the woods, and some of the best hunting is along its banks. "Water is everything for the whites," István confirms.

Mokka runs ahead on the trail, then looks back questioningly. With the slightest hand gesture, István indicates that we're headed to the left, and Mokka plunges into the woods on that side. He quickly returns long enough to drop a black nugget into István's hand before heading out again, unrewarded. He soon returns with another one. Again, no reward.

István mutters something in Hungarian, and Mokka heads off in a different direction. To my questioning look, István explains, "I told him I don't want blacks today, just whites." Black summers are so abundant in Hungary that István can collect a kilo without moving, just standing still and letting Mokka bring them, but the price is low, and this time of year, every moment spent hunting black summers is a moment not hunting whites.

Mokka stops near a poplar and turns a slow arc around it, spiraling down to a point. He marks the spot with a few scratches, then does the same thing ten yards away, then again.

"Slower, Mokka," István says, calling the dog back to the first spot. "Can you show me?"

Mokka returns to the first hole, sniffs it, digs a few inches down in one corner, then pokes his nose against a spot on the ground and lies down next to it.

"Thanks," István says, getting out his trowel, which is more like a flat-headed spoon, the simplest spade I've yet seen. It's half the length of the harpoons the Italians favor, which seems to fit István's low-key style. Instead of a jaunty mushrooming vest, he wears a red Helly Hansen windbreaker—a concession to the boar hunters who also stalk these woods in fall.

He pries one small layer loose, scrapes it away, searches the dirt for a hint, does it again, and says, "There. See?"

I don't. He clears more dirt to reveal a spot of ivory the size of a pencil eraser. "See? It's a big one."

"How do you know?"

"The way it sits in the soil." He pries dirt in a wide ring around the spot, avoiding coming too close. Slowly he tunnels down, leaving an untouched pedestal of truffle in the center. "See how it's not rocking? That means it's still connected to the soil down below. It's big."

István tunnels around the pedestal until he's confident the truffle doesn't have a surprise lobe running off to the side. Periodically, he uses the edge of his trowel to snip any microscopic roots that might tear the truffle, slicing in a big circle, as if he's a jewel thief disconnecting trip wires. After about five minutes, he's ready: he works his trowel underneath and pops out a beautiful golf ball: smooth, white, roundish, maybe fifty grams.

"Extra class," István says softly. He slips the truffle into a plain cloth shopping bag, which he hands me to carry. Mokka gets a handful of kibble. We check the next hole, where another forty-grammer awaits. And the next, which is good for another twenty-five grams. One tree, ten minutes, €300.

"This could be a good day," István muses.

For the next four hours, István and Mokka show me levels of truffling mastery I had no idea existed. Mokka crisscrosses the forest at a gentle canter, nose low, tail sweeping wide and slow.

Occasionally he'll freeze, raise his nose high in the air, sampling, then charge directly to a tree fifty meters away. Sometimes he'll mark spots faster than we can dig them, and István has to throw markers on the ground and return later. Sometimes he can tell the truffle's not ripe yet, and doesn't bother digging—they'll check again in a few days. Other times, he circles back on his path, circling, circling, ever tightening. Nose right on the ground now, left, right, tail wagging short, quicker, *there*. Only very rarely does István dig in the wrong direction, but when he does, Mokka noses his hand out of the way and starts a new hole at a better angle.

"Is he ever wrong?" I ask after a dozen successes.

"No."

Technically true, yet my favorite moments are the handful of times when Mokka signals truffle and István comes up empty-handed. Sometimes mice eat the truffles, but the scent lingers in the dirt. When István finds nothing, he calls in Mokka for a second check. When the dog realizes nothing is there, he buries his face in István's armpit in an ashamed gesture. *My bad. Let's move on.*

After our initial run of Extras, we hit a patch of smaller finds. "Still First class," István says, pulling up a lumpy, mouse-nibbled thirty-gram white, "but not so nice." He takes a sniff and wrinkles his nose. "Smells like tempera." He shrugs. "Italian quality."

That's a running joke on István's team. Top buyers in Asia only want the best quality and are happy to pay accordingly. "We have a Chinese buyer who doesn't even ask the price. 'Just send me the truffle.' He once paid seven thousand euros for one truffle." Germans and Spanish also want excellent truffles and will pay, but only up to a point. If prices get too high, or quality gets too low, they'll eat something else.

Italians, however, buy everything. They have to have their truffles or life can't go on. There are festivals. There are plates of pasta to sell to tourists. There's *tradizione!* But they also lie about the market price, István says. "They never tell you the truth." That's the hardest part of his job—what should he charge on any given day? For that, he constantly checks with a network of hunters and traders in both Western and Eastern Europe, people he's known for years, but he always wonders if he's selling too cheap, and the Italians always imply he's charging too much. "Still, I like the Italian companies. They're good customers. I have more problems with the French. They don't pay."

Through the day, the truffles keep coming. Big ones, small ones, stinky ones, but mostly nice and round ones. Spanish quality! English quality!

And not just whites. We turn up a common little rust-colored truffle called *Tuber rufum* that smells like oversmoked cheese—too strong for humans, though mice are big fans. "It's mostly something that beginner dogs dig up," István says.

Mokka also nails a small *Tuber macrosporum*, which looks like a black truffle splotched with red, like some tropical coral, and has a narcotic all's-well-with-the-world fragrance. "Best smell of any truffle," says István, echoing Imre. István has clients in Western Europe who kill for *macrosporum* ("They'd buy ten kilos a week if I could get them"), but it's never abundant.

Once, when we catch up to Mokka as he's digging, he swallows something and looks over his shoulder with an expression of pure canine guilt. "It's okay," István tells him, and the dog runs off, relieved.

"It was a *brumale*," István explains. "They're always small. He knows I don't need them, so he eats them." He shrugs. "He knows it's not ideal, but occasionally acceptable."

Tuber brumale, sometimes called the musky truffle, but more often just *brumale*, is a dead ringer for black winter truffles, and is much loathed by farmers because of its habit of infiltrating black winter plantations and outcompeting the more marketable truffle. Dealers get very unhappy if they find *brumales* in their batch of black winters.

For some reason many dogs love to eat *brumales*. When we eventually get our hands on a couple of Mokka's *brumales*, I find myself in complete agreement. The truffle smells like a smoked beetroot with musky overtones.

"Like a zoo," István says, holding it to his nose. "A wild animal."

I begin thinking of it as the ATF truffle, because it smells like alcohol, tobacco, and firearms in the best way. I wonder again at the arbitrary hierarchy in the truffle world and look forward to the moment when the traditional powers lose control of the narrative.

István has a sense for each truffle even before he starts digging. He'll assess the soil, the slope, the surrounding vegetation, and murmur "Small one" or "Could be big." Old stumps and rotting wood are good—anything that creates underground hollows the truffle can fill.

So he's already predicted that something large might lurk under a rotting tree stump, but that doesn't stop him from softly murmuring "Oh, oh, oh" as he pries it away. I can see a large truffly shoulder beneath a gnarled tree root. István pulls a knife from his belt, unfolds a small sawblade, and saws the root at both ends of the hole so he can lift it away without damaging the truffle.

This one isn't rocking at all, anchored by its own bulk. István digs a much larger perimeter. Then another. *Oh, oh, oh.* Then he goes full paleontologist, working for ten minutes to open a crater around the truffle on its earthen pedestal. He gently grabs it with his fingers, rocks it free, and lifts it out, huge and fragrant. He holds it to his nose, inhales, and cocks a mischievous smile at me. "Hong Kong quality."

I snap a photo. We later weigh it at 394 grams—the biggest Hungarian white truffle of the year.

"I think we're going to sink the price today." István laughs. "If I'd known this was going to happen, I wouldn't have brought you here."

I mumble something about the waxing moon, and István laughs again. "White truffles come in waves," he says. "A couple of good weeks, then a couple of bad ones. The Italians are very romantic. They dig, they find truffles, they look up at the sky, they get ideas."

By late afternoon, we have so many truffles that my back starts to hurt from carrying them around. We find so many that István runs out of kibble. We find so many that I begin to believe I have a pretty good handle on digging them.

"Let me have a shot at that," I propose.

István hands me the trowel and down I go, trying to mimic him. It seems like child's play. Just brush away a little at a time until you find the truffle, then carefully circle it.

And yet somehow by the time I can say with confidence yes, there's the truffle, my probings have already busted it into three chunks.

"I think you haven't quite killed it yet," István deadpans. "Maybe a couple more stabs."

I groan and fine-tune my motions, yet somehow still manage to break the remaining hunk into rubble.

"Oh, now you've definitely killed it."

Mokka averts his eyes.

I gather the bits into my hands, pose for a very sad photo, and hand the trowel back to István.

My botched truffle aside, our haul comes to 2.2 kilos. Of that, 800 grams is Extra Class and 1,400 is First. István gets €2,600 a kilo for the Extras and €2,200 for the Firsts, so it has been a €5,000 day. Even for István, who averages a kilo a day and considers anything under 500 grams disappointing, it's one for the record books.

"Who is eating all these truffles?" he can't help but wonder as we pick our way out of the woods. "Who is eating ten thousand truffle dishes per week? And I'm just one small producer."

~~~~~

The moment we're back in the car, István asks me to text him my photo of the giant truffle. "I need to sell it right away. You can't let the big ones sit. Too valuable." This one is probably worth €1,000. "But it's not always easy to sell truffles this big." He sighs. "I'm a Suzuki dealer, and I've got a Rolls-Royce."

His first thought is Zak Frost, but Zak just made a big order and is probably all set. Plus, Zak likes spotlessly cleaned truffles, and there's no time for that. István sends my photo to a German contact who's more agnostic about dirt, estimating the weight and the price. Just found this, he writes. Biggest one this year. Want it?

The German replies instantly. *Yes. Can you send today?*

Yes. Tonight.

Can I get some First Class, too? Maybe 1.5K?

Yes. They just came out of the woods with me. Really, really good.

Okay. Better make it 2K.

We don't have two kilos of First Class, but the day's truffle accretion has just begun. István is working his phone like a Wall Street trader now, an ironic necessity for a guy who escaped to the woods to be alone with his dog. He sets up a meeting with one of his best suppliers in a Spar supermarket parking lot about twenty minutes away.

As we drive, I think about how this big truffle will arrive in the German dealer's hands tomorrow and be in a restaurant that night. In a product where freshness is everything, that's transformative. In the old days, a hunter might sell to a local buyer once a week, and that buyer might sell to a big company once a week, and that company would take days more to deliver to its clients. The smartphone may be the best thing to happen to truffles since the dog.

When we reach the Spar parking lot, a gleaming black Porsche SUV awaits us in the far corner, a spiky-haired guy in a black-and-red Tommy Hilfiger tracksuit and matching sneakers standing behind the car with the hatch open.

"I guess there's money in truffles after all," I muse.

"If you're good," István says.

We shake hands with the guy, who produces a thin silver electric scale, which he places atop the dog crate in the back of the Porsche—the only flat surface around. He sets a metal bowl on the scale, resets the readout to zero, and opens a plastic box full of truffles.

István sorts the truffles by class. There's no debating; they've been doing this for years. Both parties record the details in their log books, and we all go on our merry ways.

Our second parking-lot buy is from two fathers and their assorted teenage sons, who are leaning on the hood of a mud-splattered blue pickup, waiting for us. There's already a scale on the hood. The fathers have gray mustaches, the sons tattoos and ear plugs. Everyone wears camo and smokes. Again, the exchange is pure business. Everything is weighed, cash flows, numbers are cataloged.

When we're again on the road, I ask István about the easy rapport. "Hunters like to sell to me, because I'm also a hunter," he says. "They know I know truffles. I know what conditions have been like, and I understand how much work it is to get them."

Long after dark, muddy and exhausted, we pull into a black town illuminated by a handful of wan yellow streetlights. We turn down a driveway, park next to four other mud-splattered cars, and step out.

Dogs spill out of the house and surround us. Big dogs, little dogs, yapping dogs, cool dogs. "Welcome to Truffle House," István says. "It was abandoned, so ten of us hunters bought it together." This being the wrecked corner of Hungary, it was only seven thousand euros—basically, one really nice truffle apiece.

Trailed by dogs, we step through the doorway into a truffly fog as four rough men look up suspiciously from a dirty table covered in white truffles. István greets them in Hungarian and explains who the hell I am. Handshakes ensue. Then everyone goes outside for a smoke.

The guys are middle-aged and unshaven, dressed in cargo pants and vests. They have spades like István's, carried in holsters on their belts next to their knives. Dirt streaks their faces. None of them grew up truffle hunting.

More dirt, and even some leaves, covers the cracked tile inside. Muck boots are piled in the corner near the door, but the idea seems to have been an afterthought; boot and paw prints cover the floors. The flypaper hanging from the lights is studded with corpses. There are enough open cans of beer and glasses of pálinka for everybody to have options.

At first it feels like I've just walked into a den of thieves, but as I nurse a beer someone has handed me, it all starts to feel like a familiar country scene: the piles of dirty dishes in the sink, the cots and air mattresses scattered in the back rooms, the pot of goulash in the fridge, and of course the dogs. It's deer camp, with truffles.

And like the best deer camps, it's weirdly professional. The hunters break out their bags of truffles and divide them into Seconds, Firsts, and Extras, pausing every so often to text their contacts. István's team hunts every day and ships every two or three days, so no truffle waits. There are kilos and kilos. Everything is weighed, bagged, and separated by destination into plastic bus tubs. Numbers are recorded in each of the hunters' log books and in the company book. István marveled that the Hungarian truffle market was almost white now, but I suspect he is the primary reason.

When it's all over, one of the guys loads his car with boxes and heads for Budapest, two hours away, to catch DHL for deliveries to traders across Europe. Another guy heads for Serbia to meet some Italians.

The rest of us step outside for a cigarette in the puddle of porch light. Dogs mill in and out of the darkness. It feels like my quest to get to the heart of *magnatum* is at an end. Matteo Giuliani captured the emotional essence of truffling, and Istria manifested truffle culture, but I know I'll never find a finer display of truffle artistry than what I've seen today. If this was the core of contemporary truffling, it was remarkably free of sleaze, preciousness, or even tradition. It was just a human and a dog reading the land.

That doesn't mean there aren't issues with equity, of course. As pure as the hunting had been, it was still trapped in the social dynamics of twenty-first-century Europe. Who gets to eat these truffles? Rich people, far away. It was far from a perfect setup. But it beat the hell out of fracking.

≈≈≈

Part of the reason István chose this village for his truffle lair is that it still has one bar clinging to life. Cigs stubbed out, we head for it, walking a half-mile through deserted streets with dark houses. It looms ahead, a lonely oasis lit like a Hopper painting.

Inside are four plump old-timers clustered on stools around the Formica bar, two institutional fluorescent lights flickering over a defunct ice cream chest and a working Coke machine. There's a lot of bunting, as if some festival has just been celebrated, though the dust on the bunting suggests otherwise.

The locals know the hunters and are thrilled to see us—a rare infusion of cash and, more important, novelty. Shots of pálinka all around. I click glasses with everyone, brace my gut, and knock it back.

We order Soproni beer and ask about food. Frozen chicken cutlets, they say. Take it or leave it. We take it.

István and I hold down stools while everyone cycles between drinking inside and smoking out. "Is Hungary producing a lot of white truffles?" I ask.

István hedges. "What's a lot? My guess is maybe six hundred kilos a year."

"Isn't that a lot?"

"No. The world produces ten thousand kilos, maybe twenty thousand. Nobody knows."

That's way more than I expected. "How much is from Eastern Europe?"

Another shrug. "Romania is bigger than Hungary. Serbia, too. Then there's Croatia, Greece, Bulgaria. A lot." Bulgaria alone has twenty thousand truffle hunters. It's a network as invisible as the mycorrhizal one beneath the trees, and probably as essential to the ecosystem it supports.

Late in the night, before heading back to the flophouse, where I'll hold down a cot between Mokka and a ninety-degree radiator and wait for dawn, I wind up sitting at a table in the corner with the oldest of the truffle hunters, a guy with white fuzz on his head, white stubble, and piercing blue eyes. I like his suspenders and his resigned smile, the sense that he's seen a lot of strange times come and go. We have barely any language in common, so we have to keep it simple, but it's enough.

"You like being a truffle hunter?" I ask.

"Yes." He nods. "Very much."

"Why?"

He leans forward, elbows on the table, there in that collapsed town, as his country slips further into darkness, and fixes me with that stoic gaze. "Free."

14

El Milagro

Forget woods, forget streams, forget mystery. Here's what most of the Truffleverse looks like: Pale hills stitched with neat lines of olive-green oaks. A winter sun in a white sky. An abandoned house in the distance. A skinny hound ambling methodically from tree to tree, digging holes every few meters. A bent farmhand in jeans and knee pads plodding behind with a puñal, a stainless steel truffle dagger that can rip through rocky soil, picking truffles out of the dry, red dirt as if they were potatoes.

The truffles are *Tuber melanosporum*, aka the black diamond, the black winter, the Périgord. And for all the press lavished on *Tuber magnatum*, *melanosporum* rules the roost. It's what most chefs think of when they hear the word *truffle*. After all, it's *the* French truffle, mainstay of haute cuisine.

It's also a much more cooperative little fungus. While nothing but a wild wood can grow a white, black winters have been culti-vated on oak plantations for two hundred years. And while the annual harvest of whites tops out at ten to twenty tons, black winter farms produce ten times that many. Add a superior shelf life, versatility in the kitchen, and the fact that most people prefer its gently seductive powers to the club-drug kick of the whites, and you get the truffle that defines truffle for most of the world.

~~~~~

The story begins in France, of course. By the early 1800s, truffles had expanded from the occasional royal banquet to the table of anyone who could afford them. Demand was sky-high, but supply was limited to what could be found in the wild. Not understanding the nature of a mycorrhizal fungus, numerous people had tried to cultivate truffles by planting them in fields, as if they really were potatoes, with obvious failure.

Then, in 1810, a Provence peasant named Joseph Talon put some of the pieces together. Talon owned a chunk of typically worthless land straight out of *Jean de Florette*—just hills and rocks and limestone outcroppings—and had planted a line of oaks as a windbreak. When he discovered truffles beneath the eight-year-old trees, he had an epiphany: grow oaks, get truffles. He planted more acorns on his property, and a few years later got more truffles. He was in business.

Talon covered his property in oaks, then bought up his neighbors' "worthless" land and planted acorns on that, too, creating the world's first cultivated truffiere. He got lucky: he thought the magic mojo was in the acorns that came from a truffle-producing tree. In reality, there were so many truffles and truffle spores in the area that they colonized every new oak seedling that came along.

Talon's other bit of dumb luck was to be working with *Tuber melanosporum*, a pioneering species. The truffle makes enzymes that can mine nutrients from mineral soils high in calcium, something plants and even most fungi find it difficult to do, and it specializes in teaming up with oak trees to colonize new areas. That sets it apart from the white, which prefers established forests. Talon couldn't have picked a better truffle for farming. He got rich, and word got out.

Eventually, the technique evolved from planting acorns to transplanting seedlings sown beneath truffle oaks, which came pre-inoculated with the fungus (though this was not understood by the farmers). The technique was rudimentary but effective, and trufficulture took hold in southern France to feed the insatiable demand of Paris's burgeoning restaurant scene.

In the mid-1800s the phylloxera insect, an invader from America, decimated France's vineyards. Desperate for a new crop, many growers turned to truffles for salvation. A wave of oak plantings led to a truffle boom that peaked around the fin de siècle, when France produced more than a thousand tons of truffles per year, almost entirely black winter, which were generally known as Périgords—for the region that most embraced them in its cuisine—though Provence always produced more.

That golden era didn't last long. World War I brought it to a crashing halt. The market collapsed, farmers went to war, farms were abandoned, and many oak trees were cut down for more pressing needs. Some truffle farms staggered on through the postwar wasteland, dull roots stirring a little memory and desire through the cruelest months, but World War II finished off most of the survivors. From a thousand tons per year, truffle production sank to fifty tons.

Although the wars get most of the blame, the reality is that production would have fallen anyway. Black truffles and oaks work best together when they are pioneering new territory, such as old fields and vineyards. That's when the young trees most need the fungi to mine nutrients for them. After twenty or twenty-five years, the organic matter content of the soil rises, the trees get more established, they don't need the fungus as much, and truffle production declines. France's nineteenth-century truffle boom was a one-off.

Trufficulture revived in the 1970s, when French scientists finally solved the mysteries of black truffle propagation, allowing truffle trees to be inoculated en masse in the greenhouse. Today's techniques are refinements of theirs. Oak and hazelnut seedlings are grown in purified conditions in a greenhouse, where their roots are immersed in spore-laden black truffle smoothies. (Nurseries prefer the biggest, nicest truffles for these smoothies, to get the best genetics. If you love truffles, try not to watch these perfect specimens getting atomized in a blender.) As the spores germinate, they form a fungal mantle of mycorrhizal around the tree roots, preventing any other fungi from getting a foothold. After a year or two in the greenhouse, the seedlings are ready to be planted. The fungi spread through the soil, feeding the trees and, once mature, producing an annual crop of truffles.

At least, that's how it's supposed to work. Truffle cultivation is still an art as much as a science, and each company guards its techniques and recipes. But the basics are well established, and black truffle farms have flourished since the 1980s. Today, 95 percent of the world's black winter crop is farmed. And the scale of some of these truffieres is epic.

≈≈≈

From a ridge in the center of the greatest truffle-producing region on earth, which is now responsible for half the world's

"Périgords," rows of scraggly holm oaks stretch to oblivion. Beneath them is bare ochre dirt and hay-colored grass. Stone sheds. Furrows. Van Gogh would have been all over it.

France? You'd be forgiven for thinking so. The landscape could easily be Provence, which is where I originally thought I'd head to investigate black truffles. Visit a farm, maybe hit the Saturday truffle market in Richerenches, where half a ton of truffles can change hands in a morning. Then catch the Truffle Mass on the third Sunday in January, when members of the Brotherhood of the Black Diamond march through the streets in their black-and-gold robes and gather in the church to toss truffles into the offering basket, to be auctioned off by the church. Maybe finish off the day with a roast chicken in a little bistro, black truffle bits tucked under the skin.

But the reality is that the Brotherhood of the Black Diamond and the street market itself are mostly for tourists these days. The market gets its share of local chefs, but few serious dealers are hanging out in Richerenches on a Saturday morning. Many of them are here in central Spain, in the vast depopulated highlands of Aragon, between Madrid and Barcelona. For now, France still has a lock on black truffle culture, but that culture is floated on a river of *Tuber melanosporum* coming out of Spain. It's the photo negative of the *Tuber magnatum* story, the truffle black, the flow east.

On a good year, Spain now produces eighty to a hundred tons of black winter truffles, while French production has fallen below thirty tons. Italy is third. Enfant terrible Australia produces twelve to twenty tons per year and may eventually take over the number-two spot.

Remarkably, until twenty-five years ago, not a single truffle had ever been farmed in the region, which is centered in the

Aragon province of Teruel. Back then, the area was the poster child for rural depopulation, as was much of the rest of Spain. The trickle of migration to the cities that began in the 1960s had become a torrent by the 2000s. Over that stretch, rural Spain has lost nearly a third of its population. The kids are long gone, chasing jobs. The old-timers squeak by growing wheat and other grains, but even those aren't profitable in the marginal soils of the region. About thirty-five hundred villages in Spain have been abandoned entirely. Many can be had for the price of a decent house. Parts of Teruel now have a whopping 1.6 people per square kilometer—less than Siberia.

But by the late 2000s, the truffle towns in Teruel had reversed the tide. Land is in high demand, and young farmers are working beside their parents. Today, 18,000 hectares of truffle orchards are in production. (That's about the same as in France, though a far cry from the 75,000 hectares of truffieres in France in 1890.) An additional 1,500 hectares are coming on line every year, and there are an estimated 41,000 hectares suitable for trufficulture. It's a bona fide *milagro económico*, the farmers will tell you.

And not just an economic miracle. "I never thought my children would stay in this town," says one of the old farmers who leads the Truffle Growers Association. "I never thought I'd see my grandchildren on Sundays."

The architects of this miracle are two scientists who met in the 1990s when they were grad students researching forest fungi at Oregon State University, ground zero for all things myco. Christine Fischer was from Indiana; Carlos Colinas from Spain. They fell in love, married, and moved to Spain. Now legends in the truffle community, though no longer married they still work together at the University of Lleida, in a Catalan town on the edge of the truffle zone. On a gentle midwinter day, I sit down with them at the university to learn how they did it.

Back in the early 1990s, France had thriving *melanosporum* orchards. Spain had none, but it did have a significant wild harvest. That had been going on since the 1960s, when French hunters from the Pyrenees came to Catalonia, bought small pigs from local farmers, and headed into the forests with them. Pretty soon the Catalans caught on and began looking around Spain for new hunting grounds. Christine Fischer knows one old truffle farmer in Soria who was working as a stonecutter in the 1960s when Catalan guys started arriving in cars, which were rare at the time, and leaving with big sacks filled with something from his mountain.

Pretty soon he made friends with them. *This is what we're looking for,* they explained. *Can you show us more?* He could, and he did. He also thought that looked like a lot more fun than cutting stone. Once he caught on to the environment and what to look for, he started taking buses to little villages around Soria. He found black truffles everywhere—good size, good quality. He never cut stone again.

So it went. But that was eighty years ago, when rainfall was more abundant and temperatures less extreme. In Aragon the winter wind is biting cold, but in summer the land sizzles: eight months of *invierno,* four months of *inferno,* as they say. Most of it is now too hot and too dry for wild truffles. Same story in southern France.

The woodlands, too, have changed. When the peasants burned firewood and grazed small herds of goats and sheep, the forests were like open oak parklands, which truffles like. Now the herds and the people are mostly gone, and the forests are choked with undergrowth and dead wood, as in Italy. The wild truffle harvest has all but disappeared.

That trend was already under way in the 1990s when Christine and Carlos got a grant to try to introduce trufficulture to *España vacía*, "vacant Spain." Black truffle farms had already saved France's production, the nursery science was well established, and Spain had one huge orchard in Soria, planted in 1972 with seedlings from France, that was showing signs of success. Most important, the government was willing to throw money at the problem.

Desperate, actually. Rural areas like Teruel had nothing going for them. No industry. Not pretty enough for tourism. Terrible soils choked in calcium carbonate. The farmers, who were mostly in their seventies, survived on government-subsidized cereal farming.

But those same calcareous soils were catnip to black truffles. "It's ideal truffle habitat," Christine says. You could practically drop an acorn in the soil and it would get inoculated on its own. So why not farm? "The people had nothing left to lose. The farmers had no options."

They also had no idea truffles could be cultivated, according to Christine. "Our first year was about education, education, education. We went from village to village in Catalonia and gave our little talks about what a truffle is and what kind of soil it needs and why you should grow them. We talked about subsidies and seedlings and farmer support. We handed out guides."

It didn't go well, Carlos admits. "We had many events where there were more speakers than audience. And the average age of attendees was seventy-five. The ones who'd been hunters were skeptical. The rest were downright combative." Grow a crop you couldn't actually see? That wouldn't be ready to harvest for six years, if you were lucky? Yeah, right.

What won them over, ultimately, was cash: up to €2,300 per hectare to cover the costs of putting in the orchard and surviving until the truffles came in. "They didn't have to put in any money," says Christine. "Just land, and they had plenty of that. We said that we would buy the seedlings, certify the seedlings, and plant the seedlings. All they had to do was fence it, and we were going to pay for the fencing. And they said, 'Sure, we can do that.'"

They started a few demo orchards, which began to produce in the early 2000s. That merited a little coverage in the local papers, and slowly, younger people started showing up at the presentations. One was an entrepreneur who wanted to launch a nursery, but only if he had enough local buy-in. He met with groups of farmers and made his spiel. They listened politely, but never committed. Finally, after one talk, when the old-timers trundled away, one stayed behind. He was a local leader, a smart guy. Let's have a cup of coffee, he said.

"That cup of coffee is now worth more than twenty million euros a year," Carlos says with a smile.

The orchards started hitting big-time in the late 2000s. Christine and Carlos had been right: with a little irrigation, *Tuber melanosporum* grew like weeds in the calcareous rubble of Teruel. The land yielded forty kilos per hectare. At €400 per kilo, farmers were making €16,000 per hectare—a far cry from the €300 they got for grains. A few supplemented that haul by growing lavender in between the rows of truffle trees, a technique borrowed from France.

The market took care of itself. French dealers, desperate to fill the gaps in France's faltering production, descended on

Teruel. Business was done in cash, and in bars. Farmer and buyer would have a beer, haggle, have another beer, then head out to the parking lot for the exchange. Sometimes farmers would load their vans once a week and drive to France themselves.

Deals still go down on Saturday nights in the parking lot of the local railway station, with flashlights inspecting the contents of car trunks, but Spain is making an effort to regulate the market and recoup a little tax money for its regional efforts. "Today, the market is light gray," says Carlos. "But years ago, it was pitch-black."

Only 5 percent of Spanish truffles stays in the country. The rest go to France and are granted instant citizenship. Odds are high that any Périgord is a Teruel, even if bought out of the straw basket of a cute old Frenchman.

As in Istria, until recently, no one in Teruel really cared about recognition. They were quite content to grow the truffles, sell the truffles, and be done with it. In less than two decades, Teruel's truffle towns grew quietly wealthy. It wasn't just the farmers; there were the nurseries, the irrigation companies, the dog trainers. The town of Sarrión, the center of Teruel's truffle renaissance, had to build a new school to handle the influx of families.

Now Teruel has begun to reveal itself to the outside world. Agritourism is the newest enterprise. Sarrión's annual truffle festival draws 25,000 people. A few restaurants are even beginning to play around with this new local delicacy—a level of culinary experimentation that runs against the grain of the Spanish soul.

For me, the key takeaway from *el milagro económico* is that the second golden era of the black truffle has just begun. Innovation, science, chutzpah, and plain old love are turning *Tuber melano-sporum* into an international star that is about as French as cabernet sauvignon. The truffle is being farmed in Spain, France, Italy, the United States, Chile, Australia, New Zealand, and other countries, and it is being farmed in ways that the scientists of a generation ago never dreamed of.

And while Teruel is the present of black winter truffles, it may not be the future. The perfect storm of favorable conditions, both climatic and socioeconomic, may not last. To see what's next, you have to leave the highlands and head a little closer to the Spanish coast—a little farther from *invierno*, and closer to *inferno*.

～～～

At first glance, the eight-hectare experimental truffle orchard in Batea, in the province of Tarragona, doesn't look like an existential threat to the truffle establishment. It looks a lot like the farms in Teruel: twelve-foot oak trees, tilled earth, cloudless sky, a couple of dogs working the rows. Wind howling out of the south, a line of turbines whirling on the ridge. One waits for Don Quixote to canter by. Only once I realize that the trees are too close together, the air too hot, and the orchard only half the age I estimated do I understand that something very unusual is going on.

"We broke all the rules," says Xavier Vilanova Sola, the technical director of Micologia Forestal & Aplicada (call them Micofora), the truffle research and consultation company that created this orchard as an experiment. "This place is supposed to be too hot and too dry for truffles."

Xavi (pronounced "Chavee," in the Catalan fashion) founded Micofora with Mónica Sánchez and Marcos Morcillo when the three were in university together twenty-four years ago. With his lanky hair and chin stubble, which reminds me of Shaggy from *Scooby Doo*, it's easy to see the mycology student he'd been.

Micofora has its hands in almost every aspect of truffle farming. They consult with orchards on management and design, they have a nursery with some of the most coveted truffle trees in Europe, they certify other nurseries' trees, and they produce freeze-dried inoculum that is shipped to orchards and nurseries across the globe. (€1,400 will get you two hundred grams, the equivalent of a kilo of fresh truffle.) When I visited their labs the day before, they had a hundred kilos of black winter truffles in their freezer, and the deafening sound of frozen truffles being blended filled the office.

Xavi, Mónica, two of their clients from Teruel (one old, one young), and I are watching a dog beeline down the row of trees, about two meters out from the tree trunks, digging a new hole every few meters. (The Spanish prefer female dogs, which they find less distractible, and they like mutts. They say the ugliest dogs make the best truffle hounds.)

The farm manager walks behind her, plopping golfball-sized truffles into the mesh sack on his belt, which already weighs more than a kilo. Unlike the romantic chaos of my white truffle hunts, nobody looks all that excited, not even the dogs, because this time of year they pretty much do this every day.

Farming truffles is still very new, compared to ten thousand years of plant agriculture, but we're clearly making progress. Back in the Joseph Talon days, you just built an orchard and hoped they would come. Even once scientists figured out they could precoat the roots of tree seedlings in spores and jump-start the process, they still understood little about the life cycle of the truffle or the relationship between tree and truffle. So they tried to mimic a simplified version of nature: inoculate oak seedlings, and plant them far apart in fairly arid areas with poor, rocky soils, like Provence. The idea was that the trees would depend on the fungus for water and nutrients.

But in many parts of France, that model is failing. The summers are too hot, and the rains don't come. No one expects the situation to turn around. So everyone is looking for a new model.

Micofora began breaking all the rules after seeing Australia's runaway success a decade ago, Xavi tells me. "Manjimup, the region where they grow truffles, has acidic soil, high organic matter, and it's very soft, just the opposite of Europe. I know many people who said that Australian farms would never get a single truffle. And yet they did much better than here. Their trees grew faster and produced earlier, and the truffles were amazing. They have the most productive orchards in the world." Instead of the thirty to fifty kilos per hectare they average in Spain, Australian orchards average one hundred kilos or more.

Why?

Xavi has some guesses. Australia's soil is much more acidic than the limestone-rich soils of the Mediterranean Basin, so Australian growers had to add tons of lime (calcium carbonate) to their soil, to raise the pH from 4 or 5 to a truffle-friendly 7.6 or so. They were just trying to make a nice home for *Tuber mela-nosporum*, but they wound up making the place unlivable for most native Australian organisms, eliminating competition. In Europe, by contrast, a mature orchard will eventually be infected by hundreds of other types of mycorrhizal fungi, all jockeying for position on the tree roots.

Western Australia is also hotter and wetter than traditional truffle regions. That made Micofora suspect that truffles could take the heat, as long as they had enough water to stay cool and hydrated. They chose sizzling Batea for their experimental orchard because irrigation water from a nearby river was abundant and cheap, and they watered their trees hard, in complete disregard of conventional wisdom. "Everybody thought that if you add fertilizer and water, and the tree can grow fast, then the tree won't pay the truffle," Mónica says. "But it's not true."

The trick is to plant in nutrient-poor soil, adding fertilizer in a chemical form that plants can't absorb on their own. "That way, the tree still needs the truffle one hundred percent," Xavi says. In such conditions, the trees can grow vigorously, but only by paying the truffles lavishly in sugar to keep the nutrients coming. Everybody wins.

Everything happens fast, too. The orchard we're walking through is a baby, just five years old, yet it's already producing more truffles than Micofora's ten-year-old traditional orchard, and its trees are significantly larger. They're also planted much closer together than in traditional truffieres, a trick to reduce heat stress by creating partial shade.

There's one more secret to such precocious and prolific production. It's the one responsible for the straight line the dog is making down the rows, and it's the answer to a longtime riddle: Why do some truffieres have fantastic "mycorrhization," with *melanosporum* fungi flourishing on the tree roots, and yet no truffles?

The culprit is sex, or lack thereof.

For a long time, people didn't even know that truffle fungi *had* sex. Most believed they reproduced asexually. That's in part because whenever scientists did a genetic analysis of a truffle, the DNA was an exact match of the fungus itself. The truffle didn't seem like the child of two parents. But that was because the technology of the time wasn't capable of accessing the spores within the truffle, which are protected by tough coats to allow them to pass unscathed through the digestive tract of an animal. The only thing turning up in the DNA sequences was the DNA from the structural part of the truffle (the fruit), which is just an extension of the fungus itself.

A few years ago, scientists learned how to crack open the spores and sample the DNA inside, and they discovered that truffle spores, just like apple seeds, contain the contributions of two parents: the "mother" fungus that forms mycorrhizae on a tree and grows the fruiting body of the truffle, and a mysterious father, known only by the presence of his DNA in the spores.

Since the fathers have never been found, most scientists believe they exist as microscopic spores, waiting in the ground in a state of suspended animation until some signal causes them to spring to life, mate, and die, the mayflies of the underworld. How mothers and fathers find each other is unknown, but it must be through some of the same volatile molecules they use to lure us. However it happens, truffles form only after the parents meet and mate.

Just to make things even more complicated, truffle fungi don't actually have two sexes. Any newly germinated spore can become maternal, forming mycelia and mycorrhizae and making truffles, or paternal, doing nothing but contributing a shot of DNA to a maternal host. But they do have two different "mating types," and they can only mate with the opposite type. So a "mother" of mating type 1 requires a "father" of mating type 2, and a newly germinated type 1 needs to either find an established maternal type 2 or decide to become a maternal type 1.

But that's not always an option. A newly planted truffle tree will have freshly germinated fungi of both mating types growing on it, but they don't get along. Soon one type will drive out the other. So any given truffle tree will be colonized by "mothers" of a single mating type, waiting for their gentlemen callers. Should a newly arrived spore of the opposite mating type try to grow mycelia, they'll kill it. Should it opt to mate with them instead, they'll welcome it with open hyphae.

But for that to happen, new spores of the opposite mating type need to somehow arrive. In nature, critters are constantly moving spores across the landscape, unwittingly playing cupid, but a fenced truffle orchard is a convent. And that's the problem with those barren orchards: great mycorrhizae, no sex.

The solution: "Spanish wells." Dig a trench two meters out from your row of truffle trees, add a shot of peat moss filled with spores from new truffles (which will contain both mating types), fill it back up, and let the loving begin. Two years later, you get a bumper crop of truffles, conveniently lined up in the trough.

The practice itself actually predates the science. When truffle hunters in Spain and France found truffles that were too small or too rotten to sell, they'd break them up and seed the soil in places where they'd found truffles in the past. They didn't know why it worked; they just noticed that it did. Then, when truffle farming took off in Spain, many of the farmers who had once been hunters continued the practice on their orchards, digging holes near their truffle trees and adding bits of truffle. They called them *pozos* (wells) or *nidos* (nests). After scientists discovered truffle sex about a decade ago, it all made sense.

Spanish wells are especially important in places like Australia and the United States that have no wild truffles to provide spores. When Christine Fischer introduced the concept to Australian truffle farmers in 2012, she called them "Spanish wells," and the name stuck.

In just a decade, Spanish wells have revolutionized truffle farming. New farms are shattering records. Old farms that seemed ready to expire are getting a second wind. "It's like magic," Mónica says.

With proof of concept firmly established in Batea, Micofora has surveyed potential truffle zones around the world. New Zealand, Chile, Argentina, South Africa, Mexico, and China are all growing some and could be growing more. But the real sleeper? "Turkey," Xavi says. "Huge potential. It's a Mediterranean region. And it has so much good land."

Mónica chimes in with the bigger takeaway. It's like wine. It's not about finding the perfect spot. It's about finding the right techniques for your spot. "*Everywhere* can grow truffles."

I nod gamely, but in my head, one big exception looms. I know of one country that has struggled painfully to grow truffles, despite great effort and earnestness. Explanations for its pain vary, but I already have an inkling that somewhere in the heart of that anguish lies some of the purest truffle love, so it's my next stop. And to be honest, I have to go anyway. I live there.

15

Winter People

There's a woman and a dog too, this time. Two dogs, counting Monza, a Lagotto the color of rum-raisin ice cream, in whom runs some of the same blood that ran in the founding Lagottos of Blackberry Farm, and two women, counting Margaret Townsend, who is digging some of the first black winters from her ten-year-old orchard and wiping away a tear as she says, voice thick with emotion, "I'm a truffle farmer at last."

Monza pants beside her, wearing the satisfied expression of a Lagotto who has fulfilled her destiny, at least for the day. Her human, Lois Martin, gives her a pat and a treat. Lois and Monza are one of a handful of professional-grade truffle-dog teams east of the Mississippi. Until recently, so few American truffle farms actually produced truffles that this wasn't a problem. But now that truffles are bubbling up from Maryland to the Carolinas, the calls don't stop. Lois tries to hit as many farms as she can within a few hours of her Oak Ridge, Tennessee, home, but she has a full-time job as a project manager for Bechtel, the industrial engineering behemoth, so truffling is relegated to weekends and vacations.

I'm palling around with Lois and Monza to take the temperature of American truffle farming. And at the moment that temperature is exceedingly chilly. A fine slurry of microhail pours out of an ashen January sky, bouncing off the cold ground and bare trees. It pounds my jacket and finds its way down the back of my neck.

We're in Allen County, Kentucky, a land of handsome hills and happy horses, but not somewhere I ever expected my truffle quest to take me. There are two main zones in America considered promising for *Tuber melanosporum*: the West Coast, and the middle Appalachian states of Kentucky, Tennessee, North Carolina, and Virginia. Maybe they are, but this sure as hell doesn't feel like Spain.

I can already tell things are going to feel different in America. Different climate, different soil, different people. While European truffle farming has been the purview of professional and profoundly unromantic farmers, American truffle farming tends to be the passionate pursuit of the part-timer with a little land and a lot of dream—like Margaret Townsend, kneeling in the dirt in her Carhartt jacket, trowel in one hand, a streak of mud cutting across her forehead like war paint as she holds up her truffle in her outstretched palm, flush with joy and relief—as I would be too, if I'd endured nine years of pastoral purgatory.

Smart, successful, quirky, fiftysomething, with a light Kentucky accent and a penchant for firearms and Wathen's bourbon, Margaret could be the poster child for American truffle farming. So could her mother, Miss Jane, a tiny eighty-year-old teller of Faulknerian tales that reach deep into the past to elucidate the present, who lives alone in the sprawling, book-filled farmhouse above the orchard with Scout, a towering German shepherd who never leaves her side, and Pollo (Apollo without the *A*), the emergency backup hound everyone hopes will make a good truffle dog someday.

Then there's the orchard itself, twenty-four acres of oak and hazelnut quilting the hills, a palimpsest of the human enterprise. Abandoned tobacco racks in the barn. Potsherds and arrowheads in the furrows. Below the house, one of Kentucky's great caves, two miles of passageways and antechambers harboring blind cave crickets, hibernating bats, and ancient graffiti. That morning, I'd felt my way over generations of guano, my headlamp falling on stacks of mud blocks from the War of 1812, when they leached saltpeter out of the guano to make gunpowder. Somewhere above me, truffle mycelia were threading their way through the earth, stitching it into articulation.

At the orchard's highest point, guarding it like a sentinel, sits an old yellow fire engine named Bridget and a ninety-foot wood-and-steel trebuchet that shoots flaming railroad ties. When I ask why flaming, Margaret's husband Steve says, "Because they're easier to see at night." But when I ask if we can fire it up, he gets a haunted look and says, "We've had trouble with trebuchets in the past."

The orchard's been trouble, too, and the trebuchet was no help. Nine years, no truffles, despite a massive investment of resources and laudatory maintenance. But that's just how it goes in the American truffle scene. A whole generation of orchards has come and gone without fruition. Now a new generation is hitting the ten-year mark, and things are beginning to look guardedly hopeful.

But there have been too many false starts, too many crash-and-burns where everything looked good before it went horribly wrong. American truffle farming itself has been a Faulknerian palimpsest built on the cautionary tales of the ones who came before. And whenever any of this new breed of truffle farmer finds a few black diamonds in their fields and starts to dream big, in their mind's eye rises the gentlemanly and slightly tragic figure of Tom Michaels.

〜〜〜

For a brief stretch a dozen years ago, Tom Michaels had the only truly productive truffle orchard in the country. He lost that title not because others joined him in glory but because he regressed back to them. Still, he's the golden one, the one who made it real.

The first person to successfully grow *Tuber melanosporum* in the United States was a New Age dude named Billy Griner, who inoculated a hundred hazelnut trees in Mendocino County, in the heart of cannabis country, in the 1980s. Griner got his first truffle in 1987, and at his peak in the mid-1990s produced fifty pounds in a year. His production seems to have declined after that. In 2008 he died of an infection and was found ten days later, his faithful truffle dog Ace still standing over him. There were three pounds of rotting truffles in the fridge. Today, another Mendocino type named Rye N. Flint is trying to revive Griner's aging hazelnut trees.

Griner sold to a handful of restaurants in northern California and New York, but never made much of an impact. A paranoid recluse by nature, he never shared his methods (though buried crystals were definitely involved), and was more an outlier than the beginning of a trend.

Tom Michaels is a different kind of cat—urbane, musta-chioed, an accomplished pianist. Picture a septuagenarian Clark Gable in hipster sneakers. It's hard to imagine him hip-deep in mud or slobbering over a faithful canine companion.

But he's also a mushroom man. Grew up working on his dad's mushroom farm in Illinois. Wrote his PhD (at OSU, of course) on "In Vitro Culture and Growth Modeling of *Tuber* Spp. and Inoculation of Hardwood with *T. Melanosporum* Ascospores." Cultivated button mushrooms in California for years. He knew a thing or two about farming fungi. And he knew Griner had done it.

Tom knew enough that when he moved to eastern Tennessee in the 1990s and looked around at the high-pH bedrock (Limestone, Tennessee, was just a few miles away) and the Périgord-like climate, he knew just what to do with it. He "limed the hell out of the soil"—even Limestone, Tennessee, is not alkaline enough for truffles—bought some black winter truffles, threw them in his blender, and used the slurry to inoc-ulate the roots of European hazelnuts, which are the preferred truffle tree in North America, since they yield truffles a few years faster than oaks. Tom planted his first truffle trees in 1999. Then he waited. And waited some more.

On January 3, 2007, Tom was windrowing fallen leaves in his orchard, assuming that he had at least another year to wait, when he noticed a weird "blister" in the ground. He pulled away the soil and found himself staring at the unmistakable black pebble of *Tuber melanosporum*. He shouted. He jumped around. Then he found a few more and started jumping more carefully. Then he started thinking about where to sell his truffles.

Tops: Blackberry Farm, the 4,200-acre Appalachian Elysium snuggled into the crook of the Smokies. Tom called Sam Beall, the gastronomically inclined paterfamilias, who wasn't impressed by some hillbilly kook who thought he knew what a truffle was. So Tom showed up at Blackberry with a tub of tubers packed in Carolina Gold rice. Beall took a whiff. We're in, he said. How can we help?

Well, actually, there was a little something. Tom Michaels is a cat person. Dogs, not so much. And though he'd been lucky enough to stumble across his first truffles without canine assistance, he knew that as his orchard took off, he was going to need a dog. So he proposed a swap: he would provide Blackberry Farms with truffles, and they would provide the detector.

Sam Beall (who died in 2016 at age thirty-nine in a tragic skiing accident) was never one to miss a branding bonanza when he saw it. He did his homework, learned about Lagotto Romagnolos (unknown in the United States at the time), and bought a breeding pair in Italy: Tom (no relation to Tom Michaels) and Lussi. Every week during truffle season, Tom the dog and Jim Sanford, Blackberry Farm's animal trainer, trekked up to Tom Michaels's farm to find truffles.

Blackberry Farm became famous for its Tennessee truffles (even starting its own small orchard), and even more famous for its Lagottos. Tom (the dog) sired a line of Lagottos that have fanned out across the country. Blackberry now has eight Lagottos in its breeding program and produces three litters of puppies a year. For $8,500 or so, one could be yours.

That January day in 2007 turned out to be something of a coming-out party for American truffles. Who else happened to be slumming around Blackberry Farm that day but Molly O'Neill, the *New York Times* food writer. Smitten, she published "Coveted, French, and Now in Tennessee" in the *Times* a month later. "This is it," the chef Daniel Boulud said in the article.

"The first time in America. This Tennessee truffle is the real thing."

And it was, for a few sweet years. Tom's orchards began churning out truffles, Tom sold them directly to chefs for $800 per pound, and the culinary world beat a path to his country door. In "Hillbilly Truffle," a celebrated 2009 profile in *GQ*, Alan Richman accused him of having the ideal existence, described thus: "Awaken a mile from Davy Crockett's birthplace, the sun rising over the Blue Ridge Mountains, handily visible from your back porch. Phone for a rare Lagotto Romagnolo truffle-hunting dog to be brought around in an ever available Lexus SUV. Stroll your backyard hazelnut orchard with the happy hound bounding beside you, him sniffing the soft earth for precious *Tuber melanosporum*, you gathering them up."

Richman gathered up a few of Tom's truffles and, with a few foodie friends, tested them blind against French truffles, *melano a melano*. The final score was Tennessee 10, France 0.

Tom harvested two hundred pounds of truffles that year, an American record. The profile seemed to be catching him on the cusp of breakout success. But instead it turned out to be his zenith. The following year, eastern filbert blight found him. The blight is caused by a fungus native to eastern North America that causes only minor problems for the native American hazelnut (which can't be used for truffles), but wipes out European hazelnuts, girdling the trees and cutting off their circulation. Within a few years, Tom's orchards collapsed.

So did most of the other truffieres on the East Coast. Yet the media kept falling for the same story. In 2012 NPR, apparently unaware that most orchards in Tennessee and North Carolina were dying, ran with "Truffles Take Root in Appalachian Soil," again featuring Tom, even though he was only producing a few pounds per acre by then. "Truffles are notoriously hard to farm, even in France, where Périgords originate," went the story. "Now, in the rolling hills and clay soils of eastern Tennessee and western North Carolina, a growing number of farmers are hoping to establish southern Appalachia as the new truffle capital of the world."

Aaaaaaaand . . . still hoping. Of the hundreds of truffieres in the United States, only a handful produce more than a few pounds. Most first-generation hazelnut orchards have now expired. Some owners replanted with blight-resistant hazelnut trees. Tom Michaels did not. "Been there, done that," he says. "I still have the land, but being seventy-two, do I really want to replant and wait another ten years?" He found greener pastures as a consultant to other truffle farmers, including Margaret Townsend.

Blight-resistant hazelnuts aren't entirely immune to the blight, but they can be kept alive with aggressive management. Some are now the age Tom's were when they started producing. So far, none have taken off like his. The most productive black winter truffiere in the United States is that of Jackson Family Wines in Santa Rosa, California. Ten years old, it produces about thirty pounds a year on ten acres.

No one else is close, but many seem to finally be producing *something*, and very few have functional truffle hounds. Sure, many a Lagotto was purchased as part of the midlife crisis, but it turns out those things don't train themselves. And when you don't have any actual truffles coming in, it's easy to put off the training for another year.

Now, suddenly, many orchards need a dog. And many others wonder if they might. Call it the conundrum of the invisible crop: How do you know when your first truffle arrives?

That's where Lois and Monza come in. Monza is a nine-year-old Lagotto from Blackberry Farm. Even Blackberry Lagottos do not spring from their mother's wombs looking for truffles, but Monza and Lois are all about training and follow-through.

As you'd expect from a Bechtel project manager with sensible short-cropped hair, Lois is deeply systematic. A veteran of the canine agility training circuit, she's flirted with becoming a nose-work instructor and fantasizes about having a "money dog"—the ones that can smell wads of cash in airport luggage. Detection, tracking, search-and-rescue; those are her happy places. She's even gone to chicken camp, training chickens to run an obstacle course and to differentiate between pictures of a zebra and other animals.

"What's the secret to training chickens?" I can't help but ask.

"Very short sessions," she says. "Three minutes, then you put away your chickens and go to Theory for a while. Then you get your chickens back out. Within four days, they just get it."

Truffles weren't on her mind when she got Monza from Blackberry Farm in 2011. She knew Lagottos were truffle dogs, but she thought the only action was in Italy. The following year she met a local forager in Asheville named Alan Muskat. Hey, said Muskat, looks like you got yourself a Lagotto there. Want to go look for wild truffles in the mountains? There's a spot I've been curious about.

Monza wasn't yet a year old, no training, but why not? Muskat sent Lois one truffle he'd found doglessly, and she trained Monza with it in her backyard. Then they headed for the secret spot, deep in the woods, and Monza found three individual *Imaia gigantea*, a little-known species that is either tasteless or culinary dynamite, depending on who you ask.

"It was so cool!" Lois says. "I was like, 'That's it! I gotta do this.'"

She cold-called Tom Michaels, looking for training-grade truffles. Early on a frigid January morning, the deal went down in a Weigel's parking lot. "He pulled out a scale and set it on his car. Then he pulled out these things that looked like horse turds and had me smell them." As Tom was piling a few on the scale and Lois was pulling out cash, a friend of hers pulled into the Weigel's and stared aghast, sure she was buying drugs.

She may as well have been. She was hooked. Truffles! She poked around online and found the Truffle Dog Company, a Seattle business launched a decade ago by Alana McGee, an anthropology/business major with a love of dogs and a nose for trends. Alana fell in love with hunting wild truffles in the Pacific Northwest around 2010. A skilled and classically trained dog handler, she got really good at it. She and Lolo, her Lagotto Romagnolo, began surveying the handful of West Coast truffieres, none of which had their own dogs. Demand kept rising, and requests came from farther away. In 2013 she began training others, later adding online classes as well.

Lois and Monza took Alana's online class. They were star pupils, of course, and eventually became the company's East Coast reps, part of a network of dog teams Alana hoped to build across the country, a kind of Woof Wide Web that could quickly deploy snouts on the ground where needed. Most of this web is composed of women and their dogs, which, Alana says, is not a shocker. "In general, the dog-training industry is predominantly women, especially the more relationship-based positive training that I teach. That's what drew me to it. It's not a big money-maker, but I love the relationships you form with the dogs and the people."

For a while, the Southeast's orchards were stuck in maybe-next-year mode, and Lois and Monza's duties were light. Check the occasional orchard, train the occasional pooch, do a demo each year at the Asheville Truffle Experience. Now they can't keep up. Lois is scrambling to recruit a new canine corps to service more far-flung farms. In the meantime, she and Monza have become weekend road warriors, the nexus of a notoriously secretive subculture.

And that made her the perfect person to help me answer a question that had been occupying me ever since Europe. Do truffles bring out the weirdness in people? Or do they just bring out the weird people?

≈≈≈

Margaret Townsend got the truffle bug a decade ago, when she was an executive at Microsoft. She was itching to do her own thing. Something totally different. Her parents lived in the Kentucky countryside with land to burn, so she decided to farm something. She had three criteria:

1. It had to be physical. She'd had enough deskwork for one lifetime.
2. It had to be not well understood. She wanted an intellectual challenge.
3. It had to be a snazzy product that she'd enjoy putting in front of people.

Here she was in bluegrass country. Duh, bourbon. She already had Maker's Mark and Wathen's in the blood. It seemed like a good fit. As Miss Jane says, "Around here, everyone knows what everyone did, including their grandfathers."

But bourbon wasn't exactly farming, and it wasn't exactly pioneering.

Her father, a Carnegie Mellon man, happened to read an article in the alumni magazine about a truffle farmer in North Carolina. Why not truffles?

Well, she knew squat about truffles, but she knew an online search engine that did. After a few days of recon, she determined that most of the major players in truffles were major nutballs. The one who seemed to have his head on straight was Charles Lefevre, out in Oregon. Lefevre, another product of OSU's mycology program, owned New World Truffieres, the most respected American truffle nursery. She called him that day and asked if truffles would grow in Kentucky. He told her she was in the zone. The most successful grower in the country was in Chuckey, Tennessee, not far from her. A guy named Tom Michaels.

So she drove to Tom's place and toured his orchards. He put some tree roots under a microscope and showed her how they were sheathed in mycorrhizae, like corn dogs.

She drove home and ordered 2,400 trees from Charles at $25 a pop.

Then she left Microsoft.

She flew out to Kentucky and stood at the top of her fallow fields, where the trebuchet is, and looked out at the titanic job awaiting her. The beds need to be ready when the babies come, she thought.

She rented a bunch of earthmoving equipment and bull-dozed, plowed, and trenched her fields into shape. To keep voles from nibbling on the trees, she surrounded the orchard with hawk and owl nest boxes. ("Our daytime air force and our nighttime air force.") She now keeps a taxidermied vole on her wall, a mycorrhized root still clutched in its incisors.

She rescued the fawns that fell into the trench and reunited them with their mother. As newborns they got a pass, but later, when she replaced the trench with a wire fence and the deer figured out how to shimmy under the fence and eat her trees, they would meet the fury of her .30-30 from the high deer stand above the orchard.

She tilled her subsoil so it would be fluffy and well drained. Then it was time for lime. The soil needed to be candy-sweet, with a pH of 7.6–7.9. Charles Lefevre told her she'd need to put down more lime than she could imagine, upward of forty tons per acre, and even then she'd probably have to augment later.

So she drove down to Southern States, her local farm supply cooperative. "I said I was going to grow truffles and it was going to take forever and I needed forty tons of lime per acre. They looked at me as this West Coast software person who came out here and thought she could be a farmer. They had no idea what a truffle was, and frankly, they were worried I was going to waste a lot of money on this harebrained idea. They said the most lime they'd ever put down was three tons per acre."

Go check your numbers, they said. So she called the University of Kentucky extension service, which also suggested she must have a decimal point—or something more vital—misplaced. But pH is a logarithmic scale. As you get toward either end of the scale, it gets exponentially harder to push it further. Soil with a pH of 7.6 is *one hundred times* more basic than soil with a pH of 5.6.

Margaret rechecked her math. Others rechecked her math. She needed forty tons per acre.

They still talk about the Great Liming in town. The trucks ran for three days. "It looked like Washington after Mount St. Helens," says Margaret. "It looked like a cocaine lab." Word in Allen County was that Miss Jane's daughter, the Microsoft executive, had gone crazy.

That winter, a couple of months before the tree seedlings were due to arrive, Margaret surveyed her perfect fields and worried she'd been thinking too small. Go big or go home, right? She called Charles Lefevre and doubled her order to 4,800 trees, making hers one of the larger truffieres in the United States.

The saplings landed on her front driveway in March in bundles. She spent the next five days on the back of a tree planter, plugging 4,800 trees into the ground one after the other, each thirteen feet apart.

And then it didn't rain for three months—the worst drought in Kentucky in twenty-five years. "I was frantic," she says. "I had a hundred thousand dollars' worth of trees in the ground, and there was no one to irrigate. Farmers were just letting their crops die in the field."

She called everywhere looking for water. One guy said he could irrigate her trees for $27,000. Do it, she said. But then he couldn't come up with the water.

As her baby trees began to die, a friend mentioned he'd seen that the town of North Allen was selling its old fire truck for $3,500. She bought it that day for $3,000.

Bridget (as in "Bridget of Troubled Water") saved the trees. When the drought finally eased, she assumed her station beside the trebuchet at the top of the field, where she has sat ever since, awaiting her next mission. She starts fine—just don't ask her to roll up and down the hills anymore.

Two years later, Margaret tested her soil and found she needed more lime. Back to Southern States. She'd been battling weeds, and had a new idea. "I said I wanted to use dense-grade gravel." Dense-grade is what's typically used for driveways. The proprietor seemed distressed. "He looked at me and said, 'Margaret, I'm not going to do that. Farmers do not put rocks *in* their fields.'"

He actually refused, fearing it would destroy his reputation in the community as a sensible man. She had to find a driveway guy to do it. But it worked. Sweet soil, no weeds.

At least, it worked in that the trees grew handily. They didn't make any truffles, but it was still early.

And then it wasn't so early. Year six came and went. Year seven. She checked the soil. The mycorrhizae were there; they just weren't fruiting. (What about Spanish wells, you ask? The concept hadn't yet filtered down to most U.S. growers.)

In 2018 the *Wall Street Journal* came calling, iterating on the perennial story that had been running for a decade. "The Elusive American Black Truffle" captured the angst ("Three decades after farmers first cultivated Périgord truffles in the U.S., no one has succeeded commercially") as well as the hope ("These intrepid growers are still pursuing the prize"), with Margaret as Exhibit A. "There have only been two times I sat down in the field and cried," she told them.

And then, on November 3, 2019, Lois and Monza came for an early-season check. No one expected much—the main season was December to March—and for a while Monza breezed through the orchard at the unmistakable pace of a Lagotto who isn't smelling a darned thing.

Then she stopped. Classic head check. Doubled back. Doubled back again, finding the dimensions of the scent cone. Followed that cone right to its point of convergence. And tapped the surface with her paw.

Up came a big black truffle. And Margaret cried in the field for a third time.

They found two more truffles that day. Baseball-sized truffles. Half-pounders. Four-hundred-dollar truffles. They didn't smell like much, so Margaret sent them away for DNA analysis to confirm that they were *Tuber melanosporum*. The report was good. "The little suckers went off to the lab and came back bona fide."

~~~~

Now Lois is back for a full orchard check. And Monza has just pawed the ground down below Bridget and the trebuchet, and Margaret is holding the big sucker up and hollering, "I'm a truffle farmer at last!"

I lean down in the hail for a snort and, oh yes, *that* is a black winter truffle. It's as good as that first Australian one I smelled, with the rich depth of chocolate and sorghum and the melancholy of olive. Empirical evidence that American truffles can stink with the best.

In Spain, we pulled dozens of truffles out of the ground and never even thought about sampling one. That was business. Here, we net a grand total of two nice ones, and both are immediately sacrificed on the altar of southern hospitality. While dogs tornado in and out of the kitchen, we make truffled grits, squash with truffle butter, and roast turkey with truffled gravy. I shave truffle into a blender hollandaise and pour it over asparagus.

Then Miss Jane ups the game, breaking out her 1953 copy of *Cissy Gregg's Cookbook and Guide to Gracious Living*, which includes the sainted *Louisville Courier-Journal* food columnist's scandalously thick eggnog recipe, and soon great white clouds of black-flecked eggnog (heavy on the bourbon) are floating around the house in wineglasses. Never before have I encountered truffle bonded so profoundly into the interstitial matrix of a dish.

After dinner, I sit in the library in a truffly haze, beneath the taxidermied vole, licking my eggnog-foam mustache. I think back to Sally Schneider's false memories. Somehow a black winter can trick your mind into thinking that it's the thing that was in your grandparent's attic on that perfect childhood day, or can at least get you to grant it the same emotional standing. And why not? "Everybody needs his memories," Saul Bellow wrote. "They keep the wolf of insignificance from the door." I sink deeper into the haze, the palimpsest growing ever richer.

~~~~

I'd forgotten what the Smokies smell like. That spicy musk that pools around the mountain laurel and the streams. Especially in winter.

I breathe the sharp air up on Test Farm Road, watching Monza go tree to tree. We've come four hours east from Kentucky. There was snow high in the Smokies. And then we cut through the pass and dropped down on the North Carolina side to this tiny research orchard. Here, the state of North Carolina hopes to seed a future for former tobacco farmers.

And maybe so? Monza has already flagged a dozen truffles, and Leonora Stefanile, the young horticulturalist from NC State, seems to be prying a little future from the cold ground beneath nearly every tree.

Leo researches new crops for the state. She's looked at hops, hemp, and now *T. mel*, as she calls it. She records the weight,

odor, color, condition, and location of every truffle. She notes its
distance from the mother tree and what the groundcover looks
like above it. She hopes the data will eventually point toward
some best practices for truffles, because, as she puts it, "There's no
manual for growing truffles on the east coast of North America."

The state research orchard was planted in 2010, and the first
truffles showed up seven years later, right on schedule. "There
were only three, but they were all good quality," says Leo. "One
was about a quarter pound, which was pretty exciting. The
following season, we found two big ones, side by side. We'd
hoped to find more, but that was it. But this year, the orchard
just exploded."

In truffle world, *exploded* is a relative term. They found
twelve, plus whatever Monza turns up today. But still, encouraging. For so many years, *T. mel* has thwarted them.

There were reasons for that, explains Brian Upchurch, the
trim, gray-bearded fellow in the sweater and driving cap
standing beside Leo. Upchurch is a nurseryman of some repute
and the current president of NATGA, the North American
Truffle Growers Association. (When I ask how he came to
power, he says, "It's called a vacuum.") Upchurch is a professional grower of things, and he says that many first-wave truffle
growers simply weren't. "Significant mistakes were made."

For example, plant your tree seedlings eight inches too deep,
and they die within a few years. Skimp on the lime, and you're
screwed. Those hobbyists also underestimated what was involved
with maintaining an orchard year after year. The weeds, the
pruning, the disease management. "We have so many neglected
orchards out there."

But that's how it always goes. American wine. American
oysters. American beer. The wave of dreamers plays around,

makes some mistakes, learns a little, loses a lot, burns out, and then the wave of entrepreneurs makes it real.

And if I had to place money on the entrepreneur to make that happen, it would be Davis Upchurch, Brian's eighteen-year-old son, a handsome, clean-cut kid with dark hair and intense brown eyes standing next to him. Davis knows more about the truffle business than anyone I've met. He has an almost freakish recall for names, numbers, and research. He's in daily contact with half a dozen truffle experts around the world, he's on top of the latest techniques for Spanish wells, and he and Brian are going big. Their nursery contains dozens of acres of truffle trees—all the usual European suspects, plus some native North American ones. Davis tells me *T. macrosporum* is his favorite truffle, which is like saying chenin blanc is your favorite wine grape—an insider's sign of discernment.

Davis has developed a brand-new way to inoculate trees directly with mycorrhizae instead of spores, which is going to change everything, he believes, and no, I can't come into their greenhouse to take a look, not while the patents are pending.

"Davis came up with the idea when he was fifteen," Brian says. "I'd sold my nursery business and I was pasturing animals on the farm. And Davis came to me and said we should grow truffles. I was through playing in the dirt, so my wife and I said, 'Davis, if you're serious about it, do your homework.' Two weeks later, he came back with an entire business plan. And we thought, 'Damn, this looks pretty good!'"

Standing beside Brian and Davis and Lois and me, watching Monza hunt and Leo dig, is Tom Michaels himself, who's come to check out the orchard. It feels like the high priest of American truffles is here to bless the occasion and pass the baton, and my Spidey sense starts tingling. Whatever trufflehead culture is stirring to life in America, it feels very different from the one in Europe. It has the charm of obsession and absurdity I hoped for. These are not weird people, but they've caught a whiff of the deep weirdness dangling from the end of every truffle, and, like Zelda, they're in.

Case in point: Michael Riggan, the other member of our group. A retired entrepreneur from the Raleigh area, Riggan has launched several wildly successful businesses and has more money than he'll ever know what to do with. And he's decided to devote his retirement to truffling.

Most of the truffles Monza located have been flagged and left in the ground as practice for Elora, Michael's one-year-old Lagotto puppy, who has the topiary cut of a bichon frise. Excited Elora yaps hysterically as she charges through the orchard, dragging Michael behind on a leash while Lois barks futile suggestions. No truffles are being discovered, but Michael is getting a hell of a workout.

"She's got the puppy jet fuel," Lois says, shaking her head. "I love her. No shortage of drive." Some dogs, she confides to me softly, because just maybe the owners of the dogs in question are within earshot, have the motivation of peanut butter.

The phrase is distracting enough that I lose track of the action. I begin thinking about peanut butter and its motivations, and I only snap out of it when Lois chides Michael for doing what I've seen most truffle hunters do, showering the dog in a steady stream of encouragement. "Chatter has no positive effect," Lois coaches. "She's just going to tune you out. Let her concentrate. Imagine if you'd lost your keys and were searching around your house and your spouse was walking behind you going, 'Find the keys! Find the keys! Find the keys!' Save the verbal reward for when you find the truffle."

Moments later, miraculously, Elora comes through, putting her nose to the ground like a pro right next to an orange flag. "Yes!" Lois calls. "Now talk to her. Praise her. Tell her how good she is." Michael starts to do all of the above as he digs in his pocket for a treat, but he also pulls Elora away from the spot, and Lois interjects. "Reward at source!" she calls. "Nice and low. You want obedience to odor. Not to sitting up and looking at a person."

Before the group disperses, Lois and I break out the leftover eggnog from Kentucky and share the wealth, standing there sipping from plastic cups in the icy mountain air. Michael mentions Burwell Farms, a new orchard in North Carolina's Piedmont region where he's been training Elora. He asks if I've seen what's happening there.

I haven't.

He pulls out his phone and scrolls through the photos, then hands it to me.

I gasp, flailing with my thumb and forefinger to make the things I think I'm seeing big enough for verification. "That can't be real," I blurt.

Lois, who has already seen the photo, chuckles. "That's what everybody wants to know."

16

Carolina Gold

O n a damp February morning, I walk beneath orderly rows of loblolly pine with what must be the most surprising team in the long and strange history of American truffles, trying very hard not to step on the precious nuggets beneath my feet. Nancy Rosborough—the self-described "ghetto kid" from Washington, D.C., whose wobbly startup, Mycorrhiza Biotech, might just be saved by the golf-ball-sized tubers erupting out of the red dirt—looks around, trying to contain her emotions. After fifteen years of struggle to bring her truffle-farming vision to life, she is staring at two acres of validation.

"Nobody believed in us," she says, exchanging glances with Dr. Omoanghe Isikhuemhen, the Nigerian mycologist who invented Mycorrhiza Biotech's system for truffle cultivation. "They mocked us. They thought we were just some podunk people."

She nods toward Richard Franks, the manager of Burwell Farms, standing beside her in a Duke Blue Devils sweatshirt, a ball cap pulled over his short white hair. "And then we found one person who believed in us."

Richard was expecting a few hundred truffles from this two-acre plot; instead, he's getting a few thousand, well beyond his rosiest projections. Many are breaching the surface before fully ripe, an unexpected development. The farm crew tries to cover them up with nearby dirt and mark them with little flags, but they can't keep up. The pine-needle-strewn ground is a minefield. That's what I'd seen in Michael Riggan's photos.

"Watch your step," Franks says to me, nervously eyeing my path. A lifelong Carolinian, he speaks in the clipped monotones of a Mission Control commander attempting to bring astronauts safely back to earth. "Ever seen anything like this?"

The grove is a confetti of colored flags. Michael and Elora are galloping around, practicing. Laddy, Burwell Farms' yellow-Lab truffle dog in training, is wandering the rows in a daze, nose overloaded. An old farmhand named David Crow—one half of the Crow Brothers, who caretake the property—crawls through the red clay of the plantation on his hands and knees, sniffing and calling out, "These are perfumin' right here!" as he inserts little wire flags in the ground to mark his finds.

No, I tell Richard. No, I haven't. The trees, the truffle, the people, the vibe; this is all new. There are an estimated two hundred pounds of truffles in this plot, maybe more underneath. Burwell Farms has matched Tom Michaels's best year in half the time and on one-fifth the land. It's already one of the most productive truffle orchards in the world. And it's the work of total outsiders.

I tell Richard all this, most of which he already knows. He nods slowly. At age seventy-five, he's continuously thwarted in his attempts to retire, and now this. "We did something right," he finally concedes. "Now we have to figure out what it was."

For that, I turn to Dr. Omon, as everyone calls him, who's sporting a wide smile beneath his blue kufi hat. Beatific as a Buddha, round of face and belly, Omon has an unshakable faith in the sunny disposition of the universe. "The secret is this team," he answers in English generously inflected with the honeyed tones of Nigeria. "The power is in this team that came together!"

When I ask for the source of his confidence, he says, "I don't want to blow my own trumpet, but when a blind man tells you he's going to stone you, you know that his foot is on a stone."

And that's about all I'm getting out of Omon. When I ask probing questions about technique, he gives me a cagey smile. "That's nothing to share in public." All he'll admit is that his innovation has something to do with "microbial dynamics," and something to do with the growth media he uses to inoculate the pine seedlings in the greenhouse. "It's a secret mix that grows truffles five times faster than any other media. Its composition is very abnormal. *Very.* It came to me in a dream."

I give him a raised eyebrow, and he looks me right in the eye. "It's not the first time that's happened to me. When you get such messages from the divine, you work with them."

Before I can follow up, he deflects attention back to Richard. "But again, from the time the trees got to the field, it was *this man*. He took it to the next level."

Without a doubt, this is the cleanest, most OCD truffle farm I've ever seen. The trees are vigorous, the ground pristine. Along with Omon's secret sauce, that's certainly part of the reason for the eye-popping production.

But the other factor is the truffle itself. Instead of the black winter, Burwell Farms has opted for the bianchetto ("whitish") truffle, *Tuber borchii*. The bianchetto looks a lot like the famed white, and shares certain characteristics with it—"garlic and gas" is the classic description—but unlike the white, it's easily cultivated, partnering with many different trees. It's so promiscuous, in fact, that nurseries have to go to great lengths to keep it from infecting other truffle trees.

The bianchetto especially loves pines. In Italy it's often found growing under stands of pines in sandy coastal plains. A truffle that loves pines and sand seems like an inspired choice for the Southeast. The season sets it apart, too. No other truffle comes ripe in the spring, meaning no competition in the market.

Because of all these advantages, the bianchetto is increasingly popular with farmers. It's being cultivated in Europe, Australia, and New Zealand. The United States has bianchetto farms in Washington State and Idaho in addition to North Carolina, though none has duplicated Burwell's success.

But the bianchetto has one huge knock against it. Many pros say it just isn't that good. If the black winter has the silky luxury of a Rolls-Royce, and the white the sexy rush of a Lamborghini, the bianchetto is more like a Camaro—plenty of pheromonal zip, but less sophistication.

"It's got a very strong smell, sometimes overpoweringly strong," Zak Frost told me. "Much more raw and gassy than *magnatum*, which is infinitely more refined, more perfumed and fragrant. I call it the Marmite truffle—you either love it or you hate it."

That second-tier status means the bianchetto sells for a much lower price in Europe: about €100–150 per kilo wholesale, a third that of the black winter. A proper assessment? Or Classic European Bullshit? In New Zealand, it often sells for the same price as black winters. Apparently the jury is still out.

Richard grants me permission to grab a truffle, so I follow David Crow, who seems to be crawling circles around Laddy. Burning with the conviction of the newly converted, he has red dirt on the tip of his trucker cap and the tip of his nose, his eyes shining with amazement. He'd never even heard of a truffle until about a year ago, and now he's sold. "That smell brings tears to my eyes," he says in his Carolina drawl. "You could just about bottle it."

I notice that most of the truffles are still a pale beige, a sign of immaturity. "Those don't smell as good," David Crow says. We scooch along until his nose leads him to one that has darkened to the color of scrapple. He snorts deeply and his eyes dance. "That aroma . . . I don't know what to call it, other than . . . *satisfactory.*"

It's exactly the right word, and I tell him so. I suggest he should become a food writer if the whole truffle-dog thing doesn't work out.

He grins. "I can smell 'em from my knees. I don't even need to go all the way down."

I pluck the truffle from the ground and hold it to my nose. Garlic and gas, for sure. Also mud. It's definitely a real truffle, but it has none of the dazzle of a European white. I wonder if it's still a little early in the season.

Nancy and Omon and Richard catch up to us. As word has spread about the unlikely eruption under way at Burwell Farms, they've become hot properties. A parade of agronomists is beating a path to Burwell Farms to see if American trufficulture is finally taking off, and if this is the engine to power it. If so, it will be because three outsiders from wildly diverse backgrounds were able to form a partnership as improbable and inventive as the one humming beneath our feet.

~~~

Growing up poor in Washington, D.C., Nancy Rosborough didn't know a truffle from a tricycle. But she knew a bit about farming. Her mother was raised on a small farm in Gibsonville, North Carolina, in the heart of tobacco country. The house was still in the family, and the rural landscape had always been a spiritual touchstone to the city kid, who went on to build a successful career as an IT consultant. But over the years, as tobacco tanked, Nancy watched while Gibsonville was engulfed by the New South. "Dirt roads and farms turning into subdivisions," she says. "Then you get Walmart and Ruby Tuesdays and you can't afford the taxes."

Nancy was always looking for new crops that could revitalize the region's farms, including her family's. In 2005 her mother sent her a *Washington Post* article about North Carolina tobacco farmers experimenting with truffles. "Like everyone else, I thought, well, they grow on trees, how hard could it be? Hah!"

She moved to the Gibsonville farm that same year and contacted a truffle tree supplier, who explained that after planting the seedlings she'd have to wait a decade to get a real crop. That's ridiculous, she thought. What kind of farmer could do that?

The more she looked into the truffle business, the dicier it seemed. Truffle-tree seedlings seemed to vary greatly in the amount of truffle mycorrhization on their roots, from lots to zilch, but the average farmer had no way of telling. Her IT career had taught her a lot about risk assessment, so she decided to start a lab that could analyze and certify the seedlings.

To develop the technology, she approached Dr. Omon, a mushroom expert at North Carolina A&T State University in nearby Greensboro. Omon had grown up on a subsistence farm in rural Nigeria, hunting mushrooms with his family and hawking them in the market. The first in his family to attend college, he'd gone on to get his PhD in mycology. His family thought that was hilarious ("You went to college to study *mushrooms?*"), but he'd become a respected specialist in shiitake cultivation and had helped some of North Carolina's tobacco farmers pivot to mushrooms.

Omon had watched the nascent truffle industry with skepticism. The closer he and Nancy looked at *Tuber melanosporum*, the more they decided that its prospects in America were limited. "That is a beast of a problem," Omon says. Slow growing, finicky, outcompeted by too many native organisms, it's commercially challenging. Besides, everybody was doing *melanosporum*. "Let's do something different," Omon suggested.

They were intrigued by *Tuber borchii*. Sure, it didn't command the prestige or the prices of black winters, but the promise of a bigger crop in half the time, and a spring harvest with no competition, was appealing. Most important, instead of non-native European oaks and hazelnuts, it liked to grow on loblolly pines, the standard timber tree of the Southeast.

With grants from the North Carolina Biotech Center, they set up their lab and tackled bianchetto cultivation. Omon visited bianchetto farms in Italy, observing what worked and what didn't. At some point, he had his dream epiphany about microbial dynamics.

By 2010, they were achieving mind-blowing levels of mycorrhization on pine seedlings in their lab. They advertised. They spoke at forestry conferences. They presented to truffle farmers. No dice. Everyone wanted to see examples of successful orchards. They wanted hard numbers on pounds per acre. No one was willing to take a chance on an African American woman from D.C. and a Nigerian with a thick accent.

"It was extremely frustrating," Nancy says. "We knew it worked. And nobody believed in us." Whatever the reason, the truth was that they had no proof it would work in the field. In her darker moments, Nancy worried that it was nothing but a Hail Mary.

After two years, Mycorrhiza Biotech had burned through its seed money and had nothing to show. "We had no customers," Nancy says with a sigh. "We were tired. We decided to quit." She stuck a For Sale sign on the lawn in front of the lab and called a liquidator to come get the equipment.

And that was when she received a mysterious phone message. "My employer has an interest in truffles," said the stiff voice.

She didn't bother calling back. "First of all, who talks like that?" Second, she was all too used to pretenders whose interest disappeared as soon as they learned it took $25,000 an acre to set up a truffle farm.

But the caller left a second message. His employer was still interested in truffles.

By the third call, she decided to call back. "We did our song and dance and told him it would be close to fifty thousand to set up a two-acre orchard. And he didn't flinch. And I thought, 'Who *are* these people?'"

The man on the other end of the line was Richard Franks, and his employer was a man named Dr. Thomas Edward Powell III—a very familiar name in North Carolina. In 1927, Dr. Thomas Edward Powell II, a science professor at Elon College, founded Carolina Biological Supply to provide plant and animal samples to science teachers. The company went on to become a leading provider of teaching materials worldwide.

Powell's three sons then founded a diagnostics company called Biomedical Laboratories in a hospital basement in Burlington in 1969. After various mergers and acquisitions, Biomedical Laboratories became LabCorp, which is now the largest clinical diagnostics company in the world. LabCorp processes hundreds of millions of lab tests every year. It has 61,000 employees. And it's worth an estimated $25 billion.

Nancy called the liquidator and told him not to come just yet.

~~~~~

Richard Franks had worked for the Powell family his entire life. Both he and his father spent their careers at Carolina Biological Supply. After retiring in 2007, Franks managed some of Dr. Powell's properties, including timber holdings.

One Sunday afternoon in 2010, he was settled into his den, watching a football game, when he received a phone call from the seventy-eight-year-old Powell, who'd just had lunch with his interior decorator, who'd read an article about a truffle in Italy that grew beneath pine trees. Powell owned hundreds of acres of pines in Warren County. Could he inoculate them with truffles? And could Richard manage the thing? See him at eight o'clock in the morning.

Richard spent the rest of the afternoon giving himself an online crash course in truffles. He didn't like what he saw. A lot of people had lost a lot of money. He didn't want Dr. Powell to be the next. This is crazy, he thought.

Then again, most of those early adopters weren't working with the pine truffle, and they weren't tree professionals. If there was one thing Richard knew, it was how to grow good pines.

The first seedling supplier he called laughed at him when he said he wanted to grow *Tuber borchii*. "I consider those weeds," the man told him.

Back to the internet. Up popped a single hit for a source of bianchetto-inoculated seedlings: Mycorrhiza Biotech.

Unbelievably, the company was right in Burlington, less than two miles away. It seemed like a sign.

When Richard finally got Nancy on the phone, they talked for three hours. His employer was interested in truffles. A lot of truffles. Was she interested?

Hell, yes, she was interested.

He met with Nancy and Omon and peppered them with questions about timing and yield. "We really don't know," Omon kept answering. "No one has tried these techniques on a commercial scale before."

The honesty impressed Richard. "If anybody involved with truffles doesn't use the term 'I don't know' a half dozen times in your first conversation," he says, "they probably have no idea what they're talking about."

He called Powell. "They think they can do it. I think they can do it. Do you want to do it?"

"Go for it," said Powell.

In 2012, while Mycorrhiza Biotech was growing eleven hundred inoculated loblolly seedlings in its greenhouse, Burwell Farms prepared two acres of ground, clear-cutting pines on an existing plantation. Omon showed up for a site inspection and groaned. Any existing roots would already be impregnated with their own native mycorrhizal fungi, so they all had to go, down to a depth of eight feet.

It took a bulldozer equipped with a massive steel root rake a year to comb the earth clean. Then the pH of the soil had to be raised from 5.7 to 7.3. A procession of trucks plastered the ground with fifteen tons of lime per acre.

In June 2014 they planted the year-old seedlings, along with Omon's mysterious media, watered them hard, and waited. They hoped to see their first truffles in the winter of 2018–19.

In December 2016, Omon, Nancy, and Richard made the ninety-mile drive to the farm for one of their regular site visits. On the way, Nancy and Richard confessed to having doubts. Unproven techniques, unproven truffle. They were already the laughingstocks of the truffle world.

Keep the faith, Omon told them. "If you are born to do something, every road you take leads to what you are supposed to do. And you are naturally equipped with intuition and awe to find your way there." He flashed his wide smile. "I'll bet you a hundred dollars we find a truffle next year."

They pulled up to the neat block of pine trees and stepped out into the cold. As soon as Omon looked at the pines, he grinned. They were larger and more vigorous than any three-year-old trees he'd seen in Italy. The truffles and the trees had taken to each other like long-lost siblings. He leaned over to Richard. "I take it back," he whispered. "There are truffles here now."

"How do you know?" Richard asked.

"I just know."

Then they noticed an animal trail leading from the forest into the orchard. They followed it to a spot where the ground had been scraped raw in an attempt to dig beneath the protective weed mat. Omon slashed at the mat with his machete and pulled it back. Breaching the surface was the small white rump of a bianchetto.

"Holy shit," Nancy whispered under her breath. "It worked."

Omon did some sort of a jig. Richard called Powell with the good news. From the sounds on the other end of the line, the doctor may have been doing his own jig.

They found another dozen truffles that winter. Then four pounds the following year. Then thirty pounds in 2019, well before they were ready. They had no sales-and-marketing team. They had no distribution. Laddy had been trained to be rewarded with a tennis ball instead of food, which seemed like a good idea when they were dealing with a handful of truffles, but now every time he found one he wanted to play ball for ten minutes.

What on earth will 2020 bring? Richard wondered. And that was before he knew about any of the things 2020 had in store for them.

～～～

Richard first realized something was up in October 2019, when he visited the orchard and saw the soil lumping up in hundreds of spots. Omon did his jig again when he heard the news. "I knew it!" he sang. "Destiny!" Soon the truffles started breaching the surface, far too early. Everywhere the farmhands dug up soil to cover the truffles, they uncovered other truffles on their way up. When they did pull out a truffle, they found others nested beneath.

By February, when I visit, they've flagged three thousand truffles. Most weigh an ounce or two, but one they nicknamed "The Brain" tips the scales at 9.7 ounces. The fragrance is reminiscent of white truffles, but more raw leek than golden-fried garlic. When I run a few past the North Carolina chef Andrea Reusing, queen of farm-to-table, she's underwhelmed.

It makes me wonder if there's a reason this easy truffle isn't more widely grown. My European experts had already given it lukewarm reviews.

Christine Fischer: "I've never had a bianchetto where I said, 'Wow, this is a fabulous flavor!' I'm not saying it doesn't exist, but I haven't seen it."

Xavi Vilanova: "For me, the smell depends. It smells of garlic and gas, but generally more of one than the other. I don't like garlic, so when the garlic is strong, for me it's no good. But when the gas is strong, it's a lovely truffle."

Zak Frost's biggest objection was that it sometimes gets passed off as a *magnatum*. "Some websites will just say 'white' truffles. You know, 'Very similar to Alba truffles, but at a lower price.' Chefs don't understand it, and they use it like *magnatum*, and then it's weird tasting and puts people off white truffles."

On the other hand, he sells quite a few bianchetti in springtime. "We have five or six customers that go mad for it and can't wait for it to come into season. It's good that it comes in the spring, because it goes well with other spring ingredients. So if you eat it with morel mushrooms, wild garlic, the first quail eggs, and things like that, you can make a really nice seasonal meal."

Later, I take Zak's advice almost verbatim. As the truffles come into full ripeness, the flavor deepens into what I can only describe as Garlic Cheez-It. I shave one over morels, ramps, and an egg floating atop bright-green stinging nettle soup. It's raw, punchy, vital. I'm on board.

Through the early spring of 2020, others are, too. "Chefs ordered," Richard says, "and then they ordered some more." Gary Menes, of the Michelin-starred Le Comptoir in Los Angeles, tweets that they are "Beautifully fragrant, sweet and delicious."

Thomas Edward Powell III sees enough to double down on the future. Burwell Farms now has five two-acre orchards in the ground, 5,500 trees in all. In a few years, it expects to be looking for homes for more than a thousand pounds of truffles a year. It has started to sell inoculated seedlings as well.

Meanwhile, Omon and Nancy have seen their stars rise. "They took a chance on us, but it wasn't as big a risk as they thought," Nancy says. "There's nobody smarter than Dr. Omon, and can't nobody outwork me. Come hell or high water, we were going to have truffles in this field."

Still, she gives Richard tremendous credit for his trust and openness. "It's been a good partnership for us. We've grown together. We've both learned from each other."

Omon received new grants to expand his bianchetto program from the U.S. Department of Agriculture and the Evans-Allen Program, which funds agricultural research at historically Black universities. He began a long-term project to test different sites in five different North Carolina counties to learn which micro-climates and soil dynamics are most conducive.

And Mycorrhiza Biotech went from zero customers to a full docket. Nancy bought the lot beside her lab and put up another greenhouse to try to keep up with seedling orders. If all goes well, she expects some of her new client orchards to begin fruiting by 2022. One orchard in Delaware is looking especially good. "And once that guy finds his first truffle, it's all gonna blow up."

For her, the ultimate sign of success came when she harvested twenty-five pounds of truffles from her very own bianchetto orchard. But don't expect her to eat one anytime soon. "Personally, I don't like truffles," she admits. "I'm not a fan of that woodsy-garlicky thing." Then she lowers her voice conspiratorially. "But you know how women say there's no such thing as an ugly millionaire? Well, there's no such thing as a stinky truffle."

17

The Mysteries of Oregon

I'm scrambling through a patch of Douglas fir in Oregon's Willamette Valley, holding a mystery wrapped in an enigma inside a peridium. Said peridium is knobby, beige, and pock-marked, like a runty white truffle. It looks unpromising at best. But when I hold it to my nose, an explosive scent of cedar and petrol fills my head, and little bubbles of happiness burst in my brain like Pop Rocks. It's intense, it's an Oregon white, and it's supposed to suck.

I knew that the Pacific Northwest had its own truffles, both black and white, but no one seemed to take them seriously. Everyone from professional food writers to Michelin-starred chefs wrinkled their noses when they came up. Some said they were gross. Others said they were dull, the cubic zirconia to the European diamonds.

But this little beauty has aromatics like a European white turned up to eleven. The profile is similar, but a little more mad scientist. "Why does everyone think these are lame?" I ask

Charles Lefevre, the gray-goateed mycologist scampering beside me, who has devoted the past fifteen years of his life to clearing the good name of Oregon truffles. "How did we get it so wrong?"

In answer, he points to his two four-legged friends hoovering across the forest floor like furry Roombas. "No one had dogs," he says. "They were the key."

Dante and Mocha, Charles's Lagotto Romagnolos, are bounding from tree to tree and unearthing truffles as if they'd studied a treasure map in advance, enthusiastically spraying dirt behind them and occasionally hiking truffles between their legs like tiny footballs.

More often, however, they simply eat the truffles they find, and they do it fast. "Wait, Dante, no!" Charles shouts, hurling himself in the dirt to snag a truffle from his pooch, who has hit a motherlode and is gobbling down the world's most expensive dog treats.

For the next three hours, we race after the Lagottos in a desperate attempt to minimize the carnage while Charles tries to explain how one of America's great foods could have been so overlooked, and how it just might be a godsend to the ecology and economy of the Pacific Northwest. I'm here for the Oregon Truffle Festival, which Charles started with his wife, Leslie Scott, in 2006. Over three days of truffle hunting, truffle learning, and truffle eating, Charles and some of the Northwest's best young chefs will try to convince me and other pioneering souls that America's native truffles can run with the big dogs.

Until a week ago, I was skeptical of such a notion. But then I attended the Napa Truffle Festival, which showcases black winter truffles, the variety most commonly farmed in California.

The festival includes a blind tasting. Wrapped in paper towels in separate wineglasses were six different truffles: a black winter, a black autumn, a *brumale*, a European white, an Oregon white, and an Oregon black. We all passed the wineglasses, sniffed, and made our notes before the big reveal.

It was a superb idea, and really fun, as well as thought-provoking. But if the goal was to promote black winter truffles, the organizers might want to reconsider.

I was certain the European white would be my favorite, and I'd pegged the black winter for No. 2. I expected the Oregon truffles to be firmly at the bottom. The results shocked me. I had indeed placed the Oregon black near the bottom ("Weirdly fruity, like off-gassing apples in a root cellar," according to my notes), along with the black autumn ("Almost nothing"). In the middle of the pack were the black winter ("Deep, rich, but subtle") and the *brumale* ("Nicely smoky, like lapsang souchong tea"). I'd ranked the European white No. 2. My favorite, for which I'd scribbled "Pretty, bright, smells like an Italian white except I don't feel like I need to go to confession afterwards," was the Oregon white.

Well, that got me curious, but you can't find Oregon truffles outside of the Pacific Northwest, the only region where they grow, so I've come to the Oregon Truffle Festival in hopes of finding out what the deal is. And Charles is telling me dogs are the deal. But it's a conversation held on the run and in the dirt as we tear through the mossy woods, ducking Douglas fir branches, and we're never getting to the part where he actually explains why these truffles were disdained, or what dogs have to do with it.

"No, Mocha, that's mine!" Charles shouts, diving on the ground to snatch a golden nugget from her maw. His jeans are already trashed, and yes, now they are torn. Apparently, this is how he spends his weekends.

But there's a method to the madness, he assures me. Charles rewards every find with a pat, a treat, and a high-pitched squeal of delight that his friends refer to as his Gollum voice. "Good job! Pretty truffle!"

You want to reward them instantly, he tells me. "Some people use clickers. I do it with my voice. I make a sound that I don't normally make."

Even when Mocha scarfs a truffle, she gets the treat and the squeal. "The pro trainers make fun of me for letting them eat the truffles," he admits, "but I think the trick is to make truffle hunting more fun than anything else. When they find a truffle, you lavish them with treats."

I feel my inner Yankee Calvinist squirming, but Charles says it's important to pour on the indulgence right from the beginning of training. "I recommend ribeye hot off the grill. Don't hold back! They're reading your behavior as well, so you have to be really happy. Act like it's the best thing that's ever happened in your life for the dog to have found that truffle. If your neighbors aren't embarrassed for you, then you're not happy enough."

Just then Dante uncovers a big one and Gollum returns. "Good boy! Mine!" Dante looks up at Charles and cocks his head at an adorable angle, and my inner Calvinist begins to turn into a gibbering goofball.

And now Mocha is going deep after a truffle, disappearing down the hole, just a dog butt and a fan of dirt visible, and Charles and I are jockeying for position, trying to avoid a face full of earth while we determine if maybe the truffle already shot out the back. "Sometimes I think she thinks God is on the other end of the hole," Charles mutters. (Later, when I read

Merlin Sheldrake's book *Entangled Life*, I will discover with a curse that I'm not the first writer to whom Charles has fed this irresistible line.)

Miraculously, Mocha comes out of the crater with a truffle, a big one for Oregon. Even more miraculously, she drops it into Charles's outstretched hand and sits there, panting hard. She laps at the truffle in deep satisfaction as Charles gazes at her with love in his eyes. "She's so sweet when she finds a monster truffle," he says. "She just sits there licking it. It makes my heart melt." And then his voice lowers and his arm extends dramatically, and, good heavens, there in the middle of the forest he starts singing to her. "Whatever Mocha wants, Mocha gets . . ."

And I can't help but imagine the Europeans standing beside us. Carlo Marenda. Radmila Karlić. István Bagi. Giancarlo Zigante! Not even Matteo Giuliani would be singing show tunes to his dogs. In Europe, there's always a seriousness to truffles. It's business. The dogs are working, and they know it. The romance is there, but not the hugs.

Here at the Oregon Truffle Festival, there's a whole lot of hugging going on. Chefs getting hugged. Visitors getting hugged. And, of course, dogs getting hugged. The Eugene hotel where the festival is held is a barking madhouse. Dogs in the lobby, dogs in the seminars, dogs riding the elevators.

It reminds me of the contrasts between European and American schooling. In Europe, rote learning and impersonal tests are still the norm. Spare the rod and spoil the child. Ditto for dogs. Here, an unapologetically progressive version of truffle culture is blossoming, rooted in the soils and optimism of the Pacific Northwest.

And it's hard to argue with success. Sure, we're losing a third of our truffles to the dogs, but my pockets are full of truffles.

There's plenty to go around. And I'm hanging out with the happiest dogs in the world. It's an abundance mindset, and over the three days to come, as the mysteries of Oregon truffles are revealed, I'll come to find it irresistible.

Charles is continuing to sing to his pooch, and as I look nervously around to make sure no one's watching, I feel my inner Calvinist losing out to my inner Gwen Verdon, and soon I've joined him there in the wet woods in wobbly harmony. "Whatever Mocha wants, Mocha gets . . . and little truffle, little Mocha wants *you!*"

≈≈≈

Like me, Charles Lefevre was always taught that Oregon truffles were no good. As a PhD student in mycology at Oregon State University in the late 1990s, he put himself through school by foraging wild mushrooms and selling them to local restaurants, but he never messed with truffles, which were considered more of a novelty than a coveted ingredient. The few he encountered on menus were either bland or rotten.

At that time, the native truffles had several factors working against them. First, there were no truffle dogs in the Pacific Northwest. Harvesters used rakes, sieving the soil around Douglas fir trees and pulling up every truffle in the stand regardless of size or ripeness.

Second, Oregon truffles don't start to ripen until mid-January, but what little demand there was for native truffles tended to be around the holidays, the traditional time to enjoy European truffles. The result was that the truffles that came to market had all the allure of unripe peaches.

Third, Oregon truffles have very short shelf life, so the ones that weren't underwhelming people with their woodenness were often terrifying them with their unholy excrescences.

The fourth factor was a consequence of the other three. The unloved truffles sold for about $25 per pound. At that rate, there was no incentive for better handling or more attentive harvesting, or even for learning about the truffles. Consumers and chefs just steered clear, believing the only good truffles came from Europe.

Charles, however, was fascinated by all truffles. He knew the French and Spanish had been successfully cultivating black winters for decades, but that pioneers had struggled to do so in North America. While still in grad school, he invented new ways to inoculate tree seedlings with black winter spores and launched New World Truffieres in 2000, seeding America's new wave of truffle love.

But native truffles? Charles didn't take them seriously until he began foraging for his own, also while in grad school. "Every year I wanted to find something bigger and better than what I'd found before," he says as we continue to chase Dante and Mocha. "You know, I'd found chanterelles, but then I wanted to find porcinis! Eventually I reached a point where I'd found everything except truffles. All the expert mycologists were at OSU, so I asked them."

His professors told him to look in dense stands of old Douglas fir, which was wrong. "Unbelievably, even at OSU, nobody knew what good truffle habitat was! The commercial harvesters knew, but they weren't talking."

After one typical day of failure, Charles pulled his car over to the side of the road to take a leak. He stepped into a stand of young Douglas fir, planted on what had been pastureland just fifteen years before. Bladder relieved, he decided to poke around just for the heck of it. "And there were truffles!"

They were Oregon whites. Over time, Charles figured out where they lived. "It's a very specific type of habitat," he says. "Pastureland planted with Doug fir, near existing Doug fir.

That series of events only takes place on private land, typically on smaller parcels. It's nearly always in somebody's backyard."

In other words, Oregon truffles aren't just in symbiosis with trees. They're in symbiosis with us, too. Edge species, they work with seedlings to colonize new areas, and the modern Pacific Northwest gave them a bonanza.

Charles believes the current abundance of truffles in Oregon and Washington is a result of grazing becoming less profitable in recent decades. Landowners planted their pastures in Douglas fir in hopes that Christmas trees would save them. Those open, airy, fifteen-year-old stands are truffle factories, the Pacific Northwest version of France's nineteenth-century truffle boom.

By the early 2000s, through his work with New World Truffieres, Charles had experienced truffles all over the world. At the same time, he was foraging native truffles for fun. And one day, he had a revelation. "I had these Oregon truffles that I'd harvested recreationally in my refrigerator," he says. "And even though all the experts out there suggested that they were nothing but poor, inexpensive substitutes for the real thing, every time I opened the refrigerator, this powerful blast of truffle came out. So it seemed like they were being overlooked. And it seemed like there was an opportunity to redeem this species."

Charles suspected raking had put the native truffles in the doghouse. He'd seen dogs in action in Europe, and knew they followed their noses to ripe truffles. Obviously, rakers couldn't do that, and wouldn't bother, anyway—as a general rule, the people raking truffles in the spooky forests of the Pacific Northwest have quick cash on their minds, not culinary excellence. Only dogs could redeem Oregon's truffles.

THE DIRTY DOZEN

When George Sand referred to the "black magic apple of love," she was talking about a French black winter truffle. When Alice Waters waxed nostalgic about her truffle initiation, she was reminiscing about an Italian white. Most descriptions of truffles ever written spotlight one of these two, which dominate haute cuisine and truffle travel porn. And most so-called experts will tell you that no other truffle is worth paying attention to, in part because those are often the only ones they've heard of.

But the real world of truffles is much more interesting and diverse. The two greats really are great, with amazing aromas and wonderful traditions, but neither has a lock on greatness, and no one country has a lock on them. They are joined by many other enchanting species, all of which are more available than ever before. The following is a primer on the ones most likely to be encountered. Some are wicked pricey, some are surprisingly affordable. All can be found for free by a clever canine. Happy hunting.

ISTVÁN BAGI

WHITE

LATIN: *Tuber magnatum*

ALIAS: Alba, Italian

APPEARANCE: Like tanned moon rocks, or old fossils. Knobby but smooth-skinned. The marbling has a pink, prosciutto-like touch.

SIZE: Anywhere from marbles to softballs, and even the occasional bowling ball. (The world-record holder is a 4.16-pounder found in 2014.)

SEASON: October–December, with the best coming in the second half.

HABITAT: Wild riverine forests with sandy outwash, especially under oak, poplar, and willow.

REGION: From northern and central Italy east to the Black Sea. Follow the limestone.

PRICE: Ridiculous. A 3.3-pounder, found near Pisa in 2007 by a mutt named Rocco, sold at auction to a Macau casino tycoon for $330,000.

AVAILABILITY: Ubiquitous in Italy and Istria in the fall. Easy to find in top restaurants and online.

USE: Never cook. Infuse fats and eggs in your fridge for several days, then grate raw over hot, steamy dishes like pasta or rice, or add to broths or cream sauces at the last moment. In Piedmont, traditional uses besides pasta include tartare (meh) and fonduta (yeh!).

FRAGRANCE: Intense aroma of garlic, fried cheese, and gym socks. Like a subterranean trattoria where sweaty chefs have been laboring over deliciousness for hours.

NOTES: For many the ultimate truffle, the one upon which an entire Italian tourism industry is built. Many people who don't know better (and even some who do) often generalize about truffles as if they were one thing, but the Big Two, the white and the black winter, are polar opposites in scent and elicited behavior. The black is the snuggly truffle, the one that elicits tender memories; this is the all-night-dance-party truffle. It triggers great memories, too, but tender is not the word that comes to mind.

Black Winter

LATIN: *Tuber melanosporum*

ALIAS: winter, Périgord

APPEARANCE: Black and firm, with a surface covered in tiny pyramidal bumps. The interior is all formal black-tie class.

SIZE: Generally anywhere from a golf ball to a baseball.

ROWAN JACOBSEN

SEASON: November–February in the Northern Hemisphere, June–August in the Southern Hemisphere.

HABITAT: Under oaks and hazelnuts. Today, more than 95 percent is farmed.

REGION: Native to limestone-rich soils in an arc across eastern Spain, southern France, and northern and central Italy. Now cultivated throughout the world, including Spain, France, Italy, Australia, New Zealand, China, Israel, Turkey, South Africa, Chile, and the United States.

PRICE: High

AVAILABILITY: Ubiquitous. Between the two hemispheres, there are only a few months a year when this truffle is unavailable. It also ships well.

USE: Good raw, but its subtle flavors really blossom when gently heated. This is a great truffle to play around with. And with its excellent shelf life (weeks, rather than days), it also stands a better chance of being found in good condition.

FRAGRANCE: Deep earth and forest floor, drenched in cocoa and cognac. Layers of dried tobacco, sorghum, and cured olive slowly unfold. Not piercing like the white truffles. It warms you like an old friend. Toward the end of the season, the slow maturing ones develop a rich brandy or sherry scent thanks to the fermenting microbes they harbor in their interstices. Hunters in the Pyrenees swear by the ones they uncover after a dusting of snow.

NOTES: The most popular and important truffle in the world, and the beating heart of French truffle culture. The black winter's volatiles aren't as, well, volatile as the white's, so it can stand the heat for a few minutes. It doesn't hurt that it hails from the same region of France known for ducks and foie gras, its soul mates. Slip splinters of black truffle under the skin of a bird, or let its aromas melt into duck fat or foie gras, and you begin to understand where its association with decadence came from. Although France made it famous, Spain now produces the most, and Australia's Manjimup region lays claim to the best.

ROWAN JACOBSEN

Black Summer

LATIN: *Tuber aestivum*

ALIAS: summer; *scorzone*, sometimes Burgundy

APPEARANCE: Black and warty on the outside, marbled ivory inside. Always very firm.

SIZE: Generally key lime–sized, but can be quite large.

SEASON: Summer–fall.

HABITAT: Hill forests in alkaline soil.

REGION: Abundant from Europe to the Caucasus Range. Also farmed.

PRICE: Low

AVAILABILITY: Common as dirt.

USE: Makes an excellent paperweight.

FRAGRANCE: Vanishingly light. There's a beautiful floral note, but you'll have to search hard for it.

NOTES: Harvested in massive quantities in the summer across Europe and the Near East, this truffle keeps the industry afloat. Any packaged product using truffle is likely using this one. It also looks exactly like people think a truffle should look and, being hard as a rock, has superb shelf life. What it lacks is aroma. Better to hold out for its fall variant, the black autumn.

ZAK FROST

Black Autumn

LATIN: *Tuber uncinatum*

ALIAS: Burgundy

APPEARANCE: Black and warty on the outside, with a marbled, cappuccino-colored interior. Firm.

SIZE: Plum-sized to tennis ball–sized.

SEASON: September–November

HABITAT: Hill forests in alkaline soil.

REGION: Throughout Europe and into Iran and Turkey. Also farmed.

PRICE: Moderate

AVAILABILITY: Good in fall. Once the whites arrive, everyone stops paying attention to these.

USE: Do everything you'd do with a black winter, but use more.

FRAGRANCE: Beautiful, delicate, floral; boiled corn and frying hazelnuts.

NOTES: Not really its own species (thus the Latin name should really be retired), this truffle is differentiated from the black summer by its darker interior and superior fragrance. The main factors seem to be environmental: In cooler climates (higher altitude or latitude), the truffles come later in the season and build a lot more aromatics, perhaps because the microbes they harbor have more time to develop. The best are said to come from hilly spots with rockier soil. This truffle is becoming a big deal in northern Europe and is promising for cool-climate farms worldwide.

ROWAN JACOBSEN

BIANCHETTO

LATIN: *Tuber borchii*

ALIAS: spring; spring white; March; Marzuolo

APPEARANCE: A bit darker than the white, with a skin like ginger root and an interior like bresaola.

SIZE: Anywhere from an ounce to half a pound.

SEASON: February and March

HABITAT: Sandy soil, especially under pine.

REGION: Grows wild in central Italy along the coastal plains. Now farmed in Washington State, Idaho, North Carolina, New Zealand, Australia, and Europe.

PRICE: Low in Europe; higher elsewhere.

AVAILABILITY: Used to be uncommon. Now being embraced by farmers worldwide. Expect to see more of it.

USE: Infuse olive oil in your fridge, then create a spring pasta with wild greens, peas, and radishes.

FRAGRANCE: Gas and garlic, with a resinous quality possibly derived from its partner pines. A raw, rustic attack. In late maturity, it begins to smell like a wheel of Parmesan.

NOTES: Bianchetto literally means "whitish" in Italian, and this has always been considered the poor-man's white. If the white smells like a beautiful Italian pasta sauce—sizzling garlic and mushrooms and salumi—the bianchetto is more like the raw ingredients. Some Italians love it, everyone else is happy to leave it. The price, therefore, has always been low. But it is also the easiest truffle to grow, and it has the spring season to itself and is being widely embraced worldwide for those reasons. Give it a shot.

Brumale

LATIN: *Tuber brumale*

ALIAS: winter; musky

APPEARANCE: A dead ringer for a black winter, but a bit softer. Brown to black skin with a less dense network of "veins" inside.

SIZE: Like a smaller black winter.

SEASON: November–February

HABITAT: Alkaline soil under oak and hazel.

ŽELJKO ZGRABLIĆ

REGION: Grows wild in Europe and turns up in black winter orchards worldwide.

PRICE: Low

AVAILABILITY: Everybody tries *not* to grow this truffle, so you are more likely to encounter it by accident (in a shipment of black winters) than by intention.

USE: Cook with fatty meat, adding near the end of the process. The heat drives off the tarry notes.

FRAGRANCE: I call this the ATF truffle, because it smells like alcohol, tobacco, and firearms. If, like me, you've always swooned for the flinty scent of gunpowder, this is the truffle for you. "Tarry" is a common description, but it's earthy, too, like smoked beetroot. The legendary Croatian truffle hunter Željko Zgrablić says that it smells like Karbofix, a Serbian glue used for arts and crafts that seems to have scarred the memories of generations of Balkan schoolchildren.

NOTES: I love the name of this truffle, which makes it sound like a villain from the Comedia dell'arte. It plays that role, too, infiltrating black winter orchards and outcompeting the desired truffle like a cuckoo in a nightingale nest. At one time, it was considered acceptable to have mixed orchards of the two black truffle species, and there was a market for brumale, but too many growers tried to pass off their *brumales* as black winters, which has made the truffle a pariah. It's now difficult to sell, yet many truffle insiders secretly prefer it to the black winter. Time for a reevaluation.

Oregon White

LATIN: *Tuber oregonense; Tuber gibbosum*

APPEARANCE: Like a Jerusalem artichoke, off-white and splotched with pink. Very thin skin. The inside is like gray-pink prosciutto.

SIZE: Almost always small, mostly the size of a grape or cherry.

SEASON: October–February, but the best don't arrive until January.

ROWAN JACOBSEN

HABITAT: Young Douglas fir stands.

REGION: Everywhere you find Douglas fir, i.e., northern California to British Columbia. The bulk are in Oregon and Washington.

PRICE: Moderate

AVAILABILITY: Popular in the winter in Pacific Northwest culinary hubs such as Portland and Seattle. Rare elsewhere. The annual Oregon Truffle Festival in Eugene is the highlight.

USE: Don't cook. Infuse fats and eggs in your fridge for several days, then grate raw over hot, steamy dishes like pasta or rice, or add to broths or cream sauces at the last moment.

FRAGRANCE: An eye-popping bouillabaisse of diesel and pine, mixed with garlic, salami, blue cheese, and a touch of model airplane glue. One of the more intense aromas on planet Earth. When it first comes out of the ground it has soft cedarlike notes that dissipate within minutes.

NOTES: No truffle divides people like the Oregon white, which is the most abundant truffle in the Pacific Northwest and the driving force behind the region's truffle awakening. I'm in awe of how one whiff of an Oregon white can drench you in a Technicolor emotional landscape of microfeelings that have no names. But others get paint thinner, not Roquefort, and feel that its aromatics have no place other than a toxic waste dump. Regardless, this is the only truffle that can make *Tuber magnatum* seem a little bit staid, and it looks poised for superstardom. There's a second species of white truffle in the Pacific Northwest, *Tuber gibbosum*, that looks and smells similar but lacks the red splotches. It comes in the spring.

ŽELJKO ZGRABLIĆ

OREGON BLACK

LATIN: *Leucangium carthusianum*

APPEARANCE: Fragile. A smooth, thin black coat hides a fine-grained, cake-like interior.

SIZE: A huge range, from small to quite large.

SEASON: Mostly in late winter and spring, but they can be found year-round.

HABITAT: Young Douglas fir stands.

REGION: Everywhere you find Douglas fir, i.e., northern California to British Columbia. The bulk are in Oregon and Washington.

PRICE: Moderate

AVAILABILITY: Spotty. These tend to come in small waves in many places, rather than in a few big flushes. The Oregon Truffle Festival is one of the few reliable sources.

USE: Dessert, famously. Grate into whipped cream, eggnog, custard, tiramisu.

FRAGRANCE: Ridiculously fruity. Pineapple and banana when young. Then raspberry scones, Juicy Fruit gum, and caramel. Then washed-rind cheese and barns. Then death.

NOTES: Technically, this isn't a truffle at all. It's a different genus entirely, *Leucangium* instead of *Tuber*, but hey, if it walks like a duck and quacks like a duck. . . This truffle has huge fans in the Pacific Northwest, who prefer its fruity qualities to more traditional truffle scents. I think it combines both beautifully, and a high-quality Oregon black is one of the great treats to be found in any forest anywhere in the world. But the truffle is delicate and wet and rots if you look sideways at it, so . . . don't look sideways at it.

ROWAN JACOBSEN

MACROSPORUM

LATIN: *Tuber macrosporum*

ALIAS: large-spored; smooth-skinned

APPEARANCE: Smooth black skin with distinctive red splotches and a dense network of sharply defined "veins" inside. A particularly firm and compact truffle.

SIZE: Always small.

SEASON: Autumn

HABITAT: Same as white truffles: valley forests and stream banks.

REGION: Mediterranean and Eastern Europe.

PRICE: Moderate

AVAILABILITY: Rarely makes it to market. Keep your eyes peeled.

USE: As you would a white. Grate fresh on eggs, pasta, toast, salad, vegetables.

FRAGRANCE: Gorgeous. Like an especially debonair white.

NOTES: The black truffle that smells like a white. Hunters and dealers love this truffle but can never get their hands on enough. It tends to be the occasional bonus turned up by dogs looking for whites. Ask around.

Appalachian

LATIN: *Tuber canaliculatum*

ALIAS: Michigan; yellow-furrowed; great Eastern white

APPEARANCE: Suave sienna skin with a cocoa center (when ripe). Seems to glow from within.

SIZE: Always small, reliably round.

SEASON: September and October

HABITAT: Sandy soil under spruce, pines, oak, and hickory. Roadsides are often good.

ROWAN JACOBSEN

REGION: Midwest; Eastern Canada; Northeast; down the spine of the Appalachians through Maryland and West Virginia.

PRICE: Unknown; never for sale.

AVAILABILITY: Never seen in the market, rarely found in the wild.

USE: Shave onto hot eggs or pasta so the warmth and humidity can free its volatiles.

FRAGRANCE: Not strong but beautiful, round, comforting. Combines some of the most appealing qualities of black and white truffles. If the white is the Lamborghini of truffles and the black winter is the Rolls-Royce, this is the Aston Martin: classy, subdued, intensely pleasing.

NOTES: The great hope of the eastern half of North America. A stunning truffle that grows wherever you find mixed hardwood forests, especially near pines. Only a handful of dogs have trained with this truffle, so it may be more common than we think. The secret to its cultivation has been cracked in Quebec, now several young orchards have been planted. Stay tuned.

ROWAN JACOBSEN

Honey

LATIN: *Mattirolomyces terfezioides*

ALIAS: sand; sweet

APPEARANCE: Not very truffle-like. More like a lumpy meringue with black stippling. Feels especially dense and wet compared to most truffles.

SIZE: Often baseball-sized and larger.

SEASON: September–November

HABITAT: Sandy deposits beneath black locust trees along rivers in the Carpathian Basin.

REGION: Hungary

PRICE: Low

AVAILABILITY: Uncommon, but increasing fast.

USE: Desserts only. Crazy sweet. The sweetness holds up in cooking and freezing.

FRAGRANCE: Very mild and mushroomy, like a bloomy-rind cheese.

NOTES: This is not in the *Tuber* genus and has none of the classic truffle aromas. Instead, it has a saccharine sweetness that makes it a natural for desserts. I've had it in tiramisu and in chocolate "truffles." It's impressive, but a little goes a long way. The truffle has become a sensation in Asia, and a number of operators are banking on it as the next big deal. The Hungarian truffle expert István Bagi published the first book about the honey truffle in 2021.

CHINESE

LATIN: *Tuber himalayensis; Tuber indicum*

APPEARANCE: *Himalayensis* is a dead ringer for the black winter truffle, outside and in. *Indicum* is brick red on the outside, turning to deep brown when fully ripe. It should be dark on the inside, too; if white, it's immature.

SIZE: Golf ball and smaller.

SEASON: November–February

DAVIS UPCHURCH

HABITAT: Mostly mountain pines.

REGION: *Indicum* is found throughout the plateaus of Yunnan and Sichuan in southern China. *Himalayensis* grows in the mountainous slopes of the Himalayas, near Tibet.

PRICE: Very low

AVAILABILITY: At their peak, more than three hundred tons of truffles were exported from China annually. Now that number is down to one hundred tons or less.

USE: Pass off as black winter truffles and sell to gullible chefs; get rich.

FRAGRANCE: Zero for truffles harvested while immature, which is most of them. A mature *Himalayensis* is mildly chocolatey, while a good *Indicum* is slightly gingery.

NOTES: Truffles were never particularly popular in Chinese cuisine, but in the 1990s truffle dealers in Europe began importing Chinese truffles, which look similar to black winters but could be had for a hundredth of the price, and selling them as such. This led to a harvesting boom in China and a scandal in Europe, because the Chinese truffles had no aroma. But that was because the Chinese truffles were being harvested unripe, and were too old by the time they reached Western markets. *Tuber indicum*, which accounts for more than 90 percent of the Chinese supply, has very little smell. A mature, fresh *Himalayensis* is quite nice, though no comparison to a true black winter. Today, a few people are encouraging the use of dogs in China, and local interest in high-quality truffles will likely grow.

BAGNOLI
ŽELJKO ZGRABLIĆ

. . . AND THE SCRUFFY SEVEN

A few more obscure truffles you would be fortunate to encounter.

BAGNOLI (*Tuber mesentericum*)

Sometimes known in France as the Lorraine, this is a dead ringer for the black summer or black autumn truffles, but it has intense phenolic odors (think tar and mothballs) that are too much for most people. Once those blow off, however, what remains is pleasant almond and truffle scents.

MACULATUM (*Tuber maculatum*)

A light-colored truffle sometimes mistaken for bianchetti, it grows in Europe, North America, and New Zealand. Definitely has a white-truffle garlicky note, and it has its fans, but others complain about the off-putting petrol fumes.

PECAN

ROWAN JACOBSEN

EXCAVATUM (*Tuber excavatum*)

An extremely common truffle found throughout Europe when hunting other truffles. The best dogs know to ignore it. Small, light in color, it always has a cavity in the middle, like a travel pillow. Most people consider this truffle too strong and unpleasant for polite company, but a few old-timers have a thing for it.

OREGON BROWN (*Kalapuya brunnea*)

The fourth great truffle of the Pacific Northwest. A small, elusive truffle with savory miso scents, an orange-brown skin, and a speckled interior like the breast of a thrush. Stupendously aromatic. Named in honor of the Kalapuya tribes of the Willamette Valley. Rare find!

PECAN (*Tuber lyonii*)

A small nut-colored truffle commonly found in pecan orchards throughout the Southeast. Now commercial cultivation has begun in

Georgia and Florida. Subtle but pleasing, like butter-fried sunflower seeds with an earthy, garlicky component. A good introduction to "truffly" aromas. Considering its abundance and respectable shelf life, this could be a big deal.

MELANOGASTER (*Melanogaster spp.*)

Not true truffles, but used as such by the brave on America's west coast. They are found frequently by truffle dogs. The flavor is fascinating (Alana McGee of the Truffle Dog Company says they smell like old wine), but the texture is mush, so these are best used as a flavoring accent in sauces or butters.

DESERT (*Terfezia, Tirmania,* and *Kalarituber spp.*)

When the Greeks debated the origins of truffles and the role of thunder and lightning, they were probably thinking of desert truffles, which grow in profusion throughout the Near East, Middle East, and North Africa and are considered a delicacy, a medicine, and, of course, an aphrodisiac. They can get grapefruit-sized and are often white or tan, resembling misshapen rolls. (The manna of the Bible is believed to have been desert truffles.) In markets throughout the Middle East, these truffles are sold in massive quantities, generally less than one hundred dollars per pound. Unfortunately, they have none of the classic truffle scent and are more like the tofu of the desert: A good canvas for whatever flavors you cook with them.

But how do you jump-start a culture of truffle dogs where they've never existed? Well, for one thing, you need to significantly raise the price of truffles, and the only way to do that is to convince chefs and foodies that these things are special.

With that realization, the Oregon Truffle Festival was born. It would be in late January, when the native truffles are at their peak. It would feature rigorous quality control and top-notch culinary creativity.

And it would be dog-centric.

Not only would that improve the quality of the truffles, it would also be good for the forests. Raking disturbs the soil. In a wilderness area, it can be profoundly destructive. "In an older forest, where the soil biome has developed over decades or centuries, there's so much interdependency," Charles says. "Once that's disturbed, the biome dies off, and the recovery process can take decades."

Fortunately, most truffles aren't found in those areas. "These stands of trees that are producing truffles are very young, simple systems," Charles says. "They're not wilderness. So the act of raking isn't necessarily any more destructive than what was happening when it was a pasture. I just think there's a better way to do it. When you use a dog, you get better truffles. The aesthetics are better, the prices are better, and it's less work. Besides, working with a dog in the forest is part of the mystique. There's just no reason not to use a dog."

The first festival in 2006 was a simple affair, but it has grown into a four-day blowout. It kicks off on Thursday with the Joriad North American Truffle Dog Championship, in which amateur pooches from far and wide compete to sniff out the most truffles. The first few years of competition were dominated by Lagotto Romagnolos and other scent-work specialists, but in

2018 Gustave the Chihuahua crashed the field, captivated the crowd, and turned the Joriad into a national sensation, reminding everyone that America is the land of opportunity. (For an exclusive inside account of this saga, straight from the horse's mouth, so to speak, see "The Legend of Gustave" in the appendix.)

The Joriad ends with a Parade of Dogs, an awards ceremony, and a truffle dinner. The rest of the weekend includes a grower's forum for pros and wannabes, a two-day dog-training workshop, and an evening Mercato del Tartufo, where local restaurants show off outré concoctions that would never grace a proper European table, like truffle cream puffs, truffle ice cream, truffle pizza, and truffle cocktails. There's a legit wild truffle hunt and a tour of a local truffiere. And then the whole thing culminates with the Grand Truffle Dinner: three hundred people, six playful courses, no holds barred.

What I notice after a couple of days at the OTF is the pioneering spirit, the sense of discovery and egalitarianism. With no weight of tradition, anything goes, and anyone can be a part of it. It's grassroots, it's goofy, and no one's really doing it for the money. They're doing it for the dogs.

This canine corps has transformed the reputation of Northwest truffles, and chefs have noticed. Prices for dog-harvested truffles have risen to several hundred dollars per pound, and Oregon truffles are becoming a highlight of the terroir.

A win for local gastronomy, says Charles, and for the forest economy. An acre of Douglas fir can produce thousands of dollars' worth of truffles every year, which means the trees are worth more alive than cut. Leaving the trees standing is hugely beneficial for wildlife, for carbon sequestration, and for protecting stream banks where salmon spawn, many of which have been degraded by cattle. "Those trees end up producing more value than the cows ever did!" says Charles. There are even B&Bs beginning to market themselves and their forested backyards as truffling destinations. It's all part of a remarkable awakening, a discovery of goodness that was hiding in plain sight.

Here's the essential thing to know about the Grand Truffle Dinner: five days ahead of time, Charles Ruff, the festival's culinary director, packs beef-tallow candles and Oregon white truffles together in sealed plastic tubs and lets the whole thing steep in the walk-in fridge of the hotel. The pungent emanations of the truffles slowly and irrevocably embed themselves in the waxy beef fat, until the candles are infused with more truffle essence than the truffles themselves. This detail signals a new way of thinking about truffles—what they are, what they're for, what they mean.

I catch up with Ruff in the kitchen before the dinner to get his take on Oregon truffles. This is his fifteenth festival, so he should know. He has open tubs of black winters, Oregon blacks, and Oregon whites on a table and is ducking his nose from truffle to truffle, checking for duds with Michael Baines, a long-time forager who serves as the festival's chief truffle wrangler.

Sure enough, Ruff has strong thoughts on the subject. The thing most chefs get wrong, he says, is to think of truffles as normal ingredients. "There's this spectrum of aromas and flavors in a truffle," he tells me, "and you can't get it all just by shaving truffles, and you can't get it just by infusing, and you can't get it just by steeping. But if you do all of those elements, and work them into a dish, you can create this kind of musical chord of truffle harmony."

This syncs with something that's been nagging at me since my earliest truffle experiences, and it has to do with the truffle's tendency to dance away when you try to pay attention to it. Its scent is pouring out of the earth, and just when you tunnel down to it and hold it to your nose, it disappears. Or the waiter arrives at your table with a big one, and everybody exclaims at the scent, but by the time he's shaved wafers over everyone's pasta, the volatiles have left the building.

Don't blame the truffle. A truffle is a fragrance factory. It has more in common with flowers than food, and eating it is kind of like eating flowers to get the perfume. The magic isn't in the truffle; it's constantly being made by the truffle. As soon as you slice it up, you've killed the golden goose.

Capture that fragrance beforehand, barks Ruff, who channels a sergeant major's brusque efficiency. Infuse, infuse, infuse.

Fat is your friend. Fats of all kinds readily absorb truffle volatiles, and they actually hold onto those essences better than a freshly sliced truffle, from which the gases quickly dissipate. Hence the beef tallow candles. Ruff also has twelve pounds of lardo infusing with Oregon whites in the walk-in, as well as pounds of butter, cream, and eggs, the three classic truffle buddies.

"Avocado is my favorite," Michael Baines chimes in. "Cashews are my second favorite."

Be creative with capture, says Ruff. A few festivals ago, he did a *chawanmushi*, a savory Japanese steamed egg custard. All three hundred guests were served the custard in a lidded glass box, in which the truffle gases had been slowly building. When they lifted the lid, a puff of truffle shot out.

Over the course of fifteen festivals, Ruff has probably had more truffles pass through his hands than anyone in the country, and when I ask his favorite, he doesn't hesitate. "It's a three-way tie. Oregon black, Oregon white, and *Tuber magnatum.*"

"No black winter?" I ask, surprised.

"Périgord is my least favorite truffle," he says (using the old name still preferred by many chefs). "All I get from it is olive and alcohol."

Le scandale! I scribble notes furiously while Ruff digs his hole even deeper. "After that, I think the next tier is bianchetto and Burgundy [as he calls black autumn]. They're wonderful! I'd take a bianchetto or a Burgundy over a Périgord any day of the week."

The Black Magic Apple of Love, all the way down at the bottom? Seriously? But Ruff is unbowed. He picks up an Oregon white. "*These* are the powerhouses of the truffle world. The volatile gases are off the map. In Italy, they shave seven to eight grams of *Tuber magnatum* over dishes. If you shaved that much Oregon white over a dish, people would be gagging. It's so much more intense. Right now I have heavy whipping cream in sealed, aseptic cartons next to Oregon whites, and the gases just blast right through the cartons. It also works with raw eggs in the shell and butter in the wrapper."

"I'm not sure there's a barrier they can't get through," says Michael Baines. "I had to get a second refrigerator for my place because I was told we could no longer have everything in the fridge taste like truffles."

Black winters do have their advantages, Ruff admits as he hefts a large one. "These things are basically baseballs," he says. Their shelf life is terrific—a big part of why they've conquered the world. "The Oregon whites are pretty firm, they'll hold up for ten days, but you're lucky if you get four days out of an Oregon black, especially if it's dog-harvested, because that means it's dead ripe."

In other words, outside of a few enclaves like the Oregon Truffle Festival, most of the Oregon blacks people have experienced were already compost.

I pick up a lumpy Oregon black. At first glance it resembles a black winter, but in place of black winter's thick skin, Oregon black's looks fragile. Where black winter is firm, OB is springy. When I hold it to my nose, I inhale a fruit bowl. "Pineapple!" I exclaim, surprised. Plus cocoa crumble and durian and all sorts of crazy tropical stuff.

Ruff nods. "The Oregon black is unique. There's nothing like it." He slices one open and shows me its porcelain marbling. "Early in their ripening stage they have this white interior flesh and the fruitiest flavor of any truffle. It's all banana and pineapple. When they're at this stage, I call them banana truffles, and I use them almost exclusively for sweet applications."

Ruff finds a truffle with a darker interior and holds it up so I can breathe in the beefy barnyard. "As an Oregon black goes through its ripening process, it changes. The pineapple fades, and it puts out more almond and filbert. And then, at the end of its life, it starts to take on the aromas of a French farmhouse cheese." He gives it a snort. "Wonderful in its own way, but it has to be applied to the right dish. That's not a dessert truffle."

Actually, at the *end* of its life, OB becomes foulness incarnate. Any truffle does, it just happens a lot faster with OB. That's always been the problem. Four days from Belle of the Ball to Spawn of Satan. I squeeze the truffle again. It seems like black winter's shy, artsy sibling. While black winter confidently set out into the world and became a global superstar, OB just wanted to stay home and write songs in its bedroom. I develop an instant crush on it.

By then, showtime is nigh, and Ruff boots me from the kitchen. In the dining room, the candles are lit. A fine mist of ripe possibility permeates the air, as if somebody has sprayed truffle-scented laughing gas. As the guests stream in, everyone's eyes are twinkling. The occasional nostril flares. It feels like the Eleusinian Mysteries are going to begin any moment.

And, in a sense, they do. From the first tastes—wagyu beef dipped in the white-infused tallow, then black-cured smoked salmon with burrata and black truffle–walnut crumb over the top—a strange elevation takes place. For the next three hours, the table is a tapestry of colors, shapes, and textures, a refutation of the European tradition of serving truffles against a bland canvas. It feels giddy. But maybe that's just the cannabinoids and sex pheromones talking. I rescue a last wafer of Oregon black from my plate and let it melt on my tongue like some sort of fragrant communion.

The Seattle chef Eric Tanaka brings out an abalone congee spiked with that truffled lardo and slivers of Oregon white. Thomas and Mariah Pisha-Duffly, the couple behind the Portland pop-up Gado Gado, follow with a quail-and-foie-gras wonton soup that has Oregon whites in the wonton dough and a blizzard of shaved truffle on top, soaking into the broth. After the wontons are gone, there isn't a person in the room who doesn't set down their spoons, lift up their bowls, and slurp.

The Oregon blacks tag back in for the fifth course, where Portland chef Gregory Gourdet shaves the bawdiest of them over a fork-tender beef shank in cocoa-prune jus, adding a thrilling hint of transgression. OB may be too tetchy to travel, but catch it in its hometown on the right night, and you'll never forget it.

As promised, the last course, dessert, shows off its fruitier side: a musky Baked Alaska with the young banana-scented OBs whipped into the frozen nougat, some Oregon white toasted-meringue on top for good measure.

And now it's late. The tallow candles are low. Dogs are snoozing in hotel rooms, a few at the bar. A goaty bianchetto farmer from up near the Canadian border, dressed in a beaver-fur coat, is giving free sniffs of his truffles to any takers. The cult is coalescing.

I admit, it was a lavish meal, not everyday fare. But it wasn't snooty. And it wasn't about status. It felt more like a frontier town, here on the edge of the New World, trying to put on a fancy dance with whatever we had at hand. In a sense, we were liberated by our own ignorance. We knew just enough to get everything wrong. Wrong trees, wrong truffles, wrong recipes, wrong dog training. And perhaps because of that, we got the spirit of the thing just right.

And maybe that's always the cycle. Before they were appropriated by the high priests of haute cuisine and the captains of commerce, truffles were the thing from the forest that lured peasants' animals—and then peasants themselves—to the place where the pasture met the wood. Edge species, as Charles Lefevre says. Perhaps, in a sense, every truffle re-creates that visitation in the mind. You step across into the shade, your primal senses prickling to life, and you paw at the fragrant earth, and try to remember.

18

New Tricks

W ell, who *doesn't* want their own truffle hound? Having now seen a number of kick-ass truffle dogs in action, I confess to thinking that the human part doesn't look that hard. Just pick a good area, follow behind, supply treats.

The reservoir for my fantasies is my ten-year-old cockapoo, Friday, who looks like a cocker spaniel who got shipped with a corgi's legs by accident, which makes him less than ideal for extreme truffling. And being ten, his interest in new tricks is dwarfed by his interest in the warm hearthstone directly in front of my woodstove. On the other hand, he does spend hours tracking mysterious scents outside the house, so . . . maybe.

But what to hunt? I'm stuck in the Northeast, which seems like the ultimate truffle wasteland.

Ever hopeful, I pick up a copy of *The Field Guide to North American Truffles*, published by the North American Truffling Society. The coauthor is James Trappe, the Darwin of truffle science. Now ninety years old, Trappe (pronounced "Trappee") began unearthing new truffle species while getting his PhD in the 1950s, eventually discovering and naming hundreds of new species and turning Oregon State University into the mecca of mycorrhizal research.

Unfortunately, the field guide confirms my fears. Most of the hundred or so species listed have Desirability Ratings ranging from "insipid" to "palatable" to "inedible." What turns on the red-backed vole doesn't necessarily turn on the gastronaut. The majority labeled "delicious" are limited to the Pacific Northwest—Trappe country.

In the entire Northeast, only one species looks tantalizing: *Tuber canaliculatum*, also known as the Appalachian truffle. It has a stunning burnt-orange coat, a range from eastern Canada to North Carolina, and the chef James Beard once called it "exquisite." But a rabid online search turns up nothing beyond a few accidental sightings in the woods. Even the James Beard quote can't be confirmed. The Appalachian truffle is Bigfoot by any other name.

I scale back my ambitions. I order a bottle of natural truffle oil from Alana McGee at the Truffle Dog Company, a custom blend using a broad range of truffle species that should—in theory—help dogs cue in on any true tubers they come across. What do we have to lose? Vermont fall evenings are cold and long, and Friday's dance card isn't exactly full.

The training oil arrives in a cute little green medicine bottle. It doesn't smell like truffle to me, more like toe jam, but what do I know? I douse a chunk of old sock in the oil, stuff it inside a red Kong rubber chew toy, and begin our lessons in the living room one night. "Get the truffle!" I cry, tossing the Kong to the other end of the room.

Friday looks at me skeptically. He's highly "food motivated," which is supposed to make training much easier. I hold up a box of treats and shake it alluringly. "Get the truffle!"

Success. Friday pads across the room, grabs the toy, brings it back, and drops it where I kneel. Reward at Source, I've been told, so I pick up the Kong, say "truffle," and slip him a snack.

He perks up, so we do it again. This time, when he brings it back, his tongue is hanging out in disgust. The Kong looks greasy; I may have used too much oil. Anyway, he gets another treat, and we do it again. And again.

We do it three more times and he gets three more treats. Easy peasy!

Then I get overly ambitious. I hide the Kong under a towel beneath the dining room table before returning to my spot on the living room floor, the box of treats beside me. "Get the truffle!" I say. "Truffle, truffle, truffle!"

Friday just stares at me in confusion.

"Where's the truffle?"

Friday gazes up with his sad spaniel eyes. Then he walks up to me, knocks over the box of treats with his nose, and buries his head in my lap.

Perhaps not all dogs are truffle dogs after all.

But now I'm obsessed with the Appalachian truffle, so I return to the *Field Guide to North American Truffles*. My gaze lingers over that one tantalizing word from James Beard: "Exquisite."

I burn the midnight oil online. Nothing, nothing, nothing. The few accounts of Bigfoot are old and have little to say on its exquisiteness. The trail is cold.

And then, in the wee hours, I plow into a site in French that wakes me up. It's for an agroforestry outfit in Quebec called

Arborinnov that claims to know how to cultivate the Appalachian truffle. Quebec! An hour north of me. The site looks rudimentary—a quick WordPress-style job set up by a single person named Jérôme Quirion, who, if you were not interested in the Appalachian truffle, would be happy to sell you some cedar trees—and this Jérôme has never come up in my conversations with other truffle experts, but I allow myself a little hope. Squeezed into a corner by the English-speaking populations of the United States and Canada, Quebec has always been a bit of a language island.

I write Jérôme. Is he really working with *T. canaliculatum*? Can I come visit? And oh, by the way, *HOW IS IT???*

No response. I give up on Bigfoot once and for all.

But six days later, a reply. As I read it, my excitement fades. Yes, he's working with the truffle. No, he doesn't have any on hand. Bad season. "I will try to find some." He doesn't address the subject of their merits. He doesn't even sound particularly enthusiastic. He just says sure, he'll let me know if he finds any.

It feels like a polite kiss-off, and I don't expect to hear from him again. But two weeks later, there he is in my in-box. "Do you have time in the next few days for a visit at my farm?"

I drop everything and make the ninety-minute drive to Saint-Denis-de-Brompton, an agricultural backwater in Quebec's Eastern Townships lake district. It takes some time to convince the Canadian border guards that I'm really on my way to a truffle farm, but they eventually let me through.

Jérôme's directions lead me to an apple orchard and farm stand called Les Jardins des Pommes. There's a cheerful pile of pumpkins at the entrance, a gnarled apple tree in the front yard, and shelves of apple pies and cider doughnuts in the stand.

Jérôme steps out of the shingled farmhouse, a handsome, bearded guy wearing jeans and a brown vest, an Arborinnov ball cap pulled down on his head. He grew up on the farm, which is still run by his parents, though his tree projects are slowly taking over. He says he's farming both Burgundy truffles, as he calls them, and Appalachian truffles.

My hunch about the language island was right. Jérôme figured out how to cultivate *T. canaliculatum* a few years ago, and has been selling inoculated truffle trees to a few Quebec clients. Almost no one south of the 45th parallel has a clue.

He leads me past a greenhouse filled with baby truffle trees to a small fenced plot of eight-foot hazel and oak. On one end is a simple hutch, a mud puddle, and a handful of picked-apart pumpkins. "My Burgundy truffiere," Jérôme says. "I keep it separate from my Appalachian truffiere."

Two obese geese come waddling toward us at high speed, honking.

"Watch your testes," Jérôme says.

I jump back just in time. The geese honk and hiss and size up their food prospects. I'm casting about for a peace offering when something snorts in the hutch.

"What was that?"

"Oh, that's my potbellied truffle pig."

I make a noise of great enthusiasm. "You have no idea how long I've been searching for a truffle pig."

But he's already shaking his head regretfully. "No, sorry. I wanted to try with another animal, but . . . I have no confidence in this pig." He turns away and motions for me to follow. "My dogs, however . . . you will see."

Jérôme approaches a side door of the farmhouse. It sounds like a Tasmanian devil is inside. As soon as he cracks the door, a small white meteor explodes out, parkours off Jérôme's chest, and heads for the truffiere at high speed. Jérôme sighs. "Sorry, he's crazy."

Behind the white thing, a wizened dachshund trundles out and sits. "This is Merguez. She's nine."

We head for the Appalachian truffiere, five rows of fifty trees, their leaves already turning crimson. Jérôme has managed to cultivate the Appalachian truffle on three native trees: American hazel, red oak, and American hornbeam.

The white thing, already maniacally digging under a tree, turns out to be a six-year-old Jack Russell terrier named Tofu. "Look at him go!" Jérôme says with a mix of admiration and fatigue. "I haven't said a word, and he's already looking everywhere to find them. He's the best truffle dog. But he goes so fast that he eats them all. We have to stay on him."

Jérôme pulls out a gardening pick and kneels beside Tofu, forcing him away from his hole. In seconds, he pops out a perfect little truffle the size and shape of a new potato, with glowing orange-russet skin. I hold it to my nose . . . and swoon. It combines the nutty depth of a black truffle with the aioli bite of a white. It's sensational, it's unknown, and it lives in my woods. Bigfoot is real.

Within minutes, Tofu unearths dozens of truffles and Merguez calmly adds a few of her own, sitting beside her discoveries until we're ready for her.

"How did you do this?" I ask.

Well, growing up with the apple orchard, he fell in love with trees. He studied agroforestry at the nearby University of Sherbrooke, learning to inoculate spruce and fir with *Lactarius deliciosus*, one of Europe's most prized edible mushrooms. "But what's the point? I can just go into the woods and pick some lactarius! So I decided to try *canaliculatum* on my own."

"Why?" I ask.

"The mystery," he says. "The fact that it hasn't been done before. My goal is to make the Appalachian truffle renowned worldwide."

No one thought any true truffles grew in Quebec until the 1980s, when a Quebec mycologist named Francesca Marzitelli was walking with her dog on the outskirts of Montreal. They encountered a squirrel gorging on something. Dog chased squirrel, squirrel dropped lunch and fled. Lunch turned out to be a handsome, if nibbled, Appalachian truffle.

Eventually Francesca became one of the few people skilled at finding Appalachian truffles in the wild. The truffle remained little more than myco-trivia until Jérôme came along. He knew he wanted to try growing truffles in Quebec, and had heard of the Appalachian truffle but never encountered one. At a mycology conference, he met Jim Trappe, the OSU legend and coauthor of the *North American Field Guide*. Jérôme told Trappe he was thinking about trying to cultivate *canaliculatum*. Was it actually good?

It's great, Trappe replied. Go for it.

But in order to learn to cultivate a new truffle, one needs a large supply of spores, and there was no source. Jérôme found Francesca, and she gave him his first. "I said, 'Wow! They really exist!'" Not only did they exist, they were amazing.

In 2009 they went into business together. Francesca hunted the truffles to fuel his research in exchange for royalties on future tree sales.

The work was hard. There was no manual to follow. Everything from the soil to the protocols had to be invented from scratch. After two years, the pots in Jérôme's greenhouse were filled with mycorrhizae. But was it Appalachian mycorrhizae? "For other truffles, if you want to identify mycorrhizae, you just look in books," Jérôme points out. "But no one knew what *canaliculatum* mycorrhizae looked like."

They had to do a DNA test, which confirmed that they were looking at lots and lots of *T. canaliculatum*. Jérôme had been a bit lucky, because the truffle turned out to be remarkably robust.

"It's so aggressive, it's crazy," he says as he digs through the soil around a hornbeam with his fingers, picking away crumbs of earth until he's exposed a long root hair sprouting tiny yellow corn dogs. "Look at all this mycorrhizae! So much! And so huge!"

Merguez plops down beside him and looks up suggestively. "Oh! *Cherche*," Jérôme says, pointing around the tree. "*Cherche, cherche.*" Merguez noses a spot of earth, and soon Jérôme has pulled out another truffle. "See the yellow mycelium?" he asks, pointing out the yellow threads sprouting like hair from the truffle. "Trappe's other name for this is the yellow-furrowed truffle. See how the mycelium is attached to the truffle everywhere? You never see that with other truffles. So aggressive!"

Tofu charges in beside us and attacks a new spot, making a weird hacking noise. I try to yank him away and get nipped for my efforts.

"You see how crazy he is? He bites everything. Hands, rocks, truffles." Jérôme shakes his head again. "My wife trains dogs, and she and I both agree: no more Jack Russells."

"What next time?"

He points at Merguez. "I recommend sausage dogs like this."

"Not too short?"

"No, they're great little dogs! They can get right under the trees, and their noses are already on the ground. *Dachshund* means 'badger dog.' They're like bloodhounds. Here in Quebec, guys track deer with them. They're meant for that. They work hard, and they're not crazy like that one."

Tofu is already attacking the next tree, wolfing down a truffle before the cursing Jérôme can grab him. "That's it! Let's put him inside so we can have some peace."

Back in the house, Jérôme opens his fridge and shows me his truffle collection: hundreds of them in glass jars, about an ounce apiece, all with glowing cinnamon skin and charcoal marbling. Some are a month old and still solid—superb shelf life. I stick my head in the jar, breathe in yumminess, and tell Jérôme he's brilliant.

Then I ask if I can take one home with me.

He knits his brow. "In six years of growing these, I've never given a single truffle to anyone." If his competitors got their hands on actual truffles, they could start deciphering *T. canaliculatum*'s secrets. This will happen anyway once other people's trees start producing, but he wants a head start.

"It'll be in my belly by bedtime," I promise.

And it is. Pasta carbonara, covered in Appalachian coal dust.

What's the truffle smell like? I'll crib from a Montreal sommelier's description that Jérôme sent me: Aromas of roasting and spices, like coffee, cocoa, and cloves, that evolve after a few days into black tea and dried fall leaves, and later still, crème fraîche and fresh cheese. On the palate, notes of undergrowth, dried leaves, and leather. Pair with an aged Champagne.

If I were to add a word to that, it would be . . . exquisite.

I decide to get to the bottom of the James Beard thing. I email ninety-year-old Jim Trappe. Could he point me to the source of that quote in the *North American Field Guide?*

He can. In fact, he points at himself. "I vividly recall my interaction with James Beard," he writes. It was 1977, and Trappe had organized a conference in Corvallis called "Mushrooms and Man: An Interdisciplinary Approach to Mycology." He was able to wrangle Beard into attending because the chef hailed from

Portland and still had Oregon in his blood. The scientists gave their talks, and Beard gave a cooking demo. He'd spent the fall of 1970 with Julia Child in Provence and had become one of the few truffle-literate American chefs of the time. A few days before the conference, a collector had sent Trappe "several fine specimens" of *T. canaliculatum*. Trappe gave two to Beard, who blessed them with his enthusiastic judgment.

Good enough for James Beard, good enough for me. Hiding in plain sight—well, smell—up and down the Appalachian Range. Cute as heck. Sturdy, too. The Appalachian truffle, I surmise, is going to be a big deal, and I'm way ahead of the game.

Or not, as it turns out. A while after my Quebec trip, a Maryland veterinarian named Ben Kable reaches out. He's just planted 1,500 of Jérôme's trees on his parents' Maryland farm. Jérôme alerted him to my snooping long ago. "For some reason I waited until now to introduce myself," he says.

Kable has been hunting Appalachian truffles since 2019, when he finally made contact with a secretive mushroom hunter and fellow Marylander named Jeff Long. Long is also a wine enthusiast. On a visit to Domaine Rion, one of the great wine estates of Burgundy, he happened to notice a bumper sticker on the Rion family auto: J'AIME LES CHIENS TRUFFES. The Rions, founding members of the Confrérie de la Truffe de Bourgogne, introduced him to their line of Lagottos, the first ever to be brought from Italy to France, and Long eventually went home with a puppy named Este who turned out to be a prodigy.

Long had no plans to truffle with the dog—he didn't think there were any local possibilities—but while hunting porcini in the Appalachian Mountains, Long saw Este dig up something and chew on it. He flipped the dog on his back, reached in his mouth, and pulled out two pieces of a mysterious reddish-orange truffle. He sent it off for DNA analysis and learned that it was an Appalachian truffle. Now, he and Este find a few pounds every year.

As far as I can tell, that's the extent of the Appalachian Underground. Long and Kable, plus Jérôme.

But not for lack of truffles! They're out there, these guys tell me. Your neck of the woods should be good. Look for sandy areas with spruce, oak, hickory, and especially pine.

I gaze out my window at hills of oak, spruce, and pine. And I begin to laugh. My truffle chase has come full circle. The great mysteries are everywhere, it turns out.

So I'm giving Friday another shot. His legs may be short, but they're longer than a dachshund's. This time, I've learned a few things. I use less oil on the sock. I heed Lois Martin's rules for chicken training: Very short sessions. Three minutes, then go to Theory. I throw the Kong into the woods, making sure Friday can follow its path, and squeal in delight when he brings it back. I channel my best Gollum voice. "Good boy! Pretty truffle!" My neighbors would be very embarrassed to hear me.

Then I throw it a little deeper into the woods. I follow Friday into the trees, just in case he misses it. Dogs can't see the color red, so Friday doesn't easily spot the Kong against the brown leaves, but it's painfully obvious to me. I watch him zigzag across quadrants of forest, seemingly miles off the trail. Sometimes he'll charge directly over the Kong and keep going.

But he always finds it, even if I hide the Kong under leaf litter. The process is mystifying. It looks like someone playing Twenty Questions, asking dumber and dumber questions until you lose all faith, and then suddenly Question 19 is on the nose. Friday jerks around and scampers to the proper zone, snuffles

left and right, and pops up with the Kong in his mouth. He's
hardwired to follow something older than logic.

So I'm trying to do the same. On soft fall days that make me
think of the Wiltshire Downs, we set out for the woods behind
the house, heading toward the spruce on the ridge. Friday scoots
ahead, nose to the ground, tacking back and forth across the
trail like I've seen so many real truffle dogs do. I help him over
the big fallen trees, but otherwise he holds his own. I watch him
sample the forest air the way I'll admire a sunset, then I let the
scents wash over me: musky fern, balsam fir, wayward fox. And
the more I learn to appreciate a good smellscape, the more I've
begun to wonder if dogs sniff the world mostly for the sheer
gorgeousness of it, and I've started to think of truffles as the
street artists of the forest, splashing smells across an airy canvas,
blowing the minds of passersby.

We slip deeper into the forest, the trees rustling as if they're
talking about us. I imagine the earth humming with intelligence. I watch Friday chuffing scent, etching the autumn into
his doggie memory. Somewhere out there, a truffle lurks. Our
odds, I know, are slim. We are the world's most hopeless truffle
hounds. But who knows? There are worse things than wandering
lost, senses sharp. Eventually, you always stumble upon a
thread, and find your way into the tapestry.

ACKNOWLEDGMENTS

Over two years of travels and research for this book, I had the amazing good fortune to experience the kindness of strangers, two-footed and four, in half a dozen countries. Some shared their expertise. Some shared their truffles. Some shared their mud boots. Together, they formed the extraordinary web of smells, thoughts, and stories that brought this book to fruition. In geographic order, from Greenwich Mean Time eastward, profound gratitude to:

In England: Zak Frost, Guy Manning, Mario Prati, Stanley.

In Spain: Jose Antonio Bonet, Carlos Colinas, Christine Fischer, Jose Manuel Molina, Mónica Sánchez, Xavier Vilanova Sola.

In Italy: Artu, Giuseppina Balestra, Dave Beveridge, Buk, Bruno Capanna, Ezio Costa, Giulia Costa, Emi, Matteo Giuliani, Karen MacNeil, Carlo Marenda, Miro, Julia Murphy, Anuska Pambianchi, John Paterson, Giorgio Remedia, Laura Sabattini, Ginevra Venerosi Pesciolini, Giulia Venerosi Pesciolini.

In Croatia: Hrvoje Ban, Betty, Ranko Bon, Candy, Istra, K, Ivan Karlić, Ivana Karlić, Radmila Karlić, Lela, Zdenka Majcan, David Matković, Ivan Milotić, Nero, Tomislav Pahović, Eugen Varzić, Giancarlo Zigante.

In Hungary: István Bagi, Zoltán Bratek, Mokka, Imre Lencsés, Sailor, Julia Sandor, Laszlo Sandor, Laszlo Szenye, Josef the Transylvanian.

In California, Oregon, and Washington: David Bacco, Michael Baines, Simon Cartwright, Robert Chang, Cowboy, Dante, Mike Davis, Christian DeBenedetti, Connie Green, Gustave, Kelsey Hutchinson, Adam James, Lissa James, Aaron Kennel, Sarah Kennel, Taylor Kennel, Mark Kosmicki, Charles Lefevre, Lolo, Pat Long, David Malosh, Kayt Mathers, Alana McGee, Mila, Mocha, Tiffany Norton, Staci O'Toole, Vitaly Paley, Charles Ruff, Leslie Scott, Jim Sanford, Paul Thomas, Marcy Tippmann, Jim Trappe, Jamie Ure, Aiko Vail, Bob Walker, Deb Walker, Fern Watt, Emily Wilder, Željko Zgrablić.

In Kentucky, Tennessee, and North Carolina: Jeffrey Coker, Larry Creech, the Crow Brothers, Elora, Richard Franks, Omoanghe Isikhuemhen, Antonio Izzo, Laddy, Lois Martin, Tom Michaels, Monza, Jane Newman, Pollo, Thomas Edward Powell III, Betsy Riggan, Michael Riggan, Nancy Rosborough, Scout, Susi Gott Séguret, Leonora Stefanile, Olivia Taylor, Margaret Townsend, Steve Townsend, Brian Upchurch, Davis Upchurch.

In Maryland: Este, Ben Kable, Jeff Long, Tom Mueller.

In New York: Adrienne Anderson, Elizabeth Ellis, Na Kim, Vincent Jeanseaume, Nancy Miller, Miranda Ottewell, Laura Phillips, Will Piper, Patti Ratchford, Zelda Zollyman.

In Quebec: Merguez, Jérôme Quirion, Tofu.

In Vermont: Shaun Dreisbach, Friday, Eric Jacobsen, Mary Jacobsen, Angela Miller, Helen Whybrow.

The Legend of Gustave

You are not the kind of dog who should be at a place like this at this time of year. In January, Oregon's Willamette Valley is a desolation of drizzly skies, short days, and bone-chilling fog. But that is when the truffles are at their peak, and that is when the Joriad Truffle Dog Championship takes place.

So here you are, scrambling over fallen branches and mossy hummocks in a Douglas fir forest as a chilling rain soaks the ground, racing the four other finalists to find as many truffles as possible in one hour. The conditions don't seem to be fazing the other dogs in the final round—like Ciaran, the chunky black Lab, and Autumn, the fancy Lagotto Romagnolo descended from generations of truffle hunters. But when you are a short-haired Chihuahua, it's another matter.

You've aced the first two rounds of the Joriad, where dogs search for buried plastic tubes holding truffle-scented cotton balls in the sheltered (and flat!) confines of the Lane County Fairgrounds horse arena, but here in these dark, dense woods, you're finding it very difficult to concentrate. So many distractions. Strange smells. Big dogs (never your favorite). Judges. A film crew from CBS. Squirrels!

You weigh eight pounds dripping wet. Your batlike ears are frozen. You haven't found a single truffle in thirty minutes of hunting, and it's all starting to feel like too much. Despite the hot-pink coat you're wearing, you begin shaking so badly that your human, Marcy Tippmann, has to pick you up and carry you.

The film crew finds this pretty cute, but you're not here to be cute. When you finished in the middle of the pack at last year's Joriad, that was cute. Not bad for a Chihuahua, they said. A typical backhanded compliment. But you're used to such things. The underdog jokes. The insinuation that you have an advantage because your nose is lower to the ground. You took it in stride—okay, short strides—and now you're back to win.

Yet here you are, shaking like a leaf and being carried while the big dogs race through the woods like wolves. Humiliating, honestly. Marcy tries to hide her disappointment, but you can tell. "It's okay, Gustave," she says, raking water off your fur with her hand. "It was a fun day."

At that point, a lesser Chihuahua might pack it in. But you've been through worse. Much worse.

≋

As a rescue dog, your origins are shrouded in mystery. When Marcy, a graphic illustrator from Eugene, found you online a year and a half ago, you were about nine months old. She'd been searching for the right dog for months, and as soon as she saw your photo, she knew. With that wiry tricolor coat that makes you look part jackal, you represent the more rustic end of the Chihuahua spectrum.

What else might be in the mix? Who knows. Your puppy-hood is a haze. All you really remember is that at some point you were very, very, very hungry, and you are never going to let that happen again. No piece of food will ever pass you by, including things that might serve as food in a pinch. Kibble, chocolate bars, newspaper, plastic, it all helps quiet the fear.

In October, just two months after Marcy rescued you, you fell gravely ill with an intestinal obstruction. You needed emergency surgery, but the bill was going to be $4,000— money Marcy didn't have. You endured days of crippling agony, and at some point you just lay down and waited for the end to come.

At the last minute, Marcy's relatives ponied up. The vet removed a mass of hair and toy parts from your gut, and you bounced back as only a Chihuahua can—fast enough to enter the Joriad.

There were no signs of greatness in your maiden performance, but come on, the scars were fresh. Since then, you and Marcy have been training every day. You make a game of it. Marcy drips truffle oil on a toy and hides it in the house. "Zoeky," she says (her special word for seek), burying it under blankets. It's a great way to pass the winter evenings when it's dark at 5:00 P.M. Sometimes she drops truffle oil onto kibble and scatters it in the grass outside. Yum! The truffle oil reminds you of some good part of your puppyhood from before the bad times.

When the weather's nice, you practice in the park. Marcy fans out her palm across an area of ground where she wants you to look. "Zoeky!"

It took you a while to put it all together, but eventually you learned to find the scent cones rising from the ground like streamers on the breeze. Of course! Just follow them to the point where they all converge in the earth. Then Marcy is so happy. Plus, treats.

It all paid off in the opening elimination round at the indoor horse arena, in which each dog had three minutes to walk past a line of sixteen plastic boxes filled with dirt and pick out the two that had the truffle tubes buried in them. Each team was allowed one wrong guess. Two and you were out.

Honestly, you began to shake at the start, just standing next to the other twenty-four entrants. There were several Lagotto Romagnolos, the Italian truffle-hunting breed. There were Australian shepherds and German shepherds and English shepherds. There was a bloodhound! You were seriously outgunned.

They all had different tells when they found truffles. Yours is to dig fast with both paws and then look up urgently at Marcy for a treat. Marcy calmly walked you down the line of boxes, letting you think it through before making your calls. You tried to block everything out and just stay with the smell. Nose low, tail high, you scanned your snout back and forth. Wait, that box you just passed! Scent cone! You doubled back, sniffed, confirmed, dug fast, stared at Marcy.

She glanced down at you. "You sure, Goose?"

Yes.

"Truffle," Marcy said to the judge.

The judge kneeled down and dug through the box, unearthing the plastic tube. "Truffle!" he shouted, arm pointing straight up.

The bleacher of spectators cheered, which startled you momentarily. Never in your life had such a noise been directed at you.

You shook it off and returned to the line of boxes. No. No. That one!

"Truffle," Marcy said.

The judge checked. "Truffle!"

Boom, two hits, less than a minute, no errors. As you trotted off the arena dirt, a murmur rolled through the crowd.

Only half the competitors made it through round 1 of the Joriad. In round 2, the truffle tubes are buried scattershot around the horse arena. Dogs must find five as quickly as possible, and the five best times move on to the finals.

You and Marcy received a huge cheer when you entered. Who wasn't rooting for the Chihuahua? There was also some laughter, which you chose to ignore. All that mattered was making Marcy proud. You got down to work. Calm and focused, you nailed four tubes faster than any of the other dogs, and suddenly the cheers weren't patronizing any more. "That dog's got game!" someone shouted. "Go, Gustave!"

But it's one thing to be hunting scent cones with your human in the park, and another to be doing it when a bunch of strangers are shouting your name. You lost your focus. For a full two minutes you wandered the arena in a daze, following the scents of the other dogs, hearing Marcy's pleas as if through a fog. The clock ticked toward the five-minute mark. Then—directly beneath you—scent! You scratched, Marcy shouted "Truffle!" as the clock expired, and you grabbed the last spot in the finals. The crowd cheered wildly, but it was clear they thought your luck had run out.

And maybe it had. Here you are, shivering like a Pekingese, truffleless after thirty minutes, and being carried. You are no Lagotto.

Marcy puts a second jacket on you and places you back down on the ground. "Let's get you warmed up, Goose."

A little stiffly at first, you start ambling. Fallen branches loom like boulders. All you can smell is duff and squirrel poop. But the second jacket feels good, and soon you are warm again. Now the woods feel different. The other dogs are far ahead, and the film crew got bored with you and headed off in pursuit of Autumn the Lagotto. It's just you and Marcy, a judge trailing behind.

"It was a fun day," Marcy says again, smiling down. You glance up at her, your savior, and your little heart floods with love. Snippets of your near-death experiences flash through your mind. You want to make her happy, and you know you can do it. You are a truffle hound.

There in the freezing woods on that bleak January day, with thirty minutes to go, you pull it together. Your mind is calm, your senses open. What's that over there? Some crazy scent, cutting through the fog of squirrel poop like a knife. So obvious. How could you have missed it before? You dig furiously with your paws, unearth the little white nugget, and gaze bright-eyed at Marcy. Truffle!

"Good boy! Yay!" Marcy cries, kneeling down to slide a treat into your mouth. You wolf it down and suddenly realize you would like some more of those. And, what do you know, there's a second scent cone around this same tree. Truffle!

It all begins to click. There's another on a nearby tree. And another! "Zoeky, Zoeky," Marcy says, keeping you on task. Check this tree. Then this one.

You sniff, dig, and scamper, treats surging through your bloodstream. The rest of the world fades away. You are just a nose sailing through a sea of scent cones. So many truffles. So many treats. Marcy follows behind with her tiny hand rake, scooping up the truffles and handing them to the judge.

When the hour ends, you have nailed seventeen truffles. That seems pretty great to Marcy, but who knows? The other finalists were out of sight, and the judges keep the results under wraps until the Parade of Dogs awards banquet at the hotel that evening.

You wear your best tartan plaid coat. You're feeling good in it, but the banquet is a tough scene for you. There are dozens of big dogs in the ballroom, including this year's Joriad contestants, some from previous years, and others who were at the festival for the training program. Some are on their best behavior. Others, not so much. The elevator was nuts.

Before the winners are announced, Marcy compares notes with one of the other finalists. How many truffles did she find?

Two, the woman says.

Marcy gives you a wide-eyed stare.

As it turns out, it isn't even close. Second place goes to Ciaran, the black Lab, with ten truffles. You win in a landslide. Marcy holds up the Oregon-shaped wooden plaque to wild applause. You take a little victory trot around the ballroom while the cameras flash, field a few interviews with the press, then duck out early. Long day. Your brain is fried, and your bed is calling to you.

Not long after that, you and Marcy announce your retirement from competition. The Joriad is open only to amateurs, and like many an Olympian before you, you've decided to go pro. If anyone is in need of a very small truffle hound— preference given to flat, dry terrain—just reach out. The world is full of funky nuggets, and they must be found.

RECIPES

Using Truffles
Whole Baked Truffles en Papillote
Truffletini
Tartufo Benedictus
Grilled Orange Salad with Truffle Vinaigrette
Beet Carpaccio with Truffles and Walnuts
Chawanmushi Tartufi
Cacio e Pepe con Tartufi di Nero
Seared Scallops in Truffled Butter Broth
Truffle Duck
Truffled Eggnog
Tiramisu di Tartufi

USING TRUFFLES

Truffles are ridiculously easy to use. Somehow their expensiveness has obscured this truth. That preciousness has also kept most people from having the opportunity to play around with them, which has led to a lot of myths about how to treat truffles, even among chefs. Once these myths and bad practices are dispelled, there's nothing to stand in the way of a populist uprising of home cooks taking control of their own truffle destiny. Here are some key tips:

- **Treat them like babies.** Truffles are delicate and metabolically active. They don't like to be smothered or dried out, and if things are too moist, they'll get slimy. Store them in the fridge in a sealed glass or plastic container, with a paper towel underneath for bedding. Change their bedding and give them a puff of air every day.
- **Don't dilly-dally.** Use black truffles within a week. (Their aroma actually improves several days after they come out of the ground.) Use white truffles asap.
- **Really don't smother them.** Truffles can contain the bacterium that causes botulism, but that microbe does its dirty work in anaerobic, room-temperature environments. As long as your truffles are in the fridge and get a little air, no worries. (But don't try to preserve them in oil at room temperature.)
- **Think of them like flowers.** Truffles are little fragrance factories, churning out perfume for days after they come out of the ground. Your goal is to capture as much of that fragrance as possible. Thus:

- **Infusion is the solution.** Truffle aromas are very volatile. In open air, they fly off in all directions. But fat is very good at absorbing them. Any kind of fat you place in their container is going to become impregnated with truffle essence. (With black truffles, this effect is minor. With white truffles, it's amazing. And with Oregon whites, it's insane.) This can greatly multiply the bang you get out of any truffle. The classic "truffling" media are eggs, butter, and cream, but other fatty foods work, too. Some good ones: lard, duck fat, pâté, cheese, oils, avocados, and nuts. Alcohol does this as well.
- **Don't inflame the situation.** The volatility of truffle aromatics also means they immediately dissipate when hot. That's why white truffles, which are particularly volatile, are never cooked. Always add them just before serving (or *sur la table*). Some elements of black truffles will survive light cooking, but no truffle should ever be subjected to long or intense heat. On the other hand, you do need to get those molecules into your nose, so:
- **Uplift them.** If a dish is too cold, it can be hard to smell much of anything. A little warmth or steam helps crank up the molecules. To keep them from escaping too fast, take a tip from Charles Lefevre of New World Truffieres: After adding truffle to your pizza, pasta, whatever, spritz a little oil over the top to trap truffly vapors.
- **Think like a painter, not a pornographer.** This may be the most important tip of all. Truffles are intense but subtle. They aren't there to fulfill your diners' most basic desires. They are there to add magic and mystery, to shake the snow globe for a little while. They don't need to dominate the plate. In fact, they don't need to be on the plate

at all. The most whimsical use of truffles is to truly treat them like flowers and just let them be a centerpiece on the table, uneaten. Dare you.

Many of the best ways to use truffles don't require a recipe at all. Just grate into X before serving and save a few wafers for show. Special shoutout to Thanksgiving here: the holiday seems to have been made for truffles. It falls just when the whites and black autumns are at their peak, there might even be some early black winters around, and virtually every element of it benefits from a touch of fungus: potatoes, sweet potatoes, squash, turkey, even gravy. Just don't truffle *everything*; less is more. Some other greatest hits:

Slowly shirred scrambled eggs
Egg salad
Butter
Popcorn (in the butter)
Corn on the cob (ditto)
Pasta al burro (or olio)
Whipped cream
Aioli or mayonnaise
Polenta
Fondue
Mac and cheese
Broth
Ramen
Avocado toast (truffle the avo first)
Foie gras (duh)
Chicken liver pâté crostini

WHOLE BAKED TRUFFLES EN PAPILLOTE

Domaine Rion, the Côte de Nuits wine estate known for its top Burgundies and truffle dogs, serves this to guests in season. If you don't have your own dogs and truffiere, it's an extravagance, but that's the point. How often is anyone ever going to get served a whole truffle? If you really want to make an impact, don't tell anyone what's coming; just serve the little foil surprises and wait. If you can't get lardo, guanciale or prosciutto can substitute. The following recipe is for one person. Multiply as needed.

Truffle: This is definitely not the place for that *très cher magnatum*. A nice, affordable black summer or black autumn will do just fine. Pecan truffles from the southeastern United States would serve nicely, too. *Melanosporum?* Only if you're feeling flush. If you use black summer or black autumn, you'll need to peel the thick, bumpy skin. Other truffles should be fine as is.

Serves 1 lucky duck

1 (20–40 gram) truffle
1 slice lardo (enough to wrap the truffle)
Aluminum foil in a rectangular sheet

1. Preheat the oven to 375 degrees.

2. Wrap the truffle in the lardo, then in the foil. Twist the ends of the foil to make a present.

3. Bake in the oven for 5 to 7 minutes. Serve in the foil and let your guests unwrap.

TRUFFLETINI

Class incarnate. Best to drink this in black tie. Booze is one of the best ways to capture truffle aromatics, and a martini is reserved enough to provide a nice mineral background against which the truffle can play. I prefer dry sake to any of the dry vermouths on the market, but do as you please. I'm also going with an old-school two-to-one ratio of vodka to "vermouth" here—I like the roundness it imparts—but feel free to up the vodka if you're concerned that your friends won't think you're cool. I love the truffle garnish, but it presents a logistical challenge: You need to steep the truffle in the booze for at least a week, by which point any truffle you've reserved for the garnish will be pretty much dead. One solution is to do the steeping in a jar with a lid wide enough to fish out a slice of truffle for the drink. The sporty option would be to order a second truffle for the garnish (and, one would assume, other applications). The utilitarian move is to just go with a lemon twist instead.

Truffle: Black winter is ideal. That makes for a pricey bottle of vodka, but on a drink-by-drink basis, you're still well below cocktail-bar extortion pricing. This is also a great spot for black autumn or even black summer truffles, in which case you can go harder on the truffle.

1 (750 ml) bottle vodka of your choice
40 g black truffle for bottle
1 (300 ml) bottle dry sake
Ice
Garnish: Truffle slice, lemon twist, or both

1. Infuse the vodka. Slice up the truffle and add it to the bottle of vodka, or pour vodka into a glass jar and add the sliced truffle. Cover and let sit for at least a week. Give the jar a shake every day or two just so you can feel like you're doing something.

2. Make the drink. Fill a cocktail shaker with ice (made with water you like). Add 2 ounces of vodka and 1 ounce (or less) of sake. Stir 50 or 60 times in one direction. The outside of the cocktail shaker should get really cold and frosty.

3. Strain into a martini glass. Garnish with the slice of truffle, the lemon twist, or both, and serve.

TARTUFO BENEDICTUS

Once you've had eggs Benedict with truffles, you'll start to
wonder how it ever could have been made without. Make sure
to truffle the eggs and butter a day or several in advance. I prefer
fried eggs to poached eggs, so that's what I go with here, but if
you're horrified, by all means poach away. (Hot tip: The truffle
hollandaise is also killer on a lobster roll.)

Truffle: I like the intensity of whites, Oregon whites, or
Appalachians here—or *macrosporum*, if you can find one—but
black winters would be great and classy.

Hollandaise:
2 egg yolks
salt
¼ lemon
1 medium truffle
2 sticks butter, cut into chunks

Per serving:
1 English muffin
2 slices ham, Canadian bacon, tomato, or avocado
1 tablespoon butter
2 eggs

1. Add egg yolks and a pinch of salt to a blender. Squeeze the
   lemon wedge into the blender. Grate half the truffle, until you
   get to the widest part. Shave a few nice slices (one per serving)
   and set aside for garnishing. Grate the rest of the truffle into
   the blender.

2. Place the butter in a large glass measuring cup and microwave for 30 seconds. Stir. Continue to microwave 15 seconds at a time until fully melted.

3. With the blender motor running, remove the center of the lid and pour in the butter in a slow, steady stream until fully incorporated. The sauce should be smooth and creamy. Set aside.

4. Toast the English muffins.

5. In a large skillet over medium heat, melt the butter and fry the eggs, flipping once the whites turn opaque, about 2 minutes.

6. On each plate, assemble two English muffin halves, and top each with a slice of the ham and a fried egg. Spoon a tablespoon or two of hollandaise over each egg, and top with a slice of truffle. Serve immediately.

GRILLED ORANGE SALAD WITH
TRUFFLE VINAIGRETTE

I once spent three hours at Restaurant Alveo in Lleida, Spain, with truffle guru Christine Fischer, diving deep into mycology while the chef, Jose Manuel Molina, brought out a train of brilliant truffle dishes. (Christine and Jose have been doing this for years in a midwinter celebration of truffle possibilities at the restaurant; if you can get in on it, you really should.) Jose's first dish was a grilled orange salad that opened my eyes to the perfect (and very Spanish) pairing of oranges and black winter truffles. Grilling the oranges introduces a nice charred element and provides the heat needed to lift the truffle aromatics.

Truffle: Black winter or black autumn. Oregon black might be spectacular.

Makes 4 servings

½ cup olive oil
2 oranges
1 fennel bulb, sliced into ¼-inch-thick slices (optional)
2 ounces black truffle
2 tablespoons sherry vinegar
salt and pepper
8 ounces salad greens of your choice (a little radicchio is nice
    for color)

1. Fire up your grill.

2. Pour the olive oil into a small bowl. Grate some of the zest from the oranges into the oil. Then peel the oranges, slice into half-inch-thick rounds, and set aside. Add the vinegar, salt, and pepper to the vinaigrette. Grate half the truffle into the vinaigrette and whisk.

3. Spread the salad greens on a serving platter.

4. When the grill is good and hot, grill the orange and fennel slices until nicely charred with grill marks, about 2 to 3 minutes per side.

5. Top the greens with the orange and fennel slices and spoon the vinaigrette over the top. Grate or slice the remaining truffle over the salad and serve.

BEET CARPACCIO WITH TRUFFLES AND WALNUTS

For some reason Europeans don't tend to mix truffles and vegetables very much, which is nuts, because one of the best things about truffles is how they add depth and complexity. I actually think they could be a pillar of a great vegan culinary program. Inspiration for this dish came from Vitaly Paley, of Portland's Paley's Place, who once whipped up a nice beet carpaccio after I'd been lucky enough to come into a small fortune of Oregon black truffles. Vitaly, whose cooking leans toward Eastern Europe and Russia, topped this with sour cream, but I like avocado sauce to keep it vegan, and because the colors are crazy. Use a mix of purple and golden beets (or other colors) for maximum craycray. If you don't have walnut oil, use olive oil.

Truffle: Oregon black is divine, but any white or black will do.

Makes 4 to 6 servings

4 medium beets, trimmed
1 large avocado, peeled and pitted
2 tablespoons walnut oil
¼ lime, juiced
¼ teaspoon salt
1 small truffle
½ cup walnuts, chopped
1 sprig fresh dill

1. Preheat oven to 350 degrees. Place beets in a baking dish and sprinkle them with water. Cover the dish with foil and bake until the beets are fork-tender, about 1 hour. Let them cool completely.

2. Combine avocado, walnut oil, lime juice, salt, and 2 tablespoons water in a food processor. Grate a little bit of the truffle into the mix and blend until smooth and runny. Add more water if it's too thick to pour.

3. Thinly slice the beets. Arrange them in an overlapping concentric pattern on a large platter. Drizzle the avocado sauce over the beets in a fun pattern. Sprinkle the walnuts over the beets. Shave thin slices of truffle over the top. Sprinkle tiny bits of dill all around. Serve immediately.

CHAWANMUSHI TARTUFI

If I had to recommend a single vehicle for showing off truffles, this might be the one. I got the idea from Charles Ruff, the culinary director of the Oregon Truffle Festival. But he may have snatched it from Singapore, where Truffle Chawanmushi is a Thing. Chawanmushi is a steamed, savory Japanese egg custard, traditionally served in small bowls or teacups. In Japan, there are special lidded bowls just for chawanmushi. The lid is key, as it prevents water from falling into the custard during the steaming process, but in this case it also traps the truffly vapors until the magical moment when the diner lifts the lid. It gets its savor from dashi (stock made from kelp and bonito flakes) and soy sauce, but truffle juice also packs umami, so this is the time to splurge on a good can. (Or not; you could just go with dashi and it would be excellent.) Dashi is incredibly easy to make, but can also be found dried at any good market. If possible, truffle the eggs in advance; it makes a difference.

Truffle: Anything goes. White for pizzazz; black for comfort. Both for carpe diem!

Makes 4 servings

1 cup dashi or other stock
½ cup truffle juice (or more dashi)
2 teaspoons soy sauce
1 teaspoon mirin or semi-sweet wine or sherry
3 large eggs, preferably truffled
2 ounces truffle
Toppings of your choice

1. In a small bowl or measuring cup, mix together the dashi, truffle juice (if using), soy sauce, mirin, and eggs. Don't over-whisk. Introducing too much air into the mixture will result in a spongy custard, rather than a silky one.

2. Grate half the truffle into the mixture and stir to distribute.

3. Divide the mixture evenly into 4 chawanmushi cups, rame-kins, or small bowls. Grate or shave the remaining truffle over the top. Cover the cups with lids or plastic wrap.

4. Set the cups into a large pot. Fill the pot with 1 or 2 inches of water. Cover and bring to a boil. Continue to simmer for approximately 12 minutes.

5. Turn off the heat and let the bowls sit for an additional 6 minutes. Serve with the lids on.

CACIO E PEPE CON TARTUFI DI NERO

This recipe was inspired by John Paterson, the chef and owner of La Cantina del Mercataccio, high above the Umbrian plain in the ancient stone village of Todi, who served it to me one cold night and transformed my understanding of black summer truffles. John came to Umbria twenty years ago and fell in love with the culture and the awe-inspiring local ingredients. He himself was inspired by an old Umbrian *nonna* who cooked this for him many times, though he updated it with a creamier pecorino and a gentler pepper. Summer truffles are quite mild, operating almost below the threshold of perception—but that doesn't mean they're not there. By the time your bowl is empty, you should realize that you are simmering with a subtle happiness that can't be explained by the noodles, the wine, or the company. This recipe is for two (hearty) eaters, because it's hard to get a proper emulsion with more pasta than that in the skillet. If you are doing it for more people, either use a giant pan or batch it.

Truffle: Black summer is classic. It's cheap and mild, so use a lot. Black autumn (same truffle, but later in the season, when it's stronger) would be perfect. Good spot for a bianchetto.

Makes 2 romantic servings

½ pound tagliolini or another long, tangly pasta
Salt
4 tablespoons butter
Black pepper
1 cup pecorino, parmesan, or other hard cheese, finely grated

2 to 4 ounces black truffle
Olive oil or walnut oil (optional)

1. Place pasta in a large pot and cover with just enough salted water to keep it from sticking as it cooks. (You want to make your water nice and starchy, as that's what's going to give the sauce its silkiness.) Bring to a boil, stirring the pasta periodically to keep it from sticking, and cook until al dente.

2. Melt the butter in a large skillet over medium heat. Add a healthy grind of black pepper and simmer until fragrant, a minute or so.

3. Transfer ¼ cup of the starchy cooking water to the skillet. Using tongs, transfer the pasta to the skillet. Add the cheese and swirl until everything is mixed and bubbly and emulsified. Add more cooking water as needed, one tablespoon at a time. When silky, turn off the heat.

4. Grate the truffle into the pasta and swirl again. (Reserve a little bit of truffle for the top.) If desired, add a touch of olive oil or walnut oil. (I like walnut oil with truffles, but not everybody does.)

5. Slap the pan in the middle of the table. Grate the last bit of truffle over the top. Two forks. You can use individual bowls if you're not that into each other.

SEARED SCALLOPS IN TRUFFLED BUTTER BROTH

Scallops and truffles have great affinity, and fatty broths are especially good at conveying truffle fragrance. Good fish stock is key here. You can make excellent variations of this with cod or—be still my heart—black cod.

Truffle: All good.

Serves 4

3 tablespoons butter
1 fennel bulb, finely chopped, plus a bit of frond for garnish
½ cup celery root, peeled and finely chopped
¼ cup corn kernels
1 clove garlic, peeled and minced
1 cup fish stock
Dash of absinthe
½ cup heavy cream
1 medium truffle
2 tablespoons canola oil
12 sea scallops
Salt and pepper

1. Melt the butter in a large pan or skillet over medium heat. Add the fennel, celery root, corn, and garlic and simmer, stirring, until the garlic turns golden, about 2 minutes. Add the stock and simmer, stirring occasionally, until the vegetables are tender, about 3 to 4 minutes. Add the absinthe and cream,

stir, bring back to a simmer, then grate a little truffle into the broth, cover, and keep warm over the lowest possible simmer.

2. Season the scallops with salt and pepper. Add the canola oil to a large skillet and heat until quite hot. Add the scallops and sear until they have a nice brown crust on one side. This can take 2 to 4 minutes, depending on the scallops and the heat of your pan. Flip them over and sear a crust onto the other side, another minute or so. It's okay to keep them almost raw in the middle.

3. Divide the broth into four wide soup bowls. Pile three scallops in the center of each bowl, like a little island. Grate the rest of the truffle over everything. Sprinkle with a little bit of fennel frond and serve.

TRUFFLE DUCK

Of all the substances on Planet Earth that love to snatch up truffle odors, duck fat may be the most enthusiastic. It seems ready-made for it. Using duck breasts makes the process simple, fast, and straightforward. You'll notice that the instructions call for starting the breast in a cold pan. That's a Hank Shaw innovation that delivers the crispiest skin. The apple and the mushrooms here are optional; if you think they detract from the truffle, leave them out. Serve with polenta or new potatoes.

Truffle: If ever there was a moment to break out your best black winter, this is it. And while all black truffles are especially good with duck, whites are nice and would suffice.

Serves 4 light eaters or 2 gluttons

1 (1 pound) duck breast
Salt and pepper
1 teaspoon cooking oil
1 apple, peeled, cored, and chopped into matchsticks
1 cup mushrooms, thinly sliced
¼ cup calvados or cognac
2 ounces black truffle
Chopped chervil, chives, or parsley for garnish

1. Remove the duck breast from the fridge about a half hour ahead of time. Salt and pepper both sides well. Score the skin side in a crosshatch pattern. This will allow the fat to render. Let the breast come to room temperature.

2. Add the cooking oil to a cast iron skillet. Put the duck breast on top of it, skin side down, and move it around a bit with your spatula to coat it in the oil. Turn on the heat to low-medium and cook the breast until much of the fat has rendered and the skin is nicely browned, about 10 minutes.

3. Flip the breast over and brown the other side. Not for long, maybe 2 minutes, assuming you like your duck medium rare.

4. Remove the duck to a cutting board and let it rest for a few minutes to redistribute the juices.

5. If there is an insane amount of fat in the pan, pour off the excess (and repurpose), but keep a healthy (or even unhealthy) amount. Add the apple and mushrooms to the pan and sauté, stirring frequently, until softened, about 2 minutes. Add the booze and reduce, continuing to stir, until the sauce has thickened.

6. Turn off the heat and grate half the truffle into the sauce.

7. Slice the breast and serve topped with the pan sauce and any garnish. Shave the remaining truffle over the top.

TRUFFLED EGGNOG

The Kentucky classic. There may be no finer way to celebrate the glory of *Tuber melanosporum*. Tip o' the hat to Margaret Townsend and the incomparable Cissy Gregg for inspiration.

Truffle: Nothing but black winter is going to be right here. Black autumn or Oregon black in a pinch. A honey truffle would be wildly different but really interesting.

Makes 6 indulgent servings (or 12 sensible ones)

6 eggs
2 cups milk
1 cup heavy cream
1 cup bourbon
¾ cup sugar
1 small truffle

1. Separate yolks and whites into two large mixing bowls. Set whites aside.

2. Add ½ cup sugar to the yolks and beat until smooth. Add milk, cream, and bourbon. Grate about 1/3 of the truffle into the bowl and beat until well mixed. (This can be stored in the fridge for up to a day.)

3. Add the remaining ¼ cup sugar and 1/3 of the truffle to the egg whites and beat until they are light and fluffy and peaks have formed.

4. With a rubber spatula, fold the egg whites into the main mixture, gently stirring to incorporate. Fill six glasses (wide-mouthed wineglasses work well), grate the remaining truffle over the top, and serve.

TIRAMISU DI TARTUFI

Tiramisu hails from the northern Italian town of Treviso, the original "Sin City," known for its thriving brothel business. Apparently the ladies and their clients would engage in a morning round of love, followed by an epic midday feast (this was Italy, after all), and then, to revive the johns for round two, a shot of a coffee/cake concoction. ("Tiramisu" means "Raise it up," though its unclear whether all or just part of the clients was getting raised.) So the dish has always been seen as a prelude to love, and the truffles certainly won't get in the way.

Truffle: Oregon black would be my top choice. Black winter, No. 2. Appalachian, No. 3. Then the other blacks. Wild card: honey truffle!

Makes 8 servings

1 cup mascarpone, room temp
1 cup heavy cream
4 egg yolks
½ cup sugar
1 small truffle
1 cup coffee, room temp
¼ cup oloroso sherry
24 ladyfinger cookies
Cocoa powder for dusting

1. Line a loaf pan with plastic wrap, leaving lots of overhang.

2. Whisk the mascarpone and cream together in a bowl until smooth. Don't overmix. Set aside.

3. Set a metal bowl over a saucepan of simmering water. Add the egg yolks and sugar and beat until plump and ribbony, about 5 minutes. Remove from heat.

4. Using a rubber spatula, gently fold the eggs into the mascarpone mixture until fully incorporated. Grate the truffle into the mix and stir.

5. Combine coffee and sherry in a mixing cup.

6. Dip 8 of the ladyfingers in the coffee mixture for about 1 second each, laying each on the bottom of the pan to form a layer. Spread 1/3 of the custard over the top. Repeat with another 8 ladyfingers to form a second layer, then add half the remaining custard. Add the final 8 ladyfingers to form the third layer, then the end of the custard. Cover with plastic wrap and refrigerate for at least four hours, preferably overnight.

7. When ready to serve, remove the plastic wrap from the top, invert a serving plate over the pan, and quickly flip so the tiramisu is now on the plate. Remove the pan and peel off the plastic wrap. Dust the top with cocoa powder to cover your sins and serve in slices.

RESOURCES

Not so long ago, if you wanted a real truffle experience, your only options were high-end restaurants, a few French truffle markets, or the Alba International White Truffle Fair. Now there are more ways and places to get your truffle fix than you will ever be able to check off your life list. Visit a festival or two, take home some truffles, or order them online. They are easy to ship and easy to use. Take any opportunity to go hunting with truffle dogs, even if the truffles are likely planted in advance. (You know you want to find one!) For those who want to take it to the next level, there are truffle-dog trainers and, of course, truffle-tree suppliers. The following list is by no means comprehensive. It's just a selection of some of my personal faves, as well as a few recommendations from people I trust. Happy hunting.

FRESH TRUFFLES AND
TRUFFLE PRODUCTS

Fresh truffles are incredibly easy to use. They are also light and easy to ship overnight—which they have to be, since their shelf life is short and they need to be kept cool. You want them as close to harvest date as possible, so the fewer middlemen the better. Truffles later in the season will generally be stronger.

BURWELL FARMS

burwellfarmsnc.com

The premier U.S. producer of bianchetto truffles, and the most prolific truffle grower in North America. In addition to fresh and frozen bianchetti, Burwell Farms sells pine seedlings inoculated with bianchetto mycorrhizae.

I TARTUFI DI TEO

itartufiditeo.com

One of the few sources of conserved truffle products made without synthetic aroma. Tuscan truffle hunter Matteo Giuliani uses organic and biodynamic truffles and olive oil from the Tenuta di Ghizzano estate, as well as all-natural butters, salt, and honey. Matteo also offers guided truffle hunts on the estate, which also offers guest houses and superb Tuscan wine.

MAISON DE LA TRUFFE

maison-de-la-truffe.com

Parisian institution since 1932, now with branches in Nice and Bangkok, as well. In addition to fresh truffles, all the usual truffly schlock can be had: truffle oils, chips, butters, cremes, spreads, foie gras, and so on, as well as truffle graters and shavers. Nothing you can't find anywhere else. But the logo is classic and the little cloth bags coveted, so, when in Paris . . .

REGALIS

regalisfoods.com

New York's elite supplier of wild edibles was the first in the States to honestly promote the provenance of its truffles. It gets white truffles from Italy and Eastern Europe, and black winters from Spain, Australia, and Chile. Also makes its own line of truffle products.

SABATINO TARTUFI

sabatinotruffles.com

Famous and reliable source of fresh truffles (as well as every imaginable truffle product). Sabatino carries white, black summer, black autumn, and black winter (both European and Australian) in season. They have a headquarters in Umbria that serves Europe and an outpost in Connecticut for the United States. The fake tree in their New York City retail outlet is a hoot.

TERFEZIA

terfezia.com

Chocolate bonbons made with crazy sweet Hungarian honey truffles. A unique and delicious Hungarian product.

THE TRUFFLE DOG COMPANY

truffledogcompany.com

One of the few sources for native North American truffles. Makes a specialty of Oregon whites and blacks, but can also source pecan truffles and European species.

TUCKER'S TRUFFLE OIL

etsy.com/shop/TuckersTruffleOil

A true handmade product, Tucker's Truffle Oil is one of the few made without synthetic aroma—just olive oil and Oregon white truffles. Bob and Deb Walker have long been famous in Oregon for their oil and their truffle dog training. Both worth seeking out.

WILTSHIRE TRUFFLES

wiltshiretruffles.com

The highest-quality truffle supplier in the UK, offering very fresh truffles and transparent sourcing of black winter, black summer, black autumn, white, bianchetto, and honey truffles. Also now makes a handful of extremely decadent truffle products in collaboration with UK chefs: truffle butter, truffle cream, truffle juice, truffle cheese, and truffle ham.

WOLVES & PEOPLE

wolvesandpeople.com

Brewing legend Christian DeBenedetti grew up on a filbert (aka hazelnut) farm outside Portland, Oregon, so making a beer with filberts and Oregon white truffles came naturally. Where other truffle-beer brewers have failed miserably by adding truffles straight into the kettle (flavor disappears) or using synthetic aroma (flavor gross), DeBenedetti succeeds by infusing pounds of filberts with Oregon white truffles for ten days, then using the nuts to make the beer. La Truffe is a rich, slightly sweet, and insanely aromatic stout, available only at the brewery in February and at the Oregon Truffle Festival. Beware the burps.

FESTIVALS AND MARKETS

These days, every hamlet from Aragon to Abruzzo seems to be launching its own truffle festival. What follows are some of the best, big and small, and some of the classics.

ACQUALAGNA NATIONAL WHITE TRUFFLE FAIR

acqualagna.com

An apotheosis of *Tuber magnatum* over three successive weekends in October and November in the charming Marche town
of Acqualagna, ever since 1965. Lots of demos and tastings, and
hunts can be arranged. Acqualagna also holds a black winter
festival in February and a black summer festival in August.
Don't miss the Truffle Museum. As you can tell, this town is
crazy for truffles.

ALBA INTERNATIONAL WHITE TRUFFLE FAIR
fieradeltartufo.org
The granddaddy of them all, now in its nineties and still going
strong. This fair takes over the center of Alba every October and
November. Inside the big tent, you'll discover sensory analysis
seminars, cooking demos, a pop-up restaurant, a whole lot of
wine (heavy on the Barolo), and mountains of truffles. Come for
the spectacle, stay for the smell.

ASHEVILLE TRUFFLE EXPERIENCE
ashevilletruffle.com
A February weekend of black winter wining and dining, with
visits to the Mountain Research Station in Waynesville and a
dog demo by the extraordinary Lois Martin and Monza.

BARCELONA TRUFFLE TOUR
barcelonatruffletour.com
A four-day February workshop from the experts at Micofora,
geared toward truffle growers. Learn the latest science on
growing, handling, and marketing truffles. You'll visit nurseries
and orchards and eat very well—capped by a ten-course truffle
blowout at Spain's best truffle restaurant.

BURGUNDY TRUFFLE FESTIVAL

cotedor-tourisme.com
A mid-September celebration of the Burgundy truffle (aka black autumn) in the Côte-d'Or village of Is-sur-Tille. Decent wine to be had, methinks.

CARPENTRAS TRUFFLE MARKET

avignon-et-provence.com
Cleverly held every Friday morning from November to March, this is the thing to do before you hit Provence's more famous truffle market the following day.

GOTLAND TRUFFLE FESTIVAL

gotlandstryffelfestival.se
It goes without saying that this is the northernmost truffle festival in the world, held every November on the Swedish island to celebrate the local "Gotlandic truffle," as they call it. (Black autumn, *Tuber uncinatum*, by any other name.) There's a market, a hunting demo, a banquet, and a ceremony in the cathedral.

LALBENQUE TRUFFLE FESTIVAL

tourisme-lot.com
The highlight of this southwest France town's late-January truffle festival is the digging competition, in which sixty of France's top truffle dogs compete to unearth six truffles in the least amount of time. Lalbenque also hosts one of the most famous and picturesque truffle markets, on Tuesday afternoons December to March. Truffle sellers line up with their straw baskets on one side of a rope, buyers on the other, and at 2:30 P.M. a whistle blows and the rope falls. *Bonne chance.*

NAPA TRUFFLE FESTIVAL

napatrufflefestival.com

Weekend event in January focused on *Tuber melanosporum*. Orchard visit, dog demo, science seminar, food, food, food, wine, wine, wine.

OREGON TRUFFLE FESTIVAL

oregontrufflefestival.org

The most fun truffle festival on earth, with tasting seminars, growing forums, visits to local truffieres, and an incredibly high level of food and drink. This is the only festival where you'll be able to taste native Oregon black and white truffles, as well as black winters. (It falls in late January or early February, when the native truffles are at their peak.) Arrive early enough to catch the Joriad North American Truffle Dog Championship, on Thursday before the big weekend.

RICHERENCHES TRUFFLE MARKET

avignon-et-provence.com

The most famous truffle market on the planet, held every Saturday morning from mid-November to March, featuring the black diamond in all its permutations. The Vaucluse department produces most of France's *melanosporum*, so there's still some authenticity to this market. The famous Truffle Mass, with members of the Brotherhood of the Black Diamond hamming it up in robes, as they have done for more than fifty years, takes place on the third weekend in January.

SARLAT TRUFFLE FESTIVAL

sarlat-tourisme.com

On a weekend in mid-January, the streets of this medieval town in France's Dordogne region are lined with vendors selling truffles and truffled foods. Grab a croustou, a crostini spread with foie gras and topped with wafers of "Périgord" truffle. There are hunting demonstrations, cooking competitions, and truffle workshops.

SARRIÓN INTERNATIONAL TRUFFLE FAIR
www.fitruf.es
What started as a conference for professionals in the Teruel region's self-declared "Black Truffle Capital of the World" (which, by the numbers, it is) has evolved into a weekend-long fair for everyone in early December, with dog competitions, biggest-truffle contests, culinary competitions, and lots of eating and drinking. Still heavy on the science, compared to most.

TARTUFAIA
tartufaia.co
One of the world's few excellent retail shops devoted to truffles, launched in London's Borough Market in 2006. Run by two Italian men who know their stuff, it specializes in fresh truffles from Italy (truly!) and high-quality truffled foods.

ZIGANTE TRUFFLE DAYS
trufflefair.com
The marathon of truffle festivals, Zigante Truffle Days takes over the tiny Istrian town of Livade every weekend of autumn, September through November. Fresh truffles, cooked truffles, wine, sausage, dog demos, and cool jazz. Don't miss the truffle choo-choo. If you want to take your truffle bacchanal to the next

level, Restaurant Zigante, next door to the tent, will make that happen. If you time your visit right, you can also catch the festival of truffles and local teran wine in picture-perfect Motovun (late September), or the neighboring town of Buzet's Festival of Subotina (mid-September), in which a giant truffle omelet using ten kilos of truffles and two-thousand-plus eggs (one for every year anno domini) is made in an eight-foot-wide pan that weighs a ton.

TRUFFLE HUNTS

In Europe, most truffle hunts are "demonstrations," where the truffles have been buried in advance, though the hosts may pretend otherwise. If it were me, I'd be up front about it, maybe even let everyone know in advance where the truffles were buried and pitch it as a game for the dogs, but for whatever reasons, this remains a pseudo-secret in the truffle biz. Don't let that stop you! The dogs certainly don't know the truffles were planted, so they are legit—and that's what you've really come to see. The following are some of the more authentic experiences to be had.

THE ENGLISH TRUFFLE COMPANY
englishtruffles.co.uk
Enthusiastic source for truffle trees, truffle dog training, and truffle hunts in southern England.

HUNGARIAN TRUFFLE
hungariantruffle.com
Truffle hunting in the parks of Budapest. Opt for the gastrotour options, including a truffle picnic in the park.

I TARTUFI DI TEO

itartufiditeo.com

One of the few sources of conserved truffle products made without synthetic aroma. Tuscan truffle hunter Matteo Giuliani offers guided truffle hunts on the Tenuta di Ghizzano estate, which also offers guest houses and its own biodynamic wine.

KARLIĆ TARTUFI

karlictartufi.hr

Multigeneration (and multidog) truffling family offers no-holds-barred tasting sessions in their stunning glass-walled visitor center and demo kitchen, followed by hunts in one of Istria's best truffle forests. They'll even train your pup and put you up in their hilltop villa.

SAVE THE TRUFFLE

savethetruffle.com

Carlo Marenda and Edmondo Bonelli started Save the Truffle in 2015 as a way to educate Alba and the Langhe region, as well as the greater truffle community, about the necessity of protecting truffle habitat. In addition to education seminars and consultations on how to develop a healthy truffle bed, they offer simulated hunts, which of course come with a dose of nature education as well. If you're at the Alba truffle fair, these are the guys to go out with for a holistic understanding of truffles' beauty and challenges.

SITKA SERVICES

sitkaservicesllc.com

How often do you get to go on gastronomic extravaganzas across Spain or Croatia's best truffle territories with one of the world's leading truffle scientists? Christine Fischer lives in Spain and helped invent the truffle industry there. She leads winter truffle tours to Spain's great truffle-farming regions, with generous helpings of science and cuisine, and autumn tours of Croatia's wild truffle country. Not to be missed.

THE TRUFFLE DOG COMPANY
truffledogcompany.com
Bona fide hunts for native truffles in the wild woods of Washington.

TRUFFLE HUNTRESS
trufflehuntress.com
Staci O'Toole's ranch in the foothills of California's Sierra Nevada, Tesoro Mio, is kind of a one-stop fantasy island for all things truffle. Staci and Mila, her Lagotto Romagnolo, will survey your orchard or just take you on a truffle hunt on their own truffiere. Staci will ply you with truffled foods and local wines. She'll train your dog, and if you don't have one, well, she's got some Lagotto Romagnolo puppies that might be just the ticket.

TRUFFLE DOGS & DOG TRAINING

If you've made it this far in the book and don't want your own truffle dog, I've done something wrong. The question is whether to do the training yourself (bonding) or let a pro do it (best practices).

BLACKBERRY FARM
blackberryfarm.com

The States' most legendary line of Lagottos are all trained on the 4,200-acre Tennessee estate (which has its own truffiere) by renowned animal trainer Jim Sanford. Get on the multiyear waiting list now, and save up your pennies. You're going to need a lot of them.

DOMAINE RION

domainerion.fr

This celebrated wine estate in the Côte de Nuits also raises Lagotto Romagnolo truffle dogs. The pups come pre-exposed to truffle hunting by their mothers. They are also the only truffle dogs in the world that can distinguish a Chambolle-Musigny from a Nuits-Saint-Georges.

THE ENGLISH TRUFFLE COMPANY

englishtruffles.co.uk

Enthusiastic source for truffle trees, truffle dog training, and truffle hunts in southern England.

THE TRUFFLE DOG COMPANY

truffledogcompany.com

Alana McGee has been training top truffle dogs for more than a decade. She offers field lessons, group workshops, and online training. No dog? You can still go on wild adventures in Washington State and watch Alana and Lolo, her Lagotto Romagnolo, at work. You can also buy a fully trained dog, though Alana herself will not be doing the training. ("I get too attached," she says.) Alana also makes a fantastic truffle oil for dog training and will customize the species of truffles to individual needs.

TRUFFLE HUNTRESS

trufflehuntress.com

Staci O'Toole raises Lagotto Romagnolos and trains truffle dogs at Tesoro Mio, her ranch and truffiere in the foothills of California's Sierra Nevada.

TRUFFLE TREES

Once you've got your truffle hound (see above), you'll need a truffiere to go with it. Pro tip: Plant the truffiere a few years before you get the dog.

AGRI-TRUFFE

agritruffe.eu

The granddaddy of truffle cultivation, Agri-Truffe teamed with INRA, France's National Institute for Agricultural Research, to pioneer the mycorrhization of truffle trees in the 1970s. Still a world leader.

ARBORINNOV

arborinnov.com

Currently the one and only producer of truffle trees inoculated with *Tuber canaliculatum*, the Appalachian truffle, though that may soon change. Arborinnov sells trees in Canada and works with partner nurseries in the United States.

BURWELL FARMS

burwellfarmsnc.com

North Carolina's Burwell Farms sells pine seedlings inoculated with bianchetto mycorrhizae.

CAROLINA TRUFFIERES

carolinatruffieres.com

Top truffle nursery run by Brian Upchurch (president of the North American Truffle Growers Association) with his wife, Linda, and son, Davis. State-of-the-art innovators, they are growing a wider range of truffle and host tree species than anyone else. Full-spectrum consulting services as well as inoculated trees.

THE ENGLISH TRUFFLE COMPANY

englishtruffles.co.uk

Enthusiastic source for truffle trees, truffle dog training, and truffle hunts in southern England.

MICOFORA

micofora.com

Europe's gold standard for truffle trees and inoculum. Smart hombres. They check every single truffle they use for their inoculum under the microscope, ten thousand truffles a year, and every tree in their greenhouse for mycorrhization. Their trees are only available to clients in Spain, but their freeze-dried inoculum (to inoculate your own seedlings) is shipped worldwide. Orchard consultation services, too.

MYCORRHIZA BIOTECH

mycorrhizabiotech.com

Nancy Rosborough's North Carolina lab sells loblolly pine seedlings inoculated with bianchetto mycorrhizae. It also provides truffle farmers with lab services such as analysis of the mycorrhization levels on existing trees and soil tests for competing fungi.

NEW WORLD TRUFFIERES

truffletrees.com

Charles Lefevre's truffle trees are responsible for many of America's most successful truffieres. Charles offers seedlings inoculated with *melanosporum*, *aestivum*, and *borchii*, and is even getting started on *Tuber canaliculatum*, the Appalachian truffle. He is also the expert on native Oregon truffle species.

ASSOCIATIONS

Every country that grows truffles has a professional association of growers. These are excellent sources for science, news, and contacts.

AUSTRALIAN TRUFFLE GROWERS ASSOCIATION

trufflegrowers.com.au

FEDERATION FRANCAISE DES TRUFFICULTEURS

fft-truffes.fr

NEW ZEALAND TRUFFLE ASSOCIATION

nztruffles.org.nz

NORTH AMERICAN TRUFFLE GROWERS ASSOCIATION

trufflegrowers.com

NORTH AMERICAN TRUFFLING SOCIETY

natruffling.org

INDEX

Specific truffles are also found by country.

A NOTE ON THE AUTHOR

ROWAN JACOBSEN is the author of the James Beard Award–winning *A Geography of Oysters* as well as *Fruitless Fall*, *American Terroir*, *Apples of Uncommon Character*, and other books. He has written for the *New York Times*, *Harper's*, *Outside*, *Food & Wine*, *Scientific American*, *Mother Jones*, *Vice*, *Orion*, and others, and his work is regularly anthologized in the *Best American Science & Nature Writing* and *Best Food Writing* collections. He has been an Alicia Patterson Foundation fellow, writing about endangered diversity on the borderlands between India, Myanmar, and China; a McGraw Center for Business Journalism Fellow, writing about the disruptive potential of plant-based proteins; and a Knight Science Journalism fellow at MIT, focusing on the environmental and evolutionary impact of synthetic biology. He has performed with Pop-Up Magazine, lectured at Harvard and Yale, and appeared on CBS, NBC, and NPR. He lives in Vermont.